PROGRESS FROM THE MARGINS

COLUMBIA STUDIES IN
INTERNATIONAL AND GLOBAL HISTORY

COLUMBIA STUDIES IN
INTERNATIONAL AND GLOBAL HISTORY

Cemil Aydin, Timothy Nunan, and Dominic Sachsenmaier, Series Editors

This series presents some of the finest and most innovative work coming out of the current landscapes of international and global historical scholarship. Grounded in empirical research, these titles transcend the usual area boundaries and address how history can help us understand contemporary problems, including poverty, inequality, power, political violence, and accountability beyond the nation-state. The series covers processes of flows, exchanges, and entanglements—and moments of blockage, friction, and fracture—not only between "the West" and "the Rest" but also among parts of what has variously been dubbed the "Third World" or the "Global South." Scholarship in international and global history remains indispensable for a better sense of current complex regional and global economic transformations. Such approaches are vital in understanding the making of our present world.

Marian Füssel, trans. Brían Hanrahan, *The World in Flames:
A Global History of the Seven Years' War*

Q. Edward Wang, *Staple to Superfood: A Global History of the Sweet Potato*

Pierre Singaravélou, trans. Stephen W. Sawyer, *Tianjin Cosmopolis:
An Alternative History of Globalization*

James De Lorenzi, *Feasting on History: Ethiopia and the Orientalists*

Jie-Hyun Lim, trans. Megan Sungyoon, *Victimhood Nationalism:
History and Memory in a Global Age*

Hale Eroğlu, *Muslim Transnationalism in Modern China:
Debates on Hui Identity and Islamic Reform*

Sandrine Kott, *A World More Equal: An Internationalist Perspective on the Cold War*

Julia Hauser, *A Taste for Purity: An Entangled History of Vegetarianism*

Hayrettin Yücesoy, *Disenchanting the Caliphate: The Secular Discipline
of Power in Abbasid Political Thought*

Anne Irfan, *Refuge and Resistance: Palestinians and the International Refugee System*

Michael Francis Laffan, *Under Empire: Muslim Lives and Loyalties
Across the Indian Ocean World, 1775–1945*

Eva-Maria Muschik, *Building States: The United Nations, Development,
and Decolonization, 1945–1965*

For a complete list of books in the series,
please see the Columbia University Press website.

PROGRESS FROM THE MARGINS

HUMAN RIGHTS AND DISABILITY INTERNATIONALISM SINCE THE 1960s

PAUL VAN TRIGT

Columbia University Press
New York

Columbia University Press
Publishers Since 1893
New York   Chichester, West Sussex
cup.columbia.edu

Copyright © 2026 Columbia University Press
All rights reserved

Cataloging-in-Publication Data is available from the Library of Congress.
ISBN 9780231219921 (hardback)
ISBN 9780231219938 (trade paperback)
ISBN 9780231562973 (ebook)

Cover design: Elliott S. Cairns
Cover image: Fahrul 40 / Shutterstock.com

GPSR Authorized Representative: Easy Access System Europe, Mustamäe tee 50, 10621 Tallinn, Estonia, gpsr.requests@easproject.com

CONTENTS

INTRODUCTION
1

1 JERUSALEM 1968:
BLOCKING "PROMISCUOUS SCANDINAVIA"
15

2 BELGRADE 1975:
"EQUALITY . . . NOT MATERIALIZED IN FULL"
37

3 SINGAPORE 1981:
"NOTHING ABOUT US, WITHOUT *ALL* OF US"
58

4 NEW YORK 1987:
A NEOLIBERAL UTOPIA OF DEVELOPMENT
79

5 VIENNA 1993:
"ADOPT OR ADJUST LEGISLATION TO ASSURE ACCESS"
101

6 MEXICO CITY 2002:
TAKEN BY SURPRISE
121

EPILOGUE
144

Acknowledgments 157
Notes 159
Bibliography 189
Index 205

PROGRESS FROM THE MARGINS

INTRODUCTION

During the International Year of Disabled Persons (IYDP, 1981), the British popstar Ian Dury performed the song "Spasticus Autisticus." In this song, he spoke to "Normal Land," the able-bodied world that probably did not understand disabled people like him.[1] The distance between Spasticus Autisticus and Normal Land sits at the heart of the history of the human rights of disabled persons. This book analyzes the struggle for the international recognition of disability human rights, a struggle to bridge the gap between Spasticus Autisticus and Normal Land, a struggle, moreover, that is much more than just another attempt to include and protect a "vulnerable group" by means of human rights law. Disabled people such as Ian Dury not only questioned their status as passive human rights objects, but also brought a new understanding of the subject of human rights itself.

This became particularly clear with the Convention on the Rights of Persons with Disabilities (CRPD), adopted by the United Nations (UN) in 2006. People with disabilities and their allies were involved in the struggle for and negotiation of the convention to an extent which is unique in the history of human rights law. Moreover, the convention directs member states concerning how it must be implemented, including the participation of people with disabilities as monitors. When it comes to the recognition of the freedom and equality of people with disabilities, the convention has a lot in common with other human rights treaties such as the Convention on the Elimination of All Forms of Discrimination Against Women; but in other respects the CRPD is more comprehensive and contains several innovative elements such as support in the exercising of legal capacity, which is striking given the emphasis on the autonomous subject in most human rights law.[2]

The innovative contribution to human rights law from a disability perspective may be self-evident to people working on or with disability law, but is not always noticed in the broader field of human rights and international law and certainly not in the historiography of human rights (law).[3] At the same time the insights of recent human rights historiography and the "historical turn" in international law seem rarely processed by scholars working on disability rights and law and its history. This book aims therefore to bridge the gap between two different academic fields: the study of disability (law) and the historiography of human rights. By presenting the history of disability human rights as a narrative of discontinuous progress from the margins, I hope this book will function as a useful metaphor that reshapes perception by bringing together two semantic and in this case academic fields.[4] The element of discontinuity results from a historicizing approach that reveals the shifting meanings of human rights and highlights the involvement of various actors and the influence of rival concepts often not addressed in the disability law literature. The discontinuity of the history of disability human rights makes it hard to perceive events such as the adoption of the CRPD as milestones along a clear path of progress. Nevertheless, this book maintains the concept of progress in order to uncover the significant contributions of disabled people to human rights that are still relevant and often overlooked in human rights historiography, ranging from emphasis on the nation-state's importance to human rights to the development of the notion of shared personhood. In the following two subsections I situate this book in more detail in relation to the existing literature, and in the last subsection I present its structure.

DISABILITY RIGHTS PROGRESS

Societies have often viewed people with disabilities as inferior to their able-bodied counterparts, and this has encouraged diverse attempts both to conceptualize and to combat this inequality. Since the 1960s people with disabilities have themselves increasingly taken the lead. Moreover, these attempts have acquired a more global framework: Both the grass-roots movements of people with disabilities and related policies have become internationalized. These debates have also brought together observations on the inequality of people with disabilities in concrete, local, or national settings and broader analyses of inequality as a fundamental condition occurring all over the world. In the literature, the recent history of conceptualizing the inequality of people with disabilities is often presented as developing from a welfare state approach to disability to more of a human rights and anti-discrimination one. This shift would imply turning from a focus on socioeconomic equality to a focus on status equality. In her book about disability rights Katharina Heyer states that considering disability as a human rights issue, particularly since the CRPD, was "unthinkable just twenty years earlier when most countries relied on charity, social welfare, segregated institutions, and sometimes employment quotas to incorporate people with disabilities or mitigate the suffering brought about by their exclusion." The 1990 Americans with Disabilities Act (ADA) is generally seen as the "world's first comprehensive disability anti-discrimination law," and therefore as the "first political expression" of a new approach to disability.[5]

The dominant historical narrative about the struggle for equal rights among people with disabilities connects different parts of Anglo-American disability history with what has occurred at the UN level. Before I problematize this narrative, I shall briefly present what it entails. A major shift that one encounters in almost every text on disability written in the last few decades is from the so-called medical model of disability to the social model. According to the medical model disability is an individual deficit, while the social model perceives disability as a social construct. The shift is often attributed to the Anglo-American context in the 1970s and 1980s, because at that time people with different disabilities united with one another in their struggle for emancipation. Before that time cross-disability activism aimed at equal citizenship hardly existed. People with disabilities were organized on the basis of disability type—blindness, for example—and activism focused mainly on improving social services. Society understood people with disabilities (as they also understood themselves) as belonging in a paradigm of social welfare in which medical experts played an important role in determining disability. Robert Drake summarized this point clearly: "welfare is still significantly about changing the individual to fit into the social and physical environment rather than altering the social, political, and physical contours of society."[6]

The change which the social model of disability brought about was that people with disabilities increasingly organized themselves in cross-disability groups that combatted discrimination in ways similar to those of the social movements of women, ethnic minorities, and LGBTQIA+ people. The ADA is therefore seen as a landmark event in the emancipation of people with disabilities. This shift toward the social model and a new focus on anti-discrimination are often presented as connected with a shift toward a human rights approach to disability. As Jane Campbell and Mike Oliver put it, "disabled people began to recognize that the problem of disability is externally located and that our exclusion from society is a human rights issue."[7]

The connection between the shift from the medical to social model with the shift away from welfare to human rights can certainly be observed in the history of influential disability groups in the United Kingdom and the United States. This shift has also often functioned as an inspiring example for activist groups in other countries: They wanted to realize a comparable shift in their own country. However, from a historical perspective it is questionable if the dynamisms of disability movements worldwide, let alone the history of UN disability policies, can be described by this shift. Different histories of people with disabilities are often tied together in order to create a smooth narrative with a clear teleology concluding with the worldwide implementation of the CRPD as its logical outcome. Even the more nuanced contributions tend to underline the centrality of the Anglo-American approach to disability as an issue of discrimination.[8]

An important point to make is that this narrative overlooks disability histories from other parts of the world. Moreover, not only does it ignore alternative approaches to disability, but its treatment of Anglo-American history is also rather monolithic and lacking in nuance. Gildas Brégain wrote about disability protests in Argentina, Brazil, and Spain during the period 1968–1982 and relativized the "original manner of the Anglo-American protests within the growth of disability rights movement at the international level."[9] Monika Baár has argued that "Contrary to other (capitalist) countries where the efforts of self-determination were directed against the patronising attitudes of medical and professional experts, disabled activists in Hungary were actively and wholeheartedly assisted in their emancipatory desires by these professional groups."[10] Land mine survivors in late twentieth-century Northern Uganda, as Herbert Muyinda has shown, did not take a human rights approach, but pursued the contested approach of "special needs."[11] A closer look at the United Kingdom reveals that, as Gareth Millward's work among others suggests, not only did disability activism begin by addressing welfare issues such as poverty, but social security also remained an important issue despite the rise of the social model.[12]

The observation that these and other examples problematize the "shift-narrative" does not challenge the fact that parallels and transnational exchanges between countries exist; however, disability histories as mentioned above do not support the idea that one cohesive global movement changed the understanding of disability from a medical/welfare model to a social/human rights model in the 1970s. Although the shift-narrative can be empowering, it troubles our understanding of the CRPD and its history.

In contrast to the literature that has (re)produced the shift-narrative, I do not consider human rights and disability as obvious companions. The relationship between these two concepts is contingent and in need of a precise historical explanation as to how and why these concepts have been linked or not. Analyzing the process that led to the signing of the CRPD without the assumption that a human rights perspective on disability is self-evident, as this book attempts to do, thus goes against the grain of a dominant historical narrative of disability rights. This book offers an alternative to this narrative, echoing what Dipesh Chakrabarty has coined as the "first in Europe, then elsewhere" structure.[13] This does not mean, however, that I necessarily agree with the recent "decolonial" trend among self-advocates and researchers to set human rights aside as a one-sided or useless Western idea.[14] By taking into account different actors, different meanings of rights, and different framings of disability this book will show that such criticisms do not do justice to the strong engagement of actors from different parts of the world in the emergence of the human rights perspective on disability.[15]

HUMAN RIGHTS HISTORIOGRAPHY

In order to provide an alternative and more convincing narrative, I build on insights from human rights historiography. With an historicizing approach I try to avoid what Sam Moyn critically calls the model of "truncation and fulfillment." According to this model, "once universal entitlements [like human rights] are declared, the pressure rises for remedying their original truncation" and the (metropolitan) elite cannot "keep these entitlements for themselves, they are forced by the universalism of their own claim to extend them" to "(colonial) subalterns."[16] With the "immanent 'logic'" of this model, argues Moyn, it is difficult to explain why universalisms are not always widely claimed. He therefore states that the coexistence of different concepts, the non-globalization of ideas, and the specific interpretation and context of the concept have to be taken into account.[17] Although Moyn himself is criticized for his Western focus, his historicizing approach in itself does not exclude actors in the periphery. Moyn's approach may be self-evident for historians, but in existing scholarship on the CRPD it is hardly used. As mentioned, the literature about the CRPD and its history is often focused on the drafting or on the long-awaited "fulfillment."[18] Disability is not always contextualized as a contested human rights issue in broader social and political transformations.

The results of Moyn's historicizing approach seem, at first sight, to underline the shift-narrative as discussed above. Several historians, among whom Moyn is probably the best known, have argued that human rights acquired their current meaning, namely a set of rights grounded in individual dignity that enjoy secure international protection, only in the 1970s. Before this decade human rights were understood as collective rights and/or nationally protected rights. In his book *Last Utopia* (2010), Moyn understands human rights since the 1970s as a utopia that became central to a global social movement. He explains the success of the concept and the movement since the 1970s by pointing to the fact that people around that time became disappointed in other political utopias, like anti-colonialism and socialism. Human rights, as brought to the fore by organizations like Amnesty International, became an alternative moral, minimalist utopia.[19] The breakthrough of international human rights in the 1970s went along, as several scholars have argued recently, with an increasing popularity of neoliberalism at the expense of the welfare state.[20]

Although the literature about the breakthrough of human rights and neoliberalism during the 1970s offers a relevant historical background for the emergence of the human rights perspective on disability, no empirical evidence indicates a global breakthrough of this perspective during this period. On the contrary, since this perspective was developed in the 1960s it remained marginal in the international sphere until the CRPD. Moreover, despite changes over time the focus of this perspective has always been on the improvement of the lives of people with disabilities within the framework of the nation-state. This national focus, which does not uniquely apply to the case of disability, would have disappeared after the 1970s, but—as I will argue—this "national" use of human rights seems more persistent than previously thought and is still popular today. Because the emphasis in historiography is so much on international human rights, the current backlash against human rights has been interpreted by different scholars as the end of human rights.[21]

However, this seems premature and does not do justice to worldwide human rights practices.

Nevertheless, the "breakthrough-narrative" contains much historical truth and has provoked a historiography with diverse understandings of human rights history that are highly relevant to the subject of this book. In a recent review essay Benjamin Möckel has argued that human rights historiography has recently moved from discussions about origins and/or breakthrough to acknowledging multiple chronologies of human rights. Moreover, historians increasingly approach human rights in relation to other concepts such as humanitarianism and development and with attention to particular themes and social groups.[22] By building on a selection of insights from these discussions, this book aims to provide a new contribution to the historiography of human rights.

One alternative understanding of recent human rights history in particular is relevant for disability rights: Stefan-Ludwig Hoffmann has recently argued that human rights acquired their current meaning and popularity during the 1990s. Differing slightly from Moyn, Hoffmann states that "in the 1970s and 1980s 'human rights' coexisted and overlapped with other moral and political idioms like 'solidarity' and included competing notions of rights, which were in many ways still indebted to the legacies of socialism and anti-colonialism, as in, for example, the transnational movement against apartheid."[23] This is in line with what Antony Anghie argued in response to Moyn's interpretation of the 1970s, pointing to the ongoing relevance of the utopia of development and arguing that "human rights was the last utopia for a select group of people, largely based in the West."[24] In line with Hoffmann's and Anghie's work disability human rights have often been part of and contested by other idioms, although the main competitor did not—contrary to what Anghie has suggested—come from the Global South.

Moreover, Hoffmann challenges Moyn's understanding of human rights as a utopia. He agrees with Moyn that international human rights "regained currency first as a critique of revolutionary utopias" but argues that human rights since the 1990s "is everything but future-oriented or utopian. It is not a social or political imaginary of a different, more perfect society." Human rights are "a bare human minimum," states

Hoffmann, using Michael Ignatieff's phrase. Part of the breakthrough of human rights in the 1990s is, according to Hoffmann, that "visual representations of the 'Third World' have shifted from developing nations to suffering individuals, victims of natural or man-made disasters without political agency in the international arena."[25] Interestingly, disability human rights show almost an inverted image here: The CRPD is anything but "a bare human minimum" and could be seen as offering the "imaginary" of a "different society." On top of that, people with disabilities have obtained political agency in the international arena and have introduced the innovative notion of shared personhood that challenges popular notions such as suffering individuals and autonomous human rights subjects. By addressing their agency and their perspective on structural issues, this book firmly writes people with disabilities into the historiography of internationalisms and international relations.[26]

Following a historicizing approach, I have investigated in the main UN disability policy documents since the 1960s as carefully as possible how the concept of (human) rights was used, how this changed over time, how this was related to the use of other concepts, and how we can explain this phenomenon. The UN sources do not always allow us to determine the precise actors who determined the use of particular concepts, which means that an in-depth explanation is not always possible. I have therefore taken into account additional sources such as autobiographies, grey literature, and archives of nongovernmental organizations (NGOs) and national governments.

PROGRESS FROM THE MARGINS

Based on these historiographical insights, a historicizing approach, and historical sources, I shall provide a new and hopefully more convincing narrative of the history of international disability human rights. In order to do justice to the erratic trajectory of disability human rights, each chapter will present the long-term development of a particular dimension of disability human rights as stipulated in the CRPD, varying from sexual reproduction rights to socioeconomic equality. This will show how different dimensions follow different trajectories over time and goes beyond a fixed understanding of the human rights perspective on disability. In addition to a long-term history that is focused on conceptual changes, each chapter discusses one event that was important (in a positive or negative way) for the genesis of disability as a human rights issue.[27] By analyzing events and the historical actors involved, I show how people from different parts of the world, different organizations, and different understandings of disability made an impact. Moreover, these event histories underline both the agency of historical actors and the ways in which they were influenced by broader historical phenomena such as cultural revolutions, the Cold War, and neoliberalism. Attention to different actors also sheds light on what does set the CRPD apart from some other treaties on the rights of certain groups (women, children), namely the recognition of the variety of the group.

Chapter 1 starts with Richard Sterner from Sweden, member of an association of parents of children with mental disabilities, who looks back on a conference of the International League of Societies for the Mentally Handicapped (ILSMH) in Jerusalem in 1968. He was disappointed that the ILSMH did not want to confirm all the rights of people with mental disabilities, most notably reproductive rights. His disappointment was understandable because of the progressive Scandinavian disability policies at that time, but the idea to declare internationally the human rights of people with mental disabilities was new. The 1968 conference would be a prelude to the Declaration on the Rights of Mentally Retarded Persons (1971) and the Declaration on the Rights of Disabled Persons (1975) as adopted by the UN General Assembly. These declarations would not pave the way for human rights law but inspired social policies at the global and national level: a use of human rights that is hardly mentioned in the existing literature. The idea to grant reproductive rights to people with (mental) disabilities recurred in the 1990s and after much debate was included in the convention.

Parallel to the development of an international human rights perspective on persons with mental disabilities, during the 1970s rehabilitation became the paradigm for international policies concerning people with physical and sensory disabilities. Rehabilitation was aimed at the equal socioeconomic participation of people with disabilities by adapting them to society, but not by adapting society to them or by offering them socioeconomic rights. Legislative aspects of rehabilitation were considered important by international policymakers, but equal rights hardly were. A conference on blind women in Belgrade in 1975 organized by self-advocates such as social work expert Fatima Shah from Pakistan, as discussed in chapter 2, shows that human rights were mentioned only as part of broader utopian visions. When these visions started to be abandoned around 1990, human rights did not become central in international disability policies but rather concepts such as human needs and equal opportunities—considered in the literature as neoliberal. Moreover, concepts such as rehabilitation remained central in these policies until the CRPD negotiations.

Chapter 3 discusses the first conference of the first international self-advocacy organization, Disabled Peoples' International (DPI), in Singapore during the IYDP. This is often presented as a breakthrough moment for disability rights that left a mark on the World Programme of Action (WPA), which was the main UN disability policy document during the 1980s. It is true that human rights became one of the key issues of DPI during 1981. However, the focus was on cases of maltreatment: a narrow focus without a broader interest in designing a convention. As becomes clear from the writings of DPI founding member Ron Chandran-Dudley from Singapore, the main goals of DPI were supporting self-advocacy and social development. In hindsight the IYDP must be seen as a catalyst in the development of disability internationalism. Without the IYDP the involvement of people with disabilities during the negotiations about the convention is unthinkable. This chapter will show on the one hand that the IYDP made disability a global concern and connected actors who until then had operated separately. DPI, for instance, started to function as an international platform of exchange between self-advocacy in the so-called developed and developing world. On the other hand, the IYDP did not stimulate the further development of a global framework for the human rights of people with disabilities. Human rights and the

Declaration on the Rights of Disabled Persons in 1975 were seen only as underlying disability policies.

That did not last very long: Chapter 4 starts with the negative response of UN civil servants in New York to the recommendations of the Global Meeting of Experts in Stockholm in 1987 where the idea of a disability human rights convention was discussed for the first time at the international level. By following the relationship between the secretary-general's office and a little-known North American self-advocate, Alan Reich, through the 1980s and 1990s this chapter explains the United Nations' reluctance to create a convention. From this relationship it becomes clear that one of the main reasons why it took so long before disabled people were integrated into international human rights law was the existence of an influential alternative framework: social development, a framework moreover that was considered by the United Nations as more feasible than a convention that would require political change, and as fitting the human needs approach advanced by neoliberal institutions such as the World Bank.

In order to understand why the social development framework was replaced by a human rights framework during the negotiations about the convention, chapter 5 finally turns to European self-advocates such as the German lawyer Theresia Degener. During the World Conference on Human Rights in Vienna in 1993 self-advocates were successful in demanding that disability had to be treated as a human rights issue, although the emphasis was initially on the responsibility of national governments and not so much on the development of an international instrument. In national struggles for emancipation during the 1990s disability became increasingly seen as an anti-discrimination issue, and in the case of the Deaf community as an issue of minority language recognition, but at the United Nations it hardly made any progress in the framing of disability as a human rights issue. During the 1990s, however, a collective of self-advocates and human rights lawyers became increasingly convinced that such an instrument was needed to fully protect the rights of people with disabilities. Moreover, they developed a broad understanding of human rights in which they combined the North American anti-discrimination perspective with the European welfare state perspective—against the grain of human rights as a minimalist, anti-welfarist utopia.

Chapter 6 starts with an influential statement concerning the legal capacity of people with disabilities by New York-born self-advocate and lawyer Tina Minkowitz at an expert meeting in Mexico City in 2002, just before the start of the negotiations about the convention. The way in which the human rights perspective on disability was converted into international law has surprised many: It happened relatively fast and with the substantial involvement of people with disabilities themselves. Moreover, the convention recognizes people with disabilities as subjects and agents of human rights law—a striking feature that is not self-evident in human rights policies in general and disability policies in particular. In order to explain the form the convention acquired, this chapter presents the history of the right to live independently in the community and the right to support that disabled people may require in exercising their legal capacity. This shows that the convention negotiations took a direction that cannot be considered as a logical outcome of the past, and that goes to the heart of debates about what it means to be human: During the debates about Article 12 of the convention the notion of shared personhood was developed beyond popular understandings of personhood that emphasize the vulnerability or autonomy of the human person.

In the epilogue the main findings of the book are weighed against dominant interpretations of human rights and the CRPD in the last decade. In these interpretations leading scholars emphasize the limited potential of human rights to make the world a better place because they rely more on the *(im)morality* of the international community than on (inter)national *political* communities. Without wanting to deny this, from a historical perspective the CRPD seems more likely to mark a break away from a focus on the international protection of human rights to the selective domestic implementation of human rights—a selective implementation to which Dagmar Herzog among others has already pointed. The fact that China is diligently working on its implementation and the United States has not even ratified the convention could be interpreted as a shift from using human rights as a yardstick by which to judge the bad behavior of others elsewhere to using it to show one's own good behavior to "vulnerable" others within the nation. However, it is not sure that a selective domestic implementation will save the revolutionary and innovative potential of the convention. That is why this book closes with a reflection on the concept of heterotopia as a possibility to explore new ways of continuing the path of progress from the margins and to problematize the distance between Spasticus Autisticus and Normal Land.

1

JERUSALEM 1968

Blocking "Promiscuous Scandinavia"

"We cannot conform to what was said at a symposium in promiscuous Scandinavia." This could easily have been said at one of the debates concerning the UN Declaration on the Rights of Mentally Retarded Persons (1971). It is unclear if anything like this was actually said, but it certainly reflects Richard Sterner's experience of these debates.[1] Sterner, member of a Swedish association of parents of children with mental disabilities, helped to organize a symposium of the International League of Societies for the Mentally Handicapped (ILSMH) in Stockholm in 1967. After this symposium the ILSMH published conclusions that claimed a broad range of rights to the "retarded person," including "the right to choose a place to live, to engage in leisure time activities, to dispose of property, to preserve the physical and psychological integrity of his person, to vote, to marry, to have children, and to be given a fair trial for alleged offence."[2] The right of people with mental disabilities to vote, to marry, and to have children was strongly opposed by parents and professionals at the ILSMH conference in 1968 in Jerusalem when the league adopted the Declaration on the General and Special Rights of Mentally Retarded Persons.[3] Opposition was maintained at the UN level, according to Sterner, by conservative member states.[4] This chapter contextualizes this early attempt to recognize the human rights of people with disabilities at the international level and follows UN discussions about their right to sexual reproduction until its inclusion in the Convention on the Rights of Persons with Disabilities (CRPD).

CRIP UTOPIA

In her book *Unlearning Eugenics,* historian Dagmar Herzog states that "the twenty-first century has been an auspicious time, so far, for the recognition and even celebration of disability rights." However, she continues by observing that recent decades have also seen the "ascent of a new kind of eugenics" related to the "massive spread of prenatal diagnostic testing for potential fetal anomalies and eventually the development of preimplantation diagnostics for in vitro fertilization."[5] Did this paradoxical situation, in which human diversity is at the same time fostered and undermined, also determine discussions in the late 1960s and early 1970s? Before we delve further into this question, I want to highlight the fact that it is not a given to start this book with the ILSMH conferences and the 1971 declaration. In general, the history of people with mental disabilities and their representatives has been poorly integrated within histories of the global disability movement and human rights law. The 1971 declaration is not mentioned in the CRPD because it is seen as too ingrained in the medical model of disability.[6] Moreover, representatives of people with mental disabilities have not always been included in disability movements. Only from the 1980s, when people with mental disabilities started to speak more emphatically for themselves, were they and their representatives taken seriously as part of the global disability movement.[7] However, research and activism concerning mental disabilities and their history still tends to stand apart from the disability studies mainstream. Therefore, it is no surprise that figures such as Sterner are not considered to have been at the forefront of international disability human rights. But they were.

An alternative starting point for this chapter could have been Camp Jened, a New York summer camp held in 1971 for young persons with disabilities. During the 1970s the campers, as beautifully captured in the Netflix documentary film *Crip Camp*, became activists for the American disability rights movement. Some of them, Judy Heumann for instance, went on to play a part in the global disability movement during the 1980s. American activists such as Heumann and Ed Roberts were particularly successful in spreading their independent living philosophy to other parts of the world.[8] In this philosophy people with disabilities managed their own care and lived independently with tools such as an individual health care budget and personal assistants. Thanks to the efforts of the German self-advocate Adolf Ratzska, who lived as a student in an independent living center in Berkeley, the independent living philosophy was introduced in Europe: first in Sweden, then in other European countries.[9] The CRPD also bears the marks of this philosophy, although it took some time before all the international lawyers involved in the negotiations understood what self-advocates meant by self-determination: not a group right applied to territories under colonial or foreign occupation, but "a catch-all term that included ideas such as autonomy for persons with disabilities, a right to make their own decisions and the right to be included."[10]

At the core of the society the Independent Living Movement had in mind stood equal access: If all the barriers in society were broken down and if people with disabilities could determine the assistance they needed, they would live independently as every other citizen did. We can glimpse this society in a "Tongue-in-cheek science fiction" titled *Crip Utopia*, in which Ratzka introduced his readers to Crip van Winkle, "a man of strong convictions and moral fortitude" from the United Kingdom, who "after years of putting his hopes on New Labour" became "increasingly disillusioned." In 1999 Winkle hired a company to freeze him and his wheelchair until New Year's Day in 2050. After defrosting, he met "a bearded fellow who introduced himself as a historian who wanted to interview van Winkle about life as a disabled person in the last century." During the interview Winkle found out that his country had made enormous progress toward making society inclusive and accessible. When he asked about the accessibility of public transport, the historian told him:

All conveyances, public or private, for transportation by land, air, sea and cyberspace, for individual or collective travel are naturally covered by the Universal Design principle. You don't seem to understand, van Winkle, the United States of Europe officially abolished Apartheid in the year 2024–30 years after South Africa but better late than never. Since then, Universal Design has been the law of the land and the international sign of access that you guys were so proud of, is forbidden. It singles out and stigmatizes a particular group of citizens.[11]

Although Ratzka mentioned Europe as an international institution, his utopian society is imagined as a national society. The fact that the United Nations and human rights were hardly mentioned in this Crip Utopia is telling: It would be a long time before international recognition and protection of the human rights of people with disabilities would be at the core of the Independent Living Movement. The concept of human rights was used by members of the movement, and their ideas have influenced the convention, but they did not stand at the forefront of international disability human rights. In the struggle to improve their situation, self-advocates were often focused on the national society of which they were part. As will become clear throughout this book, it took time before they gained a place at the table where global disability policies were determined, and when they did human rights were not always seen as the first priority. Ironically, the lobby for international human rights started in a field where people with disabilities for a long time had no voice at all: the field of policies for people with mental disabilities.

DISABILITY INTERNATIONALISM AND NORMALIZATION

The adoption of human rights as a central concept by the ILSMH in the late 1960s and early 1970s was a remarkable form of disability internationalism. Disability internationalism in itself was not unique at that time. Disability was part of several policies of the United Nations and its special agencies: the vocational rehabilitation policies of the International Labour Organization (ILO), the medical rehabilitation policies of the World Health Organization (WHO), and the special education program of United Nations Educational, Scientific and Cultural Organization (UNESCO) in particular.[12] As has often been the case with internationalisms, attention to disability at the international or global level was entangled with national policies.[13] Since the late nineteenth and early twentieth centuries several Western countries had developed rehabilitation and special schooling policies to (re)integrate citizens and veterans with disabilities into their societies and colonies, aiming for a healthy, productive, and disciplined nation and/or empire.[14] In these attempts, both at the national and international level, it became increasingly common to use umbrella terms such as "handicap" and "disability" instead of more specific terms such as "blindness." However, the umbrella term "disabled persons" became more popular only from the mid-1970s, until it was changed to "persons with disabilities" in the convention.[15] Organization of self-advocates at the international level has often been based on specific categories. The first cross-disability organization run by self-advocates was founded in 1981, as we shall discuss in more detail in chapter 3.

Another way in which disability was addressed by actors at the international level, although not always explicitly, was as part of eugenic policies. When people started to see the size and health of the world's population as something to be managed, internationalists with eugenic ideas stepped forward to influence international institutions.[16] Part of their strategy to keep the world's population fit was to prevent and prohibit the birth of people with disabilities and their sexual reproduction. Because of the atrocities of the Nazis against people with (mental) disabilities, eugenic policies became more contested after the Second World War. This is why for instance an attempt of Danish diplomats in 1949 and 1950 to have "forced sterilization of people with mental deficiencies" inscribed as a protected practice in the draft UN Covenant on Civil and Political Rights was not successful.[17] Moreover, the war stimulated supporters of people with mental disabilities to start (international) communities in which people with and without disabilities lived together in order to—as Dagmar Herzog has put it—unlearn eugenics.[18] At the international level, however, as Herzog rightly observes, "of all the many rights enumerated in the Universal Declaration of Human Rights of 1948 ... identifiable attention to the needs of individuals with disabilities is not there."[19] The ILSMH broke this silence. Of course, the human rights of disabled people were mentioned by international policymakers here and there. A WHO report in 1952 for instance stated that people with physical disabilities should enjoy the same "human rights" as the "able-bodied."[20] However, human rights never became the central concept intended by the ILSMH.

In order to understand how the ILSMH framed disability as a human rights issue during the 1960s and 1970s, we must consider what was going on in the world at that time. It is not difficult to see that the 1960s was a decade in which modern ideals such as freedom, equality, and fraternity were fiercely debated once more. People with disabilities increasingly asked for the same freedom and equality as everyone else. They often wanted to get rid of fraternity as it was conceived paternalistically and demanded solidarity in the form of state provisions. Amid different movements such as feminism and Third-Worldism people with disabilities did not have the loudest voice in the 1960s—let alone people with mental disabilities—although in several countries they began to be seen as people or citizens who should not be treated separately. In some cases, alternative, avant-garde communities were founded by social innovators.[21] These initiatives have not been seen as part of the global disability movement because their founders were people without disabilities. For understanding disability human rights, however, another initiative from the 1960s was more important: normalization policy.

Influenced by the well-known anti-psychiatric movement, policymakers and scientists in the field of the care and education of people with mental disabilities started to consider how they could change the prevailing treatment of mentally disabled people in separate institutions. One of the most well-known alternatives for institutionalization was the normalization principle, developed by Bengt Nirje from Sweden and Wolf Wolfensberger from the United States in the late 1960s and early 1970s. Normalization stood for approaching people with mental disabilities as normally as possible and was originally coined by Niels Erik Bank-Mikkelsen from Denmark. Through international organizations such as the ILSMH the normalization principle became popular among professionals working with people with mental disabilities, but it was not uncontested. In 1976 for instance Sterner felt the need to write "a note on some common misconceptions about normalization and integration." He responded to "a leading parent representative" who was against normalization because it was "impossible for a retarded person to become normal." That was not, according to Sterner, the point of the normalization principle. Normalization did not mean that people with mental disabilities had no special needs but highlighted that they "usually have the same needs as normal human beings." This "simple but very important fact has been disregarded in much of the traditional treatment given to them." Sterner admitted that "we are still only beginning to put it into practice." He stated that concepts such as normalization and integration "indicate the sense of direction," wherein "each individual person must be brought as far as possible in this direction."[22]

The Danish and Swedish normalization policies sparked the interest of policymakers and scientists in the United States during the 1960s, an interest that led to an intensive transnational exchange. Bank-Mikkelsen made it into the US press headlines when he remarked that "in Denmark one would not be allowed to treat cattle like this," referring to the bad circumstances in which people with mental disabilities lived in the Sonoma State Hospital in San Francisco. Another key figure in the American-Scandinavian exchange, Karl Grunewald, was once asked by a taxi driver in San Francisco if he was "the Scandinavian that said we treat people with intellectual disabilities like cattle?"[23] Anecdotes aside, from the American-Scandinavian exchange sprang the human rights approach to people with mental disabilities.

It is hard to trace exactly how human rights became part of the transnational conversation about normalization policies. An important role was probably played by Rosemary and Gunnar Dybwad from the United States, who developed close contacts with the Scandinavian network of normalization advocates. Rosemary was a sociologist and Gunnar a lawyer, and they were both involved in the US organization of parents of children with mental disabilities.[24] Since the early 1960s Gunnar had argued for recognition of the personal legal rights of people with mental disabilities.[25] Did his legal perspective trigger others within the ILSMH to organize an international symposium on the legislative aspects of mental retardation in Stockholm in 1967? It was in line with the normalization principle to grant people with mental disabilities the same rights as other citizens. Richard Sterner at least was convinced of the importance of reflection on the individual rights and legal position of people with mental disabilities. He is considered to be one of the driving forces behind the symposium, together with members of the French organization Union Nationale des Associations de Parents d'Enfants Inadaptés (UNAPEI).[26] However, human rights hardly seem to have been on the lips of the symposium participants. Its conclusions did not use the term explicitly, but instead favored the formulation of "individual rights of the retarded person as a human being."[27] What does this mean?

In the case of the conference conclusions, it is true what political scientist Benjamin Schoenfeld wrote in 1974: "At the international level, the Stockholm Symposium adopted the general principle that retarded people have the same rights as other citizens of the same country, age, and family and working status."[28] The participants did focus in the first place on citizen rights as laid or to be laid down in national law. But they did this at the international level and referred to the humanity of the rights subjects. They could have left it at that, but the ILSMH wanted to formalize the Stockholm conclusions.[29] The ILSMH drafted a rights declaration *From Charity to Rights* to be discussed in 1968 at their international conference in Jerusalem.[30] The declaration which the ILSMH adopted in Jerusalem referred to the Universal Declaration of Human Rights, but spoke in the first article about "the same basic rights as other citizens of the same country"—a formulation that was changed to "the same rights as other human beings" in the 1971 declaration. It is unclear if the ILSMH secretariat already had a UN declaration in mind during the preparations for Jerusalem. But it is undeniable that they saw the relevance of declaring human rights at the international level in order to support the fight for equal citizen rights at the national level. In that sense, this case underlines what historians such as Samuel Moyn have argued for the use of human rights in the first decades after the Second World War. The emphasis in human rights usage was not on international protection, as was more often the case since the 1970s, but on ensuring equal rights in a national framework.

An international convention was probably not on the ILSMH's mind at that time, but in Jerusalem they clearly wanted to produce an international declaration. It was Richard Sterner, who had worked with the UN Economic and Social Council (ECOSOC), who suggested asking the United Nations to take on a disability declaration.[31] Sterner was in favor of a general disability declaration, but Jacques Gemaehling from UNAPEI preferred a declaration focused on mental disabilities. Gemaehling was friends with French Foreign Minister Maurice Schuman, who brought the proposal for a human rights declaration to the United Nations.[32] The declaration as adopted by the ECOSOC and consequently the UN General Assembly in 1971 overlapped significantly with the declaration which the ILSMH had agreed in Jerusalem in 1968. Nevertheless, some members of the ILSMH were disappointed that certain elements were changed. Sterner for instance believed that it should have been made clearer that the vast majority of people with developmental disabilities should live in ordinary residential environments, even if they were adults and could not appropriately live with parents or foster parents. He also regretted that sentences about the right "to be provided with appropriate leisure time activities" and about making special services free of charge disappeared from the UN declaration.[33] Renée Portray, secretary-general of the ILSMH, wrote to Esko Kosunen, chief of the UN Rehabilitation Unit for the Disabled, asking to no avail if "to the maximum degree of feasibility" could be left out from the article that stated that "the mentally retarded person has the same rights as other human beings."[34]

In addressing the differences between the final 1971 declaration and earlier versions, the ILSMH members did not mention that articles about implementation and monitoring were also left out. The draft declaration did state that "legal and administrative measures should be adopted to ensure protection of the rights of the mentally retarded and to provide for the necessary assistance in achieving the goals set forward in this Declaration" and an "exchange of experience and information on services for the mentally retarded at the international level is required in order to facilitate the implementation of the standards set forth in this Declaration," but these articles were dropped by the ECOSOC.[35] However, the reluctance of the United Nations to encourage implementation and monitoring of the declaration did not stop the ILSMH: They followed up the declaration with a policy instrument, called *Step by Step*, that according to Peter Mittler explained "how each of the seven articles of the Declaration could be implemented at the national level."[36] Human rights came to be used by the ILSMH and its member organizations as a concept to support national policies aimed at the normalization of people with mental disabilities.

REPRODUCTIVE RIGHTS

Can we draw a historical line from this declaration and the preceding discussions to the convention as adopted by the United Nations in 2006? Article 23 of the convention, concerning the right of people with disabilities to have a family, recalls the desire of Sterner and others to grant people with disabilities the right to marry. This convention article provides that "States Parties shall take effective and appropriate measures to eliminate discrimination against persons with disabilities in all matters relating to marriage, family, parenthood and relationships, on an equal basis with others, so as to ensure that: a) The right of all persons with disabilities who are of marriageable age to marry and to found a family on the basis of free and full consent of the intending spouses is recognized."[37] It is not hard to imagine that this "right of *all* persons with disabilities," including people with cognitive disabilities and persons with genetically transferable impairments, "to marry and to found a family" was highly contested.

That is why we cannot draw a simple line of progress from the ILSMH declaration to the CRPD. The (eugenic) tradition of prohibiting the reproduction of people with disabilities, practiced for instance by sterilizing people with intellectual disabilities, never disappeared completely and was critically addressed by self-advocates during the negotiations.[38] From a disability perspective sexual reproduction has been a sensitive topic anyway, especially because legalization of abortion and development of prenatal screening in many (Global North) countries have increasingly prevented the birth of people with disabilities. That became clear for instance in the discussions about convention Article 25, which states that "States Parties shall: a) Provide persons with disabilities with the same range, quality and standard of free or affordable health care and programmes as provided to other persons, including in the area of sexual and reproductive health and population-based public health programmes." As (conservative) critics pointed out, in some countries abortion was included in such programs.[39]

Given these developments, it would be interesting to delve further into the history of the right of all persons with disabilities to have a family and to see how this right was included (or not) in UN policies since the late 1960s. What does a history of discontinuous progress from the margins look like in this case if we cannot draw a simple line from the ILSMH initiative to the convention? In the remaining part of this chapter, I shall analyze how and why this right was discussed and formulated at key moments in the history of UN disability policies. As will become clear, the 1990s was a crucial decade in the development of this right. Recent literature about Article 23 has shown that the CRPD had a more "narrow approach to sexuality" (read: heterosexual approach) than the so-called Standard Rules from 1993.[40] This change can be explained by the influence of conservative figures during the CRPD negotiations, but—as I shall show—has to be understood also as a shift to a human rights-based approach in which the emphasis was laid more on negative than on positive freedom.

HUMAN RIGHTS BEFORE HUMAN RIGHTS

The right of people with disabilities to have a family, as already mentioned, was never included in the Declaration on the Rights of Mentally Retarded Persons in 1971. It was blocked by parents and professionals during the drafting of the ILSMH Declaration of General and Special Rights of Mentally Retarded Persons in Jerusalem in 1968.[41] A few years later the Declaration on the Rights of Disabled Persons (1975) was adopted by the UN General Assembly. This short declaration stated that disabled persons had "the same fundamental rights as their fellow-citizens of the same age, which implies first and foremost the right to enjoy a decent life, as normal and full as possible." The declaration did not explicitly deal with reproductive rights, and the family was mentioned only as follows: "Disabled persons have the right to live with their families or with foster parents."[42]

How these declarations were applied at the global level can be seen in the United Nations' observance of the International Year of Disabled Persons (IYDP) in 1981 and the International Decade of Disabled Persons (1983–1992), two initiatives which called attention to the situation of people with disabilities worldwide and sought to improve the often-disadvantaged position of people with disabilities, especially in the so-called developing countries. Since 1959 the United Nations has been dedicating years, days, and decades to particular topics in order to influence the global agenda; and following a proposal by Libya the General Assembly chose 1981 as the IYDP.[43] The central theme of the year was identified as "full participation and equality" and announced with the following formulation: "'full participation' of disabled persons in the social life and development of societies in which they live, 'equality,' meaning living conditions equal to those of other citizens in their society, and an equal share in the improvement of living conditions resulting from social and economic development."[44] National governments and international organizations were asked to initiate activities that supported the main objectives linked to this theme: giving disabled people what they needed for their full participation in society, investing in the prevention of disability, and "educating and informing the public of the rights of disabled persons to participate in and contribute to various aspects of economic, social and political life."[45] As in the case of the declaration, the right to found a family was implicitly included, but not explicitly. At the same time prevention of disabilities was one of the priorities of the year, although this seems not to have included prenatal prevention.

During the IYDP, as was often the case during international years, a World Programme of Action was drafted.⁴⁶ The so-called World Programme of Action Concerning Disabled Persons (WPA) had almost the same aim as the international year: "living conditions [of people with disabilities] equal to those of other citizens in their society." The relevant terms of action proposed in the WPA were defined as prevention, rehabilitation, and equalization of opportunities. Alongside the WPA the United Nations decided to launch a Decade of Disabled Persons covering the years 1983–1992 that "could serve as a time-frame for the implementation of the World Programme of Action."⁴⁷ In the WPA documents there were references to human rights; but human rights, let alone the right to have a family, were certainly not a central notion of the program. Prevention, on the other hand, was one of the priorities. The declarations of 1971 and 1975 were thus initially not an encouragement to elaborate further on the human rights of or international law concerning people with disabilities, but as a document that underlay social policies aimed at improving societal participation and living conditions of people with disabilities. This is no surprise since the main responsibility for UN disability policies belonged to the ECOSOC and not to the Commission on Human Rights.

Moreover, the way in which the declaration of 1975 was used reflects what historian Stefan-Ludwig Hoffmann states about human rights in the 1970s and 1980s: They were part of other visions of the future and not a utopia in themselves. The way in which the ILSMH had made human rights central to their policies approached being a human rights utopia, although the ILSMH was not focused on international protection in the way for example Amnesty International was, but on national implementation of its declaration. Different from the ILSMH, the United Nations did not make human rights central, but their equalization policies were similar to what the ILSMH wanted to achieve and lacked a more radical understanding of disability human rights as expressed by Sterner and others.

Nonetheless, during the 1980s we can also observe increasing interest in an international human rights and international law perspective on disability—although the right to have a family received no special attention. In 1984 the Commission on Human Rights recommended a "thorough study of the causal connection between serious violations of human rights and fundamental freedoms and disability as well as of the progress made to alleviate problems."[48] It took a while before this study was undertaken and published, but it was the dawn of a new approach; and during an expert meeting about the implementation of the WPA in 1987 in Stockholm the idea of a convention emerged. It was recommended that "the General Assembly convenes a special conference on the rights of persons with disabilities, with the mandate to elucidate such rights and to draft an international convention on the elimination of all forms of discrimination against disabled persons."[49] The governments of Italy and Sweden submitted proposals to the UN General Assembly, but to no avail. Ultimately in 1993, at the end of the Decade of Disabled Persons, an agreement was reached on a nonbinding instrument, the Standard Rules on Equalization of Opportunities for Persons with Disabilities, "promoting disability-sensitive policy design and evaluation, as well as technical cooperation."[50] As will become clear in the next section, we can see in hindsight the beginnings of a rights-based approach in the Standard Rules, although the social-policy approach followed during the IYDP and Decade of Disabled Persons was still prominent at the beginning of the 1990s.

FROM PLANNING POLICY TO CLAIMING RIGHTS

With the declaration of 1975 reproductive rights more or less disappeared from official UN policies concerning people with disabilities, but in the Standard Rules they were addressed again. Rule 9 was about "family life and personal integrity" and stated that national states had to "ensure that laws do not discriminate against persons with disabilities with respect to sexual relationships, marriage and parenthood." Moreover, "persons with disabilities must not be denied the opportunity to experience their sexuality, have sexual relationships and experience parenthood" and "states should promote measures to change negative attitudes towards marriage, sexuality and parenthood of persons with disabilities, especially of girls and women with disabilities, which still prevail in society."[51] The right to found a family has never been so strongly addressed in UN disability policy.[52] In Rule 9 of the Standard Rules we can observe a mix of what philosopher Isaiah Berlin has described as positive and negative freedom.

Negative freedom concerns the question: "What is the area within which the subject—a person or group of persons—is or should be left to do or be what he is able to do or be, without interference by other persons?" Meanwhile, positive freedom is involved in the answer to the question: "What, or who, is the source of control or interference that can determine someone to do, or be, this rather than that?"[53] This distinction is relevant for the reproductive rights of disabled persons, because human rights in their current meaning are often focused on negative freedom. However, according to Tom Shakespeare, that is only one side of the coin: "Restrictions on negative freedom arise when states legislate for who can get married and have children." But, he asks, "what more can states do positively to enhance the opportunities for disabled people?"[54] The promotion of "measures to change negative attitudes" by the Standard Rules could be read as a more positive incentive, but in general the emphasis in Rule 9 was on eliminating the interference of others.

The attention to sexuality in the Standard Rules seems to have been part of a global trend. It was probably AIDS and increasing awareness of the importance of the provision of information about sex during the 1980s and 1990s that stimulated concern about the sexuality of people with disabilities. This concern was further accelerated by the deinstitutionalization of people with disabilities: People with disabilities were often for the first time seen as independent citizens who could develop their own (sexual) relationships without institutional mediation. Therefore during the 1990s sexuality was addressed in the academic discipline of disability studies more extensively than before.[55] In disability activism and studies, as developed during the 1970s and 1980s, priority was given to other issues, but in the 1990s—according to Tom Shakespeare—sexuality rights were recognized as central in the struggle for emancipation.[56] Of course, the attention to sexuality was not entirely new: In one of the founding texts of the American disability movement, the book *Missing Pieces: A Chronicle of Living With a Disability* (1982), sociologist and activist Irving Kenneth Zola had addressed the topic. In his analysis of "Het Dorp" (The Village), a Dutch neighborhood designed and built in the 1960s for people with physical disabilities, he observed how sexuality was denied: Sexual counseling was "not a part of the services for residents nor were any housing provisions made for married couples."[57]

It is also no accident that Rule 9 about the family followed a rights-based approach. In 1993 a statement comparable to this rule was made during a Conference on Population Development, where participants argued for the "recognition of the needs of disabled persons concerning, inter alia, sexual and reproductive health, including family-planning services and elimination of the specific forms of discrimination that disabled people may face with regard to international migration, reproductive rights and household and family formation."[58] Attention in both population and disability policies to restrictions of negative freedom was relatively new, but reflects a broader tendency to protect the individual from the interference of others. According to Marta Schaaf a paradigm shift took place in the 1990s: "Reproductive autonomy was recast as an objective, in contrast to earlier population control or pro-natalist orientations."[59] As Matthew Connelly has shown in his book *Fatal Misconception* (2010), this shift had its roots in the 1970s, when the desire to plan other people's families was increasingly replaced by recognition of the rights of reproduction for individuals and in particular women.

The increasing attention to human rights also seems to have been part of a broader desire to view the situation of "vulnerable groups" through the lens of human rights and international law. In the case of women's rights for instance the 1990s experienced not only the rise of the ideal of reproductive autonomy, but also increasing attention to the vulnerability of women, especially as victims of physical violence. Women, as Zain Lakhani states, "have been written, essentially, into international law predominantly through their experience of harm."[60] People with disabilities were also approached in this way, as can be seen in the 1993 report *Human Rights and Disabled Persons* of the Argentine human rights lawyer Leandro Despouy, commissioned by the Human Rights Commission in 1984, in which it was stated that "persons with disabilities are going to find themselves at a legal disadvantage in relation to other vulnerable groups such as refugees, women, migrant workers ... unlike the other vulnerable groups, they do not have an international control body to provide them with particular and specific protection."[61]

Despouy's suggestions, however, were only partly followed up in the Standard Rules. As Gerard Quinn and Theresia Degener have observed, the "traditional preoccupations of prevention and rehabilitation have been relegated [in the Standard Rules] to the background in favor of the rights perspective."[62] However, we should not exaggerate this point, as the intention of the Standard Rules was not to develop new international law. After the failed attempts of Italy and Sweden in the late 1980s, realization of a convention seemed unfeasible in the short term. The Standard Rules stated that "the purpose of the Rules is to ensure that girls, boys, women and men with disabilities, as members of their societies, may exercise the same rights and obligations as others," but also that "existing human rights documents seemed to guarantee persons with disabilities the same rights as other persons."[63] During the negotiations the representative of the United States had explicitly stated that the "draft Rules should also be amended to eliminate the suggestion that they were likely to become customary international law."[64] Although some self-advocates continued to strive for a convention, as will be discussed later, the United Nations aimed at improving societal participation and living conditions of people with disabilities mainly by means of social policy and not by making international law.

As Rule 9 showed, however, the human rights approach was seen as relevant for family life and personal integrity. In his report Despouy had already noted that the family rights of disabled persons were violated in some countries by preventing people with disabilities from marrying for eugenic reasons, sometimes with compulsory sterilization practices. Such human rights violations attracted more attention during the 1990s, as can be seen from the pivotal study by the disability-human rights experts Quinn and Degener, *Human Rights and Disability* (2002). They noted that "many restrictions are still placed on family and privacy rights for people with disabilities, especially those in institutions, throughout the world. Their right to adopt children on an equal footing with others is a virtually unrecognized issue on which little has been written."[65] To some extent existing international law provided protection, "but a clear statement that disability per se should never be regarded as a legitimate ground for sterilization and restrictions on marriage would have been even more helpful."[66] With this and other arguments the authors made a plea for a specific disability convention, which became a reality a couple of years after their investigation.

NEGOTIATING THE CONVENTION

The fact that Mexico was successful in 2001 in proposing to the UN General Assembly the drafting of an international convention can be explained partly by its framing "in light of the Millennium Development Goals" (see figure 1.1). Disabled people were not identified as a target group for action and "only a disability-specific convention would ensure that people with disabilities would not be left behind in the fight against global poverty."[67] When we compare Mexico's success with the failed attempts in the late 1980s, we must also search for an explanation in the 1990s: What changed in this decade? In addition to the trends mentioned in the previous section, I should say that three developments contributed to making the UN soil more fertile for a convention than it had been in the late 1980s. First, the disability movement at the local and global levels increasingly framed its struggle for emancipation in terms of human rights, and different groups worked together more than before.[68] Second, several countries included disability in their anti-discrimination law and came to see disability as an equal rights issue.[69] Third, the Standard Rules and their monitoring produced data about the situation of disabled persons worldwide and a stronger institutionalization of the disability movement at the UN level.[70] Despite these developments in the 1990s the adoption of a human rights convention on disability in the early 2000s was far from certain, as I shall explain in the coming chapters.

FIGURE 1.1 Gilberto Rincón Gallardo, President of the National Council to Prevent Discrimination in Mexico, addresses the signing ceremony of the United Nations Convention on the Rights of Persons with Disabilities at UN Headquarters in New York City in 2007. (UN Photo/Paulo Filgueiras)

With the adoption of the CRPD in 2006 human rights became the leading principle for the United Nations' disability policy. Unlike other international human rights law the convention explicitly deals with the way in which rights must be implemented and guaranteed, including setting out the duties of member states toward people with disabilities. Moreover, the convention is sensitive to "issues of structural power and oppression."[71] If we focus on Article 23, we can see that it is in line with Rule 9—with the difference that the CRPD articles are binding, and the Standard Rules were not. However, as Schaaf has pointed out, the draft text for the convention article was closer to Rule 9. The proposed text read:

> States should promote the full participation of persons with disabilities in family life. They should promote their rights to personal integrity and ensure that laws do not discriminate against persons

with disabilities with respect to sexual relationships, marriage and parenthood.... Persons with disabilities must not be denied the opportunity to experience their sexuality, have sexual relationships and experience parenthood.... States should promote measures to change negative attitudes towards marriage, sexuality and parenthood of persons with disabilities, especially of girls and women with disabilities, which still prevail in society.

On account of opposition from the Roman Catholic Church and a couple of countries and nongovernmental organizations (NGOs) during the negotiations, sexuality was deleted, because this word with its "numerous cultural concerns" did not appear in any other convention. Moreover, the article text—according to this coalition—needed to avoid any mention of sexual relationships and parenthood out of the context of marriage because that "would mean that the CRPD went into 'uncharted and controversial directions.'"[72]

With the CRPD the right of people with disabilities to have a family became internationally protected, but the negotiations show that this right was less clear for non-heterosexual and unmarried people—especially compared with the nonbinding Standard Rules of 1993. Moreover, Felipe Jaramillo Ruiz has argued, based on his analysis of the so-called concluding observations of the Committee on the Rights of Persons with Disabilities, that the committee "has sustained a protective, medical, and gender binary model to address the sexual and reproductive rights of persons with disabilities."[73] These critical evaluations of the right to have a family in the CRPD often focus on the conservative influence in the drafting process. Equally important and not attributable to conservative influences like the Catholic Church and its allies at the global level is the difference between the CRPD and the draft text and Standard Rules regarding negative and positive freedom. The CRPD focused on restrictions on negative freedom, but by using the term "promote" the Standard Rules challenged states to contribute in a positive way to the reproductive and sexual rights of people with disabilities. Again, we can observe what Hoffmann has written about human rights since the 1990s, namely that the concept is increasingly used in a presentist way as a "bare minimum" and not as (part of) a utopia. With the CRPD individuals with disabilities could protest the interference of others (claiming their "bare minimum"), but does the convention really foresee societal structures that guarantee a more inclusive society?

The international history of the right of people with disabilities to have a family shows that there were attempts in the run-up to the Declaration on the Rights of Mentally Retarded Persons in the early 1970s to include this right. However, at the ILSMH conference in Jerusalem in 1968 this attempt had already been blocked. During the 1970s and 1980s the United Nations gave priority to advancing the participation of people with disabilities in their respective societies, without focusing on reproductive rights. Human rights underlay this policy, but international human rights law was not something the United Nations aimed to promote. This changed somewhat during the 1990s, when disability was increasingly approached from a (human) rights perspective. The United Nations' disability policy did reflect a broader trend here: Where human rights before the 1990s were often part of larger utopian visions, during the 1990s the concept came to the fore in different policy areas and was often more oriented to the present and the past than the future. In the case of the right to have a family, this means that in the beginning of the 1990s we can observe in the UN Standard Rules (1993) a serious attempt to approach reproductive rights in a positive way and to challenge societies to change their attitudes. However, with the emergence of a new paradigm of human rights in the 1990s emphasis was placed increasingly on eliminating interference by others. During negotiation of the CRPD it was also easier to agree on negative freedom. Given the violence directed at people with disabilities, it is a great gain that their reproductive rights are now part of international law. At the same time, we can ask whether the CRPD is sufficient to ensure that people with disabilities not only have the right, but also the opportunity and means to have a family. Does the CRPD really provide tools to challenge societal attitudes and structures? In light of the historical trajectories presented in this chapter we can ask whether we do not need a more future-oriented utopia to change the present. Before I return to this question in the Epilogue, I shall investigate in the following chapters if other rights have followed a trajectory comparable to reproductive rights or if they have other histories and open other possibilities for the future.[74]

2

BELGRADE 1975

"Equality . . . Not Materialized in Full"

*Ladies and gentlemen, comrades, although in Yugoslavia
women and men are equal, this means that equality of
blind men and blind women exists, still formal legal
equality of men and women, at least among the blind,
is not materialized in full.*

In his speech to the first international conference of blind women in 1975 Milan Bobinski, president of the Union of the Blind in Yugoslavia, put his finger on an urgent issue.[1] Even if legal equality had been formally realized, this did not mean that equality had been achieved. This was as true for equality between men and women as it was for people with and without disabilities. In Bobinski's opinion, colored by the fact that he was speaking on behalf of a socialist and nonaligned country in the context of the Cold War, the solution was an approach that addressed different dimensions, including material or socioeconomic equality. This perspective was not uncommon at the time. It reflected the attempt of the nonaligned movement to realize a world more equal in the socioeconomic sense: a "worldwide welfare state" as one scholar has put it.[2] However, due to the increasing popularity of neoliberal economic policies and the rise of a human rights perspective which focused less on socioeconomic issues the ideal of material equality would lose its appeal beyond the 1970s. In the case of the 1975 conference, we can also observe that its legacy was hardly influenced by Bobinski's perspective. The limited influence of this approach to global disability policies cannot be explained by increasing popularity of a narrow human rights perspective, but by the influence of alternative perspectives. Understanding this will help to add new insights to the existing literature on human rights and socioeconomic (in)equality.

REHABILITATION AND THE COLD WAR

At first sight there seems to have been a breakthrough of human rights in global disability policies when in 1975 the United Nations adopted the Declaration on the Rights of Disabled Persons. But in fact, nothing could be further from the truth. The declaration was never fully embraced by people with disabilities because their involvement in the creation of the 1975 document was limited.[3] In chapter 1 we saw that in the 1960s and 1970s global policies concerning people with cognitive disabilities were not determined by those people themselves. The situation of people with physical and sensory disabilities at that time was slightly different. They had in some cases already founded international organizations, such as the World Federation of the Deaf, which were also recognized by international institutions such as the United Nations. Nevertheless, the most dominant nongovernmental organizations (NGOs) in global disability policies were run by people without disabilities, and the diplomatic influence of people with disabilities was still limited. However, the lack of representation of self-advocates is not the main reason for denying the importance of the declaration and the 1970s as a breakthrough decade for human rights. Global disability policies in the 1970s were determined by another concept: rehabilitation.

In the first decades after the Second World War "rehabilitation" became the keyword for global policies concerning physical disabilities.[4] Rehabilitation was used by policymakers as an umbrella term for a set of different practices which aimed to train people with disabilities in such a way that they could participate in society.[5] During the 1970s we can see growing interest among international actors in the legal aspects of disability policy, most notably by Rehabilitation International (RI: before 1972 the International Society for the Rehabilitation of the Disabled). This wider international interest in disability law was probably related to the 1971 declaration lobby as discussed in chapter 1. At the same time growing legal interest among international rehabilitation policymakers also has to be considered as a development in itself. It shows how human rights remained a marginal perspective in global disability policies and how different perspectives on (in)equality in the Cold War context were visible in the development of global disability policies.

In hindsight we can see that a worldview in favor of material equality, as was articulated by people such as Bobinski, would be heard less and less in global disability policies beyond the 1970s.[6] Historian Gildas Brégain has argued that global disability policies since the Second World War had already been generally in favor of "the North Atlantic project of rehabilitation" characterized by a "liberal legality" with an individualized concept of rights, a primacy of civil and political rights over economic rights, and standards that "exempted large private companies from their legal responsibility for organizing work based on solidarity." However, he also shows that this liberal legality did not remain uncontested. Policymakers at the global level in particular during the 1970s did discuss different legal approaches to disability.[7] In this context RI presented itself as standing outside the Cold War division and as "one of the very few western-based non-governmental organizations, which continued to maintain an effective East-West dialogue." The organization took, according to anthropologist Nora Groce, "an uncompromising stance against making rehabilitation a political issue" and "argued again and again" that rehabilitation was a "humanitarian endeavor and knew no political or ideological boundaries"—although she also points to ways in which rehabilitation projects were framed as US "foreign policy through the dramatization of the high values we in a democracy place upon human dignity and the worth of the individual."[8] Groce's and Brégain's observations indicate that rehabilitation did for disability policies what human rights did for other policy domains: It was a concept that could be seen as politically neutral and therefore relevant for the First, Second, and Third Worlds. A closer look at the 1970s will also show that rehabilitation was not yet the "North Atlantic project" it would become in the future.

Under the leadership of Norman Acton, who was elected secretary-general of RI in 1967 after he had worked for the United Nations International Children's Emergency Fund (UNICEF), the organization not only widened its scope to the so-called developing world, but tried also to make disability issues part of "broader social and economic discussions beyond the medical realm."[9] Part of this widening focus was increasing interest in legislation, stimulated by specific events such as the 1971 declaration and the passing of the Chronically Sick and Disabled Act in the United Kingdom in the same year. RI organized, together with Teresa Serra, an Italian mother of a child with cerebral palsy, an international conference on disability legislation in 1971 in Rome.[10] The conference agreed that the state had the main responsibility for rehabilitation services and stated that "this responsibility should be defined in the legislation of the nation." However, legislation alone was "not a sufficient means of solving the problems of the disabled." The conference emphasized the importance of the broad "application of rehabilitation principles and practices." Legislation had to support this application and "must be based on respect for the personality and human rights of the individual."[11] The conclusions of the conference made clear that introducing human rights law was not on the agenda. The main message was that the situation of people with disabilities had to be improved by rehabilitation policies supported by national legislation. Human rights were mentioned as something to be respected, but not as something to be (internationally) protected. The conference saw rights in a national framework: "Legislation should form an integral part of the general legislation protecting the rights of all citizens."[12]

Although the conclusions of the conference hardly mentioned human rights and international law, they did mention social security. The conference recommended that "every country should enact legislation to protect the rights of all disabled persons and to assure the provision of the educational, medical, social, vocational and other services needed" and legislation should include "provision of social security."[13] Although the conference did not strongly underline the importance of socioeconomic rights, it did not favor civil and political rights to the detriment of social security. What does this mean for the "liberal legality" that Brégain sees at work in the 1970s?

In his book *Pour une histoire du handicap au XXe siècle* Brégain focuses for the 1970s on the genesis of the UN declaration in 1971 and the UN Declaration on the Rights of Disabled Persons in 1975. The latter was inspired by the former: The Belgian National Collective Action for the Handicapped used the 1971 declaration to draft a new text that declared the rights of *all* people with disabilities and submitted a draft declaration to the United Nations via Belgian diplomatic channels.[14] During the negotiations a proposal of the Icelandic representative, Mr. Olafsson, to include a paragraph on the civil and political rights of persons with disabilities was successful. Socioeconomic rights did not enjoy the same general approval. A proposal of the representative of the German Democratic Republic, Mr. Richter, to mention the unconditional right to work was not included in the declaration text. The Soviet delegation was disappointed that the exercise of cultural, social, and economic rights on an equal basis with other people was not mentioned.[15] By pointing to the contributions of the Eastern bloc Brégain shows that a more radical approach to socioeconomic rights, including for instance the right to strike, was unsuccessful. However, the declaration did mention these rights in a more moderate form and did recognize, in line with the conclusions of the RI conference in Rome, "the right to economic and social security and to a decent level of living." Despite the dominance of "liberal liberty," socioeconomic rights were nevertheless acknowledged at the global level. Moreover, they were stimulated at the local or national level, as would become clear from the so-called Manila Statement.

In January 1978 RI again organized an international conference on "legislation concerning the disabled," this time in Manila because Charlotte Floro, president of the Philippine Foundation for the Rehabilitation of the Disabled, was the "prime mover."[16] This gathering resulted in the Manila Statement. The main aim of this statement was to stimulate disability law in developing countries: "Every developing country should legislate before 1981 (the International Year for Disabled Persons) to ensure the right of access to and the provision of educational, medical, social and vocational services needed to enable all disabled persons to enjoy their rights and develop their full potentials."[17] Here we can clearly see a tendency to use global disability policies and international exchange in order to transfer the welfare state model from the Global North to the Global South. This transfer was one of the main goals of the conference, with paper titles such as "The French Experience of Rehabilitation and Its Lessons for Developing Countries." The Manila Statement went beyond interventions from "the North Atlantic project of rehabilitation" into the Global South because the statement aimed to encourage structural improvement by changing national disability laws. Rights were thus mainly understood in a national framework and not as international human rights as we know them today.[18] This was also the case during the conference in 1971 and in the global policies concerning people with cognitive disabilities as discussed in chapter 1. The main difference between the conferences in 1971 and 1978 was the emphasis of the latter on improving the situation of people with disabilities in the developing world.

When disability policymakers at the global level used human rights language, they used it to support social and development policies that were mainly directed toward people with disabilities in the Global South. This did not go unnoticed by developing countries in the United Nations, and it was the delegate from Libya, Mansur R. Kikhia, who proposed an international year dedicated to disability. Kikhia had worked with organizations of blind people in his country. After hearing Norman Acton speaking about global disability policies during a UN Economic and Social Council (ECOSOC) meeting on disability in the mid-1970s, Kikhia invited Acton for lunch to discuss the idea of an international year. Acton was positive and, as he said later, "there followed a series of luncheons where we worked out the details of a resolution for him to present to the 1976 session of the General Assembly. It was adopted with modifications, proclaiming 1981 the year."[19] Because Kikhia later became a human rights advocate and was probably killed for that reason, it might be natural to think that the international year was from the beginning about human rights. However, I have not found evidence for this in the UN archives.

DISABILITY, WOMEN'S RIGHTS, AND THE GLOBAL SOUTH

The turn to the "developing world" was partly a turn of the "developed world" but cannot be understood without taking into account the increasing initiatives of actors from the Global South.[20] Decolonization after the Second World War not only went along with increased activity by new actors in the international sphere, but also with increased activity by self-advocacy organizations in the Global South—although scholarly awareness of this is still limited. Self-advocacy in the Global South emerged regularly from exchanges with actors from the Global North, but it often took different forms. This is particularly clear in the story of Fatima Shah (1914–2002), who was one of the organizers of the international conference of blind women in 1975.

Shah was born in Bhera and lived in Pakistan from 1947. She was raised in a highly educated family and worked as a physician until she became blind in the 1950s. She then did social work. In 1949 she was one of the founding members of the All Pakistan Women's Association, and in 1960 she founded the Pakistan Association of the Blind (PAB). The founding of the latter was stimulated by a meeting between Shah and Isabella Grant, a blind American woman who visited Pakistan during a tour to several countries in Africa and Latin America in the late 1950s. Grant challenged her to "form an association of the blind in this country [Pakistan] which will work on the basis of self-help rather than accept handouts. From such a platform, you can work towards your own welfare and progress without having to depend on charity. Such an organization already exists in the States and is doing marvelous work."[21] Grant was making her world tour because of dissatisfaction within the World

Council for the Welfare of the Blind (WCWB) about the representation of blind people from the Global South: "The blind in many developing countries were being represented in the meetings and conferences of the WCWB by sighted people who worked in the national agencies for the blind in the countries concerned."[22] According to Shah, PAB was the first organization of the blind in the Global South.

The national self-advocacy organized by Shah was thus from the beginning informed by transnational exchange. Shah and other self-advocates from the Global South soon started to play an important role at the international level. When the WCWB failed to adopt a resolution "requiring fifty per cent of all national delegations to WCWB meetings to consist of blind representatives," a new international organization based on the principle of self-help was founded by representatives of seven countries: the United States, Guatemala, Sri Lanka, Hong Kong, Malaysia, India, and Pakistan. Shah became second vice president of this organization, the International Federation of the Blind (IFB), together with Jacobus Tenbroek (United States) as president, Rienzi Aliguana (Sri Lanka) as first vice president, and Isabella Grant as third vice president.[23]

Within the IFB and the WCWB, in which Shah remained involved, we can see attention to legislation concerning disabled people running parallel to the interest of RI in this issue. Shah and others studied and exchanged information about legislation in several countries and used this for their national self-advocacy.[24] Moreover, Shah contributed to reflection on the intersection of disability and women rights. In 1975, the International Year of Women, the IFB and WCWB cooperated to organize the already mentioned international conference on the situation of blind women. This interest in women's issues was, according to Gildas Brégain, probably linked to the presence of women in the governing bodies of the IFB (Fatima Shah) and WCWB (Dorina de Gouvea Nowill).[25] How was this conference, that took place in a nonaligned country and was partly directed by actors from the Global South, informed by the different and often conflicting perspectives on equality at that time?

The proceedings of the conference make it clear that human rights language was rarely used. The 1975 declaration was not mentioned, probably because it was not yet known. The introduction to the proceedings mentioned the unequal position of women worldwide and stated that "it is not difficult to conclude what is the position of blind women, not to mention the social position of women in certain parts of the world where they have yet to win a place in the sun, to win the right to live and [to] some human warmth, the basic human right." However, improvement in the social position of blind women was not in the first place framed as a legal or human rights issue. The conference participants stressed the importance of dealing with "questions related to general education, professional training, employment and family life."[26]

Nevertheless, during the conference (human) rights were mentioned occasionally. In her opening address Zora Tomič, president of the federal committee for health and social welfare in Yugoslavia, stated that "in the contemporary world the question of the position of women is no longer presented as a question of the legal acknowledgement of her equality, because in a large number of countries legal obstacles have, in general, been surmounted."[27] Tomič, positioning herself as speaking from the point of view of "self-managing non-aligned Yugoslavia," pointed to "the social causes because of which the political, economic and social rights of women, including blind women, develop so slowly, if at all." According to her these causes "are linked to the position of each individual in the socio-economic and political system of a country, and are also conditioned by international and political relations."[28] From her point of view "the struggle for social progress, for human rights, for peace in the world—a part of which is the equality of women—are inseparably connected."[29] Tomič put disability and human rights in perspective by pointing out the importance of political change. How was this perceived by other participants?

Fatima Shah used her words of welcome to express her hope that "from this platform a collective call will go out to the conscience of the world to tell it the time has come for blind women to achieve the basic human rights which have been denied to them for centuries."[30] She was thinking of women in the developing world and, as she further explained in her paper, among them blind women in rural areas in particular. Shah did not expect the situation to improve by means of new legislation, but by social policy interventions.³¹ Social policy was based on and served human rights. This approach was close to that followed by organizations such as RI and was more popular at the conference than Tomič's political approach. The resolution formulated by the conference participants framed the "special needs of separate groups including the blind and visually handicapped" that had to be integrated in women's rights "appreciating the fact that blind women cannot exercise their rights as human beings without adequate provision for education, rehabilitation, employment and action to remove obstacles to their integration with Society."³² Although this conference was innovative in its intersectional approach, the conference and resolution reflected an approach to disability that was at that time common in global policies and was still focused on rehabilitation. With this approach Shah and others seemed to avoid "liberal legality" on the one hand and a socialist perspective as presented by Tomič on the other.

An issue that arose during the conference that would increasingly concern self-advocates at the global level, as will be discussed in chapter 3 in more detail, was equal representation. During the conference Shah noted "with dismay that the whole of Asia was represented by no more than four women, an indication of how far behind the rest of the world our continent was." In the years after the conference Shah was committed to changing this situation by stimulating projects in favor of the leadership skills of disabled women in the Global South.³³ During the International Year of Disabled Persons (IYDP) she was involved in three seminars: one for Asian women in Malaysia, a second for African women in Ethiopia, and a third in Latin America.³⁴ She also visited the Disabled Peoples' International (DPI) conference in Singapore, which will be discussed in the next chapter, and became a member of the board of DPI, representing Southeast Asia. Collaboration with people with disabilities other than blindness within DPI was new to her: A challenge because "no organization existed in the Third World from which one could learn."³⁵ Inspired by global collaboration and convinced by the shared interest "to enforce the adoption of a national legislation that would protect our basic economic and social rights" and the wish "to be treated like first class citizens," Shah started a cross-disability organization in her own country: the Disabled Peoples' Federation of Pakistan.[36]

WORLD PROGRAMME OF ACTION CONCERNING DISABLED PERSONS

Although rehabilitation can be understood as a means to render people with disabilities equal to other citizens in their ability to function in society, the concept of equality or equal rights does not appear to have been the central concept in global disability policies during the 1970s, either in terms of material equality or in terms of human rights.[37] This is not what the "official" UN narrative of their disability policies tells us. That narrative echoes almost exactly the shift that came to dominate the Anglo-American disability movement from the 1970s, namely from welfare toward anti-discrimination and human rights.[38] Indeed the ample literature on UN disability policies before the 1970s shows two things: 1) that disability was hardly ever explicitly mentioned in the fundamental human rights documents; and 2) that the United Nations were involved in (development) programs focusing on disability prevention and rehabilitation.[39] But did this change after the 1970s? In the remaining part of this chapter I shall answer this question by analyzing how human rights and socioeconomic equality were addressed at important moments in the making of global disability policies.

If we start with the IYDP in 1981, we encounter an approach to disability that echoes that of the UN Declaration on the Rights of Disabled Persons in 1975. On the one hand this declaration emphasized the equality of people with disabilities, but on the other hand its underlying approach to disability was that of the medical model.[40] It focused on the social services that would ensure the right "to enjoy a decent life, as normal and full as possible."[41] The declaration framed disability as primarily a welfare issue rather than a human rights issue. That is why the Centre for Social Development and Humanitarian Affairs, part of the ECOSOC, took responsibility for organizing the year.[42]

The theme of the IYDP, "full participation and equality," reflected the shift in the self-understanding of Anglo-American disability groups from a focus on welfare and rehabilitation to participation and equality. Initial preparations for the IYDP became contested, and because of vigorous protests the concept of equality was incorporated in the documents. Moreover, tellingly, "year for" in the title was replaced with "year of."[43] The significance of this seemingly minor change should not be underestimated: People with disabilities should no longer be a passive object of UN policies. During the IYDP disability activists in different countries organized their own activities and protested against the official celebrations because precisely the issues they found to be important were insufficiently addressed by politicians and policymakers.[44] The year 1981 also experienced a "revolutionary" development: At a meeting in Singapore disabled representatives from across the globe founded the first international cross-disability organization, the already-mentioned DPI. The aim of this brand-new organization was "to become the voice of disabled people," and it asserted "that disabled people should be integrated into society and participate with the same rights as everyone else."[45] However, this countermovement was only partly effective at the UN level. Although the UN Centre for Social Development and Humanitarian Affairs used the words "participation" and "equality," the emphasis remained on prevention and on the ways disabled people could be supported in their participation in society, including rehabilitation. The question as to how society (and law) could be changed (structurally) in such a way that disabled people became equal citizens remained largely absent from the UN agenda. The IYDP thus stimulated, as an unintended consequence, disability activism and alternative approaches to disability, but this did not immediately result in a shift at the global level or in the perception of international organizations.

This becomes clear when looking at how the case of people with disabilities was addressed in the so-called World Programme of Action Concerning Disabled Persons (WPA), developed during the IYDP and later linked to the proclamation that declared the period from 1983 to 1992 as the UN Decade of Disabled Persons. The WPA was described by the member of DPI Henry Enns from Canada as "a declaration of emancipation." According to him, DPI was "largely successful in having its views incorporated into the WPA," particularly in recognition of people with disabilities as "citizens with rights" and viewing organizations of people with disabilities as "the voice of disabled people." Enns argued that the first draft from 1980 was still medical-model oriented, but that the final version from 1982 affirmed that "disabled people are first and foremost citizens with rights, and second, clients of social services."[46] In the documents of the Dutch committee responsible for the national observances of the IYDP in 1981 as well as the international negotiations it was mentioned that the draft version of the WPA was criticized by countries such as Canada and Sweden because it followed excessively the "traditional line of helping the disabled" instead of "creating conditions which ensure that people with disabilities integrate in society." Canada ensured that the following paragraph on human rights was added to the plan:

> Full participation in the basic units of society—family, social groups, and community—is the essence of human experience. The right to equality of opportunity for such participation is set forth in the Universal Declaration of Human Rights and should apply to all people, including those with disabilities. In reality, however, disabled people are often denied the opportunities of full participation in the activities of the socio-cultural system of which they are a part. This deprivation comes about through physical and social barriers that have evolved from ignorance, indifference, and fear.[47]

In all likelihood the integration of such statements was not automatic but was fought for vigorously. Such amendments opened a new societal perspective on disability. However, the question arises as to whether they also justify framing the WPA as "a declaration of emancipation" and a shift toward a new approach.

A closer look at the WPA shows that the general tendency was the same as the broader aim of the IYDP: "Living conditions equal to those of other citizens in their society." The relevant terms of action proposed in the WPA were defined as prevention, rehabilitation, and equalization of opportunities. It is clear from the documents that disability was first and foremost considered a development issue, something that often seems to be overlooked in the literature. Already during the IYDP national committees in the Global North, as in the Dutch and Scandinavian cases,[48] decided to spend money and time on the Third World. The prevailing view was that the more developed countries had already secured "various social rights of disabled persons."[49] On December 7, 1981 Princess Juliana, the former queen of the Netherlands, spoke to the UN General Assembly on the occasion of the official closing of the IYDP and underlined the moral obligation of welfare states to do their utmost to support other countries in their efforts to improve the often bad situations of people with disabilities.[50] The WPA, therefore, gave priority to developing nations since they "have a bigger share of disability problems relative to the developed nations because of malnutrition and other poverty-related diseases, poor sanitation and lack of efficient communications systems."[51]

It would be a misunderstanding if we interpreted this emphasis on development merely as a paternalistic attempt by the Global North to contribute to the development of the Global South. The WPA resonates with the ideal of global equality put forward by representatives of the Global South in the 1970s: Problems of people with disabilities were viewed as "closely connected with overall development to a large extent on the creation of adequate international conditions for the faster socio-economic development of these countries. Accordingly, the establishment of the new international economic order is of direct relevance to the implementation of the objectives of the year."[52]

The reference to the New International Economic Order (NIEO, 1974) shows that disability in the WPA was framed in a broader vision of equality between countries and within societies. This framing does not, however, mean that disability became systematically included and mainstreamed in UN policies other than in the disability policies of the Centre for Social Development and Humanitarian Affairs. That would occur only around the year 2000.[53] Moreover, neither socioeconomic equality nor socioeconomic rights of people with disabilities were central aims of the WPA. Instead, the assumption was that people with disabilities should experience equal advantage from their societies' development.[54]

The overarching aim of the United Nations at that time—and the ECOSOC in particular—was therefore for structural change, although not focused on disability alone. This scenario was thus significantly different from the (more restricted) notion of "social change" which representatives of the Anglo-American model advocated. Moreover, organizations such as the World Health Organization (WHO) for which the medical model was still relevant were more influential at the UN level than were activist organizations such as DPI. It was for these reasons that rehabilitation and prevention could remain important points in the WPA and would continue to be a cornerstone of UN disability policies for much longer.

Nevertheless, we can observe another perspective on disability in the WPA under the heading of "equalization" and a focus on anti-discrimination law: "Some countries have taken important steps to eliminate or reduce barriers to full participation. Legislation has in many cases been enacted to guarantee to disabled people the rights to and opportunities for schooling, employment, and access to community facilities, to remove cultural and physical barriers and to proscribe discrimination against disabled persons."[55]

Overall, however, the emphasis was not on human rights and anti-discrimination. Inequality of disabled people for the purposes of the United Nations meant mainly inequality in living conditions and participation in society, which could be improved by services. The concept of equal rights played a role, but no real joint effort was undertaken to challenge member states to change their legislation or to develop new international legislation.

STANDARD RULES ON THE EQUALIZATION OF OPPORTUNITIES FOR PERSONS WITH DISABILITIES

Another key moment in the "shift-narrative" from welfare to anti-discrimination and human rights is the formulation of the Standard Rules on the Equalization of Opportunities for Persons with Disabilities in 1993. Before taking a closer look at these rules, I shall briefly discuss how disability rights were addressed during the UN Decade of Disabled Persons (1983–1992). One can observe a human rights approach to disability growing at the United Nations during this decade. Next to a broader reference to human rights as underlying principles of disability policies, human rights came to be used as an (international) yardstick for the maltreatment of people with disabilities.[56] Already in 1978 a WHO staff member, Einar Hollander, had tried to convince the UN Commission on Human Rights that a special initiative was needed to address the maltreatment of people with disabilities and children in particular, but it would take a long time before this was picked up.[57] Only in 1984 did the Commission on Human Rights recommend to undertake a "thorough study of the causal connection between serious violations of human rights and fundamental freedoms and disability as well as of the progress made to alleviate problems." It took another couple of years before this study was carried out.[58]

The idea of a human rights convention on disability was, as mentioned in chapter 1, discussed officially for the first time in 1987 in Stockholm during a Global Meeting of Experts about the implementation of the WPA. On this occasion the relevant documents stated, far more explicitly than the WPA documents, that "the basis of this guiding philosophy must be the recognition of the human rights of disabled persons, first as full citizens of their countries with the same rights as those of other citizens, and only secondary as users of social and other services."[59] This did not mean that social services were not deemed important: "Social security systems providing services and support for disabled people and their families should be extended to allow disabled people to achieve their full potential in society."[60] The experts, among whom people with disabilities were relatively well represented, recommended the drafting of an "international convention on the elimination of all forms of discrimination against disabled persons."[61]

The report initiated by the UN Commission on Human Rights and published in 1993 did not overcome the reluctance of the United Nations toward the drafting of a convention. In his report *Human Rights and Disabled Persons* Special Rapporteur of the Sub-Commission on

Prevention of Discrimination and Protection of Minorities Leandro Despouy observed that specific disability rights "do not appear in any formal listing but are scattered throughout a number of legal instruments, or have been recognized by the courts. In fact, what might be termed the specific rights of disabled persons are only the material and legal expression of the minimum contribution that the community or the State should make towards ensuring that such persons can enjoy on an equal basis all the human rights enjoyed by individuals in general."[62]

Despite all that was undertaken during the Decade of Disabled Persons, "persons with disabilities are going to find themselves at a legal disadvantage in relation to other vulnerable groups such as refugees, women, migrant workers" and "unlike the other vulnerable groups, they do not have an international control body to provide them with particular and specific protection." Therefore, Despouy stated that "the establishment of an international body or mechanism to supervise respect for the human rights of disabled persons is one of the most cherished aims of the non-governmental organizations."[63] Despouy's report had a more narrow focus on human rights as a yardstick for the maltreatment of people with disabilities compared with the recommendation to draft a convention put forward by the experts in 1987. This did not immediately change the United Nations' disability policies under the ECOSOC, but the focus on human rights as a yardstick for maltreatment did become significant when the idea of a convention was discussed in the early 2000s.

These developments show an increasingly human rights-based approach during the decade. At the same time, they also reveal that the meaning of the concept was contested and that it was only one of several approaches that influenced the evolution of UN disability policies in that period. Prevention, rehabilitation, and development remained influential concepts, and "with deep concern" a document noted that "many developing countries are facing enormous difficulties in dealing with increasing numbers of disabled citizens."[64]

That a human rights approach to disability had not been universally accepted by the end of the international decade is also shown by the Standard Rules, the nonbinding instrument on which the UN General

Assembly ultimately reached agreement and which was intended to promote "disability-sensitive policy design and evaluation, as well as technical cooperation."[65] In hindsight the Standard Rules were an important step toward what in 2006 became the UN Convention on the Rights of Persons with Disabilities (CRPD). In the Standard Rules, as legal scholars Quinn and Degener have stated, the "traditional preoccupations of prevention and rehabilitation have been relegated to the background in favor of the rights perspective."[66] However, if we take a closer look at the Standard Rules, we may question if this really was the case.

The Standard Rules document does state rather obviously that their purpose was "to ensure that girls, boys, women and men with disabilities, as members of their societies, may exercise the same rights and obligations as others" and also that "existing human rights documents seemed to guarantee persons with disabilities the same rights as other persons."[67] With this last phrase the idea of a convention was deemed superfluous, and was ultimately rejected by the United Nations in 1993. Moreover, rights were framed as needs: "The principle of equal rights implies that the needs of each and every individual are of equal importance."[68]

The Standard Rules were about "equalization of opportunities," and in that sense they built upon earlier policies that "emphasized the right of persons with disabilities to the same opportunities as other citizens and to an equal share in the improvement in living conditions resulting from economic and social development."[69] Furthermore, the situation of people with disabilities in developing countries was considered as urgent as before, and prevention and rehabilitation remained presented as "fundamental concepts in disability policy."[70] In contrast to suggestions in the current literature, there was thus a significant degree of continuity with earlier policies within the Standard Rules. Human rights appeared to be interpreted in terms of needs and opportunities rather than in a legal sense of (status) equality, which is the dominant approach in the CRPD and means that "no one ought to be treated differently because of the kind of person they are."[71]

We can observe a certain degree of discontinuity on other issues. The Standard Rules for example covered more aspects of life than the WPA.

They also more strongly underlined the importance of the involvement of people with disabilities themselves. In addition, the social model of disability was better integrated in the Standard Rules than in earlier UN documents. This manifests in the section on terminology, which explains the need to recognize "the necessity of addressing both the individual needs (such as rehabilitation and technical aids) and the shortcomings of the society (various obstacles for participation)."[72] Owing to the prevalence of the social model in previous years, an issue such as accessibility received more attention than ever before. In comparison with the WPA, socioeconomic equality was addressed more extensively in the Standard Rules. Rule 7 for example was concerned with the (human) right of employment, while Rule 8 informed states that they were "responsible for the provision of social security and income maintenance for persons with disabilities."[73] An important difference was that there were no longer any references to the NIEO or to an alternative global vision of social justice.

The Standard Rules seem therefore to have been part of a broader shift in the United Nations and other international institutions away from a policy aimed at changing global inequality structures. The United Nations has had difficulties since the 1990s, according to Stefan-Ludwig Hoffmann, with responding to the increasing global discrepancy between rich and poor. Hoffmann reveals a major change in perspective: "Visual representations of the 'Third World' have shifted from developing nations to suffering individuals, victims of natural or manmade disasters without political agency in the international arena."[74] This statement does not hold entirely true for disability policies, because self-advocates became increasingly involved in UN policies, and their role in drafting the CRPD is a unique phenomenon in international lawmaking. At the same time, however, people with disabilities were often considered as one of the "vulnerable groups" addressed in UN human rights policies—as we already observed in Despouy's report. In that sense the framing of people with disabilities as a separate group in the world community that was explicitly vulnerable and deserved special attention was strengthened by the Standard Rules (in which the appointment of a special rapporteur was included). In contrast to the WPA the Standard

Rules aimed at reaching an approach to disability that was all-encompassing but also unconsciously tended to stand apart from other policies.

The Standard Rules and increasing attention to "vulnerable groups" in the 1990s can explain the decision of the UN General Assembly to support Mexico's proposal in 2001 to develop a special convention on the rights of people with disabilities. With the international convention UN disability policies finally became rights-based, but this development can hardly be seen as an uncontested endpoint. Already at the stage of negotiation critics expressed concern that disability was insufficiently integrated into the Millennium Development Goals.[75] The convention is increasingly criticized from a Global South perspective, with socioeconomic inequality and poverty being the main concerns. This begs the question of whether "a redistribution of power and wealth both between rich and poor countries and within poor countries could have more impact on the lived experience of disabled people in the global South than would human rights legislation."[76] Current debates among disability experts on the limited use or even uselessness of the human rights framework in the Global South reflect broader discussion about global economic inequality and critical evaluation of other types of inequality that have become prominent in recent decades, most notably status inequality.

This chapter has shown that what the research literature has described as a shift in global disability policies and the global disability movement from welfare to human rights since the 1970s is much more complex and contentious than is often suggested. Based on investigation of several key moments in global disability policies, I have argued that the human rights perspective on disability was far from uncontested or dominant until the United Nations decided to develop a convention in 2001. Although several actors highlighted the importance of socioeconomic equality during the 1970s and early 1980s, disability was mainly conceptualized by global policymakers as an apolitical issue of rehabilitation and development. The assumption that people with disabilities would and should have the advantage of global equality as envisioned in the NIEO was almost absent in 1993: The Standard Rules as adopted by the United Nations in that year reflected an increasing attention to "vulnerable groups" in development and human rights policies. The focus on "vulnerability" did not so much reflect the concern with structural socioeconomic inequalities. Rather such an approach was meant to ensure "that the needs [and opportunities] of each and every individual are of equal importance." Therefore, the presumed shift from welfare to human rights in global disability policy during the 1980s may perhaps be better understood as a shift to human needs, followed by a shift— although contested from the start—to human rights around 2000.

Analysis of international disability policies informs the larger debate on global inequality in at least two ways. First, it suggests a more complex chronology: Attention to socioeconomic inequality was not waning after the 1970s as is suggested in the literature. Only in the 1990s did socioeconomic inequality come to be seen as less urgent and a human needs approach begin to dominate. Global inequality seems to have multiple chronologies. Second, my analysis sheds new light on the supposed relationship between increasing attention to status inequality and neglect of material inequality. During the 1990s the situation of "vulnerable groups" like people with disabilities came to be seen as a policy area in itself and was approached less as part of a general policy aimed at changing global inequality structures. However, increasing attention to the status equality of "vulnerable groups" did not mean that economic inequality necessarily lost importance. The CRPD includes socioeconomic rights and compared with other international law is sensible to "issues of structural power and oppression."[77] I return to these features of the convention in chapter 5 but shall first discuss the main developments in global disability policies in the 1980s and 1990s in chapters 3 and 4.

3

SINGAPORE 1981

"Nothing About Us, Without *All* of Us"

The minor importance of international human rights for the global disability movement in the early 1980s could not be seen more clearly than in the choice of Disabled Peoples' International (DPI), the first global cross-disability organization run by disabled people themselves, to have its founding conference in Singapore. According to DPI, Singapore was "perceived as a country that bridges the gap between the developing and developed regions, and it is noted for its political stability."[1] This quotation indicates that, as I already started to show in chapter 2, the connection between the "developed" and the "developing" world and the concept of development itself were highly relevant for self-advocates at that time. Moreover, it shows that they were willing to ignore the fact that they gathered in a country that did not give high priority to the political rights of its citizens.[2] Nevertheless, rights language was not totally absent: "A tremendous movement," wrote DPI during the International Year of Disabled Persons (IYDP, 1981), "is gaining momentum all over the world of disabled people speaking out for their own rights."[3]

As I argue in this chapter, the IYDP, including the Singapore conference in 1981, must be seen as a catalytic moment for the "speaking out together" of disabled people all over the world, rather than for the recognition of their human rights. In the end, these two elements were united in the Convention on the Rights of Persons with Disabilities (CRPD, 2006), which gives, in comparison with other international law, an extraordinarily large role to people with disabilities as human rights subjects in the implementation and monitoring of the convention.[4] Their role goes beyond that of people to be consulted, as becomes clear from Article 33.3: "Civil society, in particular persons with disabilities and their representative organizations, shall be involved and participate fully in the monitoring process." This convention article can be traced back to 1981: It was from this time that the involvement and participation of people with disabilities in international policies was no longer ignored, as I shall show on the basis of the relevant UN documents. On the other hand, the struggle for involvement and participation was not always framed by self-advocates as a struggle for human rights recognition. Moreover, paper is patient: Achieving real involvement and participation has remained a struggle until today and is, as I shall argue, a more accessible reality for some than for others. For instance, it is not clear that self-advocates from "developing" countries have been included, despite the promising start in Singapore.

RIGHTS, REHABILITATION, AND PROTEST

The preparations for the Singapore conference show that "social and economic issues" were considered "of immediate relevance to the world's disabled population of 450,000,000," in particular those living in "underdeveloped and developing countries."[5] However, this was not the main reason for which DPI was founded. It was born out of dissatisfaction with the policies of Rehabilitation International (RI), an organization *for* people with disabilities in which *they* were not very well represented. In a lecture in 1981 one of the founders of DPI, the Canadian self-advocate Henry Enns, explained how within the rehabilitation paradigm of RI the disabled person was expected to "overcome his/her problem" by yielding to "the advice and instruction of a physician, vocational rehabilitation counsellor or some other professional." In response disabled people had developed the independent living paradigm in which the "problem" was not situated in the individual but in the environment. Disabled people were, according to Enns, not patients or clients, but consumers: "advocacy, peer counselling, self-help, control by disabled people, and barrier removal are the trademarks of the Independent Living Model." In his lecture Enns mentioned rights mainly as citizen rights; he only once referred to existing human rights law.

Enns's lecture is exemplary. Human rights did not belong among the explicitly expressed main concepts of DPI: "full participation, equal opportunity, justice, integration and equal responsibility."[6] In the manifesto that DPI adopted in Singapore, the concept of "fundamental values" was used to ground disability policies: "We maintain that all people are of equal value. This conviction implies that disabled people have the right to participate in every sphere of society." The fundamental concepts of the manifesto were for the most part the same as those of the UN's IYDP, although DPI had added a paragraph about basic rights (education, rehabilitation, employment, economic security, independent living, participation in social, cultural and political activities, influence).[7]

Because of the tensions between RI and DPI and their models, as explained by Enns, the foundation of DPI in Singapore in 1981 is often interpreted in the literature in terms of the shift narrative discussed in the Introduction. Seen from this point of view, the foundation of DPI appears as part of the wave of protests in 1981 by disability self-advocates against the paternalistic attitudes of the United Nations and other organizations and their models and concepts, with the protest song of Ian Dury serving as a famous example. Already during the preparations for the IYDP, self-advocates, probably from Canada or the United States, were successful in asking the UN General Assembly to change the international year "for" disabled persons to "of" disabled persons because "disabled persons themselves must participate actively in the Year."[8]

Because the most well-known founders of DPI, such as Henry Enns, were from the Global North, scholars and self-advocates tend to see the IYDP as a moment that stimulated the spread of disability perspectives from the Global North to the Global South. In her book about DPI, Diane Driedger has described how after the Singapore congress the organization "enacted a Development Program as its main vehicle" with "Self-Help Leadership Training Seminars" as an important tool: DPI would train "disabled people in the developing world, where many begged for a living, to help themselves."[9] In an influential book, *Nothing About Us Without Us* (1998), disability activist James Charlton wrote: "1981 was very important to the DRM [disability rights movement] in the periphery. In many cases, it was the first-time efforts were made to involve people with disabilities in disability-related projects and programs." According to Charlton, "most of the organizations of the DRM [Disability Rights Movement] were founded between 1979 and 1986."[10]

When it comes to cross-disability organizations, in which people with different disabilities worked together, Charlton may be right, although this has not yet been systematically investigated globally. My main problem with his analysis, however, is that he constructs a disability rights movement that started in the Global North and then spread across the globe, a narrative that he illustrates with stories such as from Narong Patibatsarakich, who said about the IYDP: "When I heard Ed Roberts [an important disability activist from the US] speak, he had a big impact on my ideas. When I came back to Thailand, I was committed to starting DPI-Thailand." Charlton's narrative does not stand on its own and is still influential in different forms today.[11] Of course, I do not deny the worldwide influence of US activists or the relevance of differences between "developed" and "developing" countries, but based on a case study of the IYDP in the Dutch Caribbean I shall question this "first in Europe, Canada and the US, then elsewhere" narrative and argue that it does not really help us to understand the self-organization of people with disabilities worldwide and the emphasis on development in the 1980s.

THE INTERNATIONAL YEAR IN THE DUTCH CARIBBEAN

Historiography concerning UN days, years, and decades (such as the IYDP) is in its infancy, although the gender-related observances are relatively well documented.[12] Recently, Adaly Rodriguez's book about the rise of women's rights in Curaçao, one of the islands of the Dutch Caribbean, gives an impression of the meaning of the IYDP and Decade of Women in the Dutch Caribbean. She shows how women of Curaçao actively participated in these observances and used them to improve the position of women in their society and in particular to fight against the discrimination and oppression of women.[13] After the celebration of the International Women's Year (1975), Rodriguez argues, women's issues were considered more seriously in Curaçao.[14] How did this work out in the case of the IYDP?

In the European Netherlands, the Department of Public Health established in 1980 a national committee for the Dutch celebration of the IYDP. First, the committee decided to spend money and time on the "Third World" and the situation of people with disabilities there, inspired by the message of the United Nations. This decision resulted in support for two projects, a prevention program in West Africa and a rehabilitation program in India. Second, the committee subsidized many projects in the Netherlands, often intending to change existing negative attitudes toward disability in society. Third, the committee had different working groups in which several issues were discussed.[15]

In their discussion about the Third World, Surinam was suggested by one of the committee members as a possible area in which to develop a project; but the minister of Development Aid, who was consulted, did not want to focus on Surinam or the Antilles "because the services [for people with disabilities] there were already very good," and he preferred to create new projects rather than add to existing programs. Nevertheless, the Dutch committee did support the observation of the IYDP in the Dutch Caribbean or Antilles (*de Nederlandse Antillen*). When this decision was made in 1980, the committee had to appoint a representative of the Antilles. Minister R. A. (Ronnie) Casseres was asked and agreed to join the committee. Casseres's first task was to make an inventory of the state of care for people with disabilities on the islands and to formulate a plan of action. To do this, Casseres organized a meeting with care organizations in Curaçao on November 8, 1980 to discuss the ways in which the islands could participate in the IYDP, and asked people to assist with making an inventory.[16]

At that moment the IYDP had already been started by the "Council of the Handicapped." This council was founded in 1978, inspired by Norman Philip, who worked as an expert on vocational rehabilitation for the International Labour Organization (ILO), after an attempt to establish such a council earlier in the 1970s. The council intended to promote the rehabilitation of disabled persons in the Dutch Caribbean and Curaçao in particular. The members of the council were mainly organizations for people with disabilities, among them organizations like Totolica, run by the parents of disabled children. Other organizations were Sociedad di Ciegunan, Stichting Hulp aan Auditief Gehandicapten, Vereniging voor lichamelijk Gehandicapten, and Stichting Zorg voor Geestelijk Gehandicapten.[17]

The launch of the IYDP by the council took place in Curaçao in January 1980 in the garden of Consul-General of the United States in Curaçao Alta Fowler. The council presented its plans for the IYDP, and Ingeborg Zielinski (Stichting Hulp aan auditief gehandicapten) and Aminta da Costa Gomez-Sprockel (Oudervereniging Totolica) gave speeches. They said that the emphasis in 1980 would be on providing information about people with disabilities, and in 1981 on the stories of people with disabilities themselves. Aminta da Costa Gomez-Sprockel stated that Curaçao was further on its way to including disabled people in society than the (European) Netherlands, although there were more advanced services on the other side of the Atlantic.[18]

When Casseres began his work on behalf of the Dutch IYDP committee, the council had already started and would determine Casseres's agenda. In February 1981, Casseres sent the IYDP program made by the council to the Dutch committee. In an enclosed explanatory letter, the council stated, with a tone more critical than during the launch of the year, that:

> People with disabilities make in our country a not negligible percentage of the population and no doubt their position is far from satisfactory, both with regard to the material and immaterial aspects. People

with disabilities are predominantly forced and kept in isolation and their integration is hindered by prejudice and misunderstanding of society. The Council of Disabled Persons will celebrate the International Year of Disabled Persons, in particular through providing information and education. The starting point is that 1981 is not an end but a beginning, a first step which should create the opportunities for continuation of actions in the years that follow.

A month later Casseres sent the committee a wish list from the Dutch Caribbean. This contained requests varying from practical aid to projects providing information about disability—all submitted by existing organizations for people with disabilities.[19]

The list does not hide the fact that collaboration did not come naturally. The council at Curaçao's idea to sell a special stamp was not without success but became contested because the Arubian partners protested. They felt excluded by this "handicap-imperialism" from Curaçao. According to the representatives of this island, Aruba had refused to join the initiative. The Arubian representatives continued in their objection to the one-sided communication but decided in the end to join the initiative.[20]

When halfway through 1981 Casseres was asked by the Dutch committee to report about observation of the IYDP in the Dutch Caribbean, he said that it was difficult to meet the goals of the committee because too few people were involved. People from civil society organizations were the most active, but according to Casseres the Antilles at the state level did nothing. The committee agreed with the short and incomplete project descriptions and budget plans and was willing to provide a 50,000-guilder subsidy (the amount of money that was available for each province of the Netherlands in the year's budget). The final report of the Dutch committee summarized the IYDP in the Antilles with some paternalism:

> The particularity of the disability issues in the Dutch Antilles and the "small scale" of this society have brought with them, that the

National Committee not dogmatically held at the standards and criteria. The enthusiastic commitment of the people, who, always on voluntary basis, could reach their goals with the subsidies, guarantee a perfectly responsible use of the funds. The National Committee has repeatedly received expressions of heartfelt gratitude from the Antillean population.[21]

In the Dutch Caribbean newspaper *Amigoe* a more critical voice was heard: Jos de Kok (member of the council and the board of Totolica) and Ed Eleonora (working for a mental health organization) were happy with the attention on disability during the IYDP, but skeptical about the effect. They had tried to improve existing services and to stimulate new attitudes toward people with disabilities, but without much success. From this interview it becomes clear that the year had also not strengthened the unity of the council: According to De Kok the interests of the participants diverged too much.[22]

As far as I can see, the skeptics were right: The IYDP does not seem to have effected much change. In 1982 the newspaper reported a meeting of the council during which a booklet about the prevention of disability was presented. According to the chair, Mirtha Leetz-Cijntje, this was in line with the main goal of the council, the rehabilitation of disabled people, a goal pursued by doing research and providing information to the population.[23] By the end of 1982 the council participated in an advice meeting initiated by the minister of social care, Margo Croes, who stated that the situation of disabled people in the Dutch Antilles was in what she saw as a stage of care, while it ought to be in a stage of emancipation. According to Croes it was the common responsibility of the state and citizens to work in that direction.[24] After 1982, however, the council fell silent, and the ideas of the IYDP received little attention—although at the United Nations' level the World Programme of Action Concerning Disabled Persons (WPA) and the related UN International Decade of Disabled Persons (1982–1993) were launched. Maybe organizations such as Totolica had had a new impulse, but in contrast to gender policies the IYDP in general seems not to have had a legacy.[25]

HISTORICIZING DISABILITY

The case of the Dutch Caribbean seems not at all in line with the narrative of Charlton, let alone the shift-narrative or Enns's paradigm shift. In this case a cross-disability council was initiated before the IYDP, inspired by the advice of an ILO expert and consisting of members without a disability. If there existed organizations *of* people with disabilities, they seem not to have raised their voices during the year. Moreover, the IYDP did not bring people with different disabilities closer together and did not lead to the introduction of new notions of disability—in 1982 the council still used the contested medical terms "prevention" and "rehabilitation," and the people involved did not always see the need for support from the Global North. Can this perhaps be explained by the fact that there was no exchange with self-advocates from the Global North? In another Caribbean case, Jamaica, the IYDP did not lead to a big change in disability policies, but activists did become involved in DPI (where they may have met activists like Ed Roberts) and in 1981 set up a national cross-disability self-advocacy organization.[26]

Limited Anglo-American influence could be a factor, but the Dutch Caribbean is not so exceptional a case as it seems. That is why it enables us to question Charlton's narrative. In countries such as Hungary, Zimbabwe, and Thailand the IYDP resulted in the creation of a cross-disability self-advocacy organization; but in the (European) Netherlands, Kenya, or the Soviet Union this was not the case.[27] Moreover, public protests against the IYDP were organized in countries such as West Germany and the United Kingdom, but hardly at all outside Western Europe.[28] At the same time the IYDP stimulated awareness and new modes of acting and thinking about people with disabilities that did not follow the Anglo-American example. In China, for instance, the IYDP was initially taken up by the government as a challenge to collect data about an until-then unknown group, to be used by people with physical disabilities to organize themselves.[29] There were also many countries in which what I have argued elsewhere for the Netherlands and what De Schutter writes about the IYDP in Kenya was also true: "The IYDP thus acted as a thrust to continue and maybe intensify the programmes that were already in place."[30] The Dutch Caribbean also fits this description.

These examples show that it does not make sense to imagine a rigid distinction between the "west" and the "rest" as assumed by Charlton and others, let alone to use a "first, then" narrative. If we want to understand how people with disabilities and their allies were influenced by the IYDP, we must take into consideration—although it may sound very obvious to historians—that disability is a very unstable category that can be shaped in very different ways. A consequence of this insight is, surprisingly, that observance of the IYDP in a context of development such as the Dutch Caribbean or Kenya had a lot of similarities to that in "developed" countries such as the European Netherlands or Belgium. In all these countries the state, either a strong welfare state or a minimal developing state, had no particular interest in translating the IYDP into new policies, as was the case in China, for instance.

Moreover, these countries have in common the fact that people with disabilities did see the possibility of improvement in their situation, but in the reform of existing practices rather than in adopting a new paradigm. This could mean, for instance, that they decided to organize themselves around a single disability or with the geographical focus on one island.[31] The Dutch Caribbean case helps us, together with other cases, to highlight the different "landings" of UN policies on the ground and to understand why the Anglo-American approach did not always resonate among self-advocates, policymakers, and diplomats at the international level and in the countries they represented.

The Dutch Caribbean was at that time not represented at the international level, but local realities and choices in this and other cases probably informed disability internationalism as it took shape in the 1980s. This does not mean that the relation between developments at the local and global level was straightforward. In human rights historiography this point is made, for instance, by Steven L. B. Jensen when he demonstrates the importance of Jamaican diplomats for the development of international human rights, but also points out that domestic policies in Jamaica were not always in line with these international developments.[32] In the case of disabled diplomats, scholars have observed comparable discrepancies, but also other ways in which activities on the global and local level were related. As Maria Cristina Galmarini has shown in her book about international blind activism, countries such as the Soviet Union and East Germany did not live up to the ideal of social progress that their diplomats presented at the international level. Moreover, socialist diplomacy enabled the empowerment of a selected group of activists and left others "hidden and segregated either in their homes or in the many not-so-exemplary institutions that populated the socialist world."[33]

In other cases, such as Sweden, the relation between policies and persons at the global and local level seemed to be more harmonious—at least if we follow the activities of the blind activist Bengt Olof Lennart Lindqvist. He became involved in Swedish disability activism during the 1970s, combining the domestic struggle for equal rights with involvement in international disability organizations. Lindqvist was one of the founders of DPI. During the 1980s he became a member of Parliament for the Swedish Social Democratic Party, and in 1985 he was appointed deputy minister for social security. He used his position not only to improve disabled people's lives in Sweden, but also to influence Swedish foreign policies in favor of the emancipation of disabled people. As we shall see in chapter 4, he was instrumental in the organization of the Global Meeting of Experts in 1987 and the adoption of the Standard Rules in 1993.[34]

It is beyond the international scope of this book to investigate the varied interactions between the global and local level in more detail. It is, however, possible to say something concerning the way in which the people involved in global policies dealt with differences between countries and regions. Several testimonies of disabled self-advocates from the Global North have shown that they directed their international activities to improving the situation of disabled people in the Global South. For instance, Kalle Kustaa Topias Könkkölä from Finland wrote in his autobiographical *The World Became My Room* about his "miniature dream: a mud hut in Kasama, North Zambia. Above is a plaque: Independent Living Centre. . . . Gradually Independent Living Centres have been established all over the world. Their looks vary, but their goals are the same: to provide a life worth living for the disabled irrespective of the wealth or poverty of the state."[35] However, we know less about the way in which self-advocates from other parts of the world perceived the differences between "developed" and "developing" countries.

In order to do justice to the 1981 "momentum," I shall now focus on a historical actor who in a way bridges the Global North and South and whose story may help us to understand why the language of the official manifestations of DPI in 1981 was less polarizing and had significant overlap with the policy language of RI and the United Nations. DPI seems not always to have seen different perspectives as mutually exclusive. In the next section I shall look closely at Ron Chandran-Dudley from Singapore: a less well-known founder of DPI responsible for organizing the founding conference.

ANOTHER MAN WITH A MISSION

Ron Chandran-Dudley (1934–2015) was raised in a middle-class family and, after studying social anthropology at the London School of Economics, became general secretary of the Singapore Association for the Blind (SAB).[36] He also studied in New York on a Fulbright scholarship, specializing in the field of rehabilitation counseling.[37] When in 1964 a subcommittee of the Association for the Blind was considering registering itself as an independent organization run by blind people alone, Chandran-Dudley was asked to advise: "Being no stranger to progressive ideas after his university years in London, Mr. Chandran-Dudley recalls: 'I thought that rather than a revolution, I would like an evolution,'" and "I said that it may be worthwhile for us to give our blind members the right to be members of the association." While Chandran-Dudley's advice led in the 1960s to a solution, in 1982 self-advocates nevertheless founded a new independent organization of the blind separate from the SAB. Chandran-Dudley was at that time president of the SAB.[38] His involvement in the foundation of DPI at the international and national level did not affect his participation in an organization where people without disabilities still played a role. At the international level he also remained active in RI.

Unsurprisingly, Chandran-Dudley did not criticize the paradigm of rehabilitation as Enns did. In a speech during the opening of the IYDP in Singapore, for instance, he even seems to remain within this paradigm. As chairman of the National Co-ordinating Committee for the IYDP he pointed out to visitors at the opening ceremony that 10 percent of the world's population was estimated to be disabled and mentioned that "the majority of the numbers of disabled persons quoted in the United Nations' statistics are to be found in the African and Asian regions." In Singapore probably less than 10 percent was disabled, Chandran-Dudley stated, but nevertheless "disability groups are unable to exercise their fundamental rights to contribute to their own or their families' well-being or to the progress of the nation." According to Chandran-Dudley, rehabilitation was key for solving this "socio-economic problem." Moreover, he hoped for a role reversal in which disabled people would become active and productive citizens instead of "passive receivers of services and goods," and stated that "disabled persons in Singapore should look upon 1981 as a time for reaffirmation of our citizenship and of our pride as Singaporeans."[39]

The story of Chandran-Dudley shows that not every DPI member was thinking in terms of opposition between rehabilitation and independent living. Not for nothing did he prefer the word evolution instead of revolution. In countries such as Singapore it was simply the best strategy to collaborate with the government and service providers in order to improve the situation of people with disabilities. Chandran-Dudley's approach has probably been more representative of disability self-advocacy than the more antagonistic Anglo-American approach.[40] What united members of DPI at the international level was their wish to have a say in disability policies, which did not always exclude collaboration with people without disabilities, as the story of Chandran-Dudley shows. The title of the conference in Singapore was *A Voice of Our Own: Unity in Cultural Diversity*, because decisions concerning people with disabilities had for too long been made about them without them: "Disabled people have the right to make their own decisions and insist on equality of opportunity. The concern is for both developing and developed countries."[41] DPI united people with disabilities who wanted to have a say in disability policies, but seemed aware that people with disabilities in different cultural contexts could take these policies in different directions. In that sense DPI did not provide a single blueprint for a better world or society. DPI wanted a voice in decision-making processes and accepted cultural diversity.

This explains the policy language used by DPI and is the reason why different members could highlight different concepts. At the same time, we could observe that during the Singapore conference and thereafter improvement of the situation of people with disabilities in the developing world received priority above disability as a human rights issue or other framings. Members of DPI could probably more easily agree on the importance of social development policies than the more sensitive topic of human rights. Moreover, with development DPI could better connect to the United Nations, which treated disability in the first place as a social development issue. Only in the late 1990s did many organizations of self-advocates decide to unite in a rights-based alliance, and the development approach has remained highly relevant, as we shall see in the following chapters.[42] The global disability movement has never been one (human) rights movement but always a heterogeneous family of organizations with different interests. Only with the CRPD have human rights been embraced by self-advocates on a larger scale.

PARTICIPATION

In hindsight the fact that in 1981 people with different disabilities claimed their own international voice has had a lasting impact, since the IYDP organizations run by people with disabilities have almost always been referenced in UN disability policy documents. This is obviously not the same as real involvement, but the participation of people with disabilities was at least on the agenda, and DPI became in 1983 an acknowledged organization within the UN structure.[43] As we saw in chapter 2, DPI was involved in negotiations about the WPA. This program confirmed the importance of self-advocates: "All over the world, disabled persons have started to unite in organizations as advocates for their rights to influence decision-makers in Governments and all sectors of society. The role of these organizations includes providing a voice of their own, identifying needs, expressing views on priorities, evaluating services and advocating change and public awareness.... In view of their vital importance in the process of participation, it is imperative that their development should be encouraged." Moreover, the WPA stated that "disabled persons and their organizations should be consulted in the further development of the World Programme of Action and in its implementation" and wanted the United Nations and its specialized agencies "to hire more disabled persons and to make their facilities and information more accessible to disabled persons." The program also encouraged states to "increase their assistance to organizations of disabled persons" and "provide channels for them to influence government policies and decisions in all areas that concern them." Although the influence of DPI was limited, they did for instance support the idea to review "the follow-up of the International Year of Disabled Persons" with a Global Meeting of Experts "consisting largely of disabled persons."[44] This meeting would take place in 1987 and stimulate the idea of a human rights convention.

The Global Meeting of Experts in 1987 also showed that participation of people with disabilities in UN policies was still far from being achieved. Lack of participation by disabled persons was identified by the experts as one of the "obstacles" to the implementation of the WPA. They stumbled upon "the fact that disabled people were not an integral part of the decision-making process or the administrative machinery of intergovernmental bodies, regional entities, Governments and organizations." Moreover, they considered the "numbers, coverage, effectiveness and funding" of organizations of disabled people insufficient. They therefore recommended establishment of an advisory council of experts with an "appropriate participation and representation of disabled persons." Moreover, they stated that "in recognition of the fact that they have personal experience in the disability field, disabled people should participate in and should be represented at all United Nations expert group meetings on disability and all United Nations sponsored meetings at the regional and national levels." Funded consultation with organizations representing disabled people "to allow them to monitor and evaluate within each body all plans, projects and activities concerning disabled people" was also marked as a priority by these experts.[45]

Participation of people with disabilities would remain an urgent issue during the 1990s. The Standard Rules on the Equalization of Opportunities for Persons with Disabilities, adopted by the United Nations in 1993, were not really focused on participation at the international level, but highlighted the role of nation-states to foster the participation of organizations of people with disabilities. Rule 18 stated that "states should recognize the right of the organizations of persons with disabilities to represent persons with disabilities at national, regional and local levels" and "states should also recognize the advisory role of organizations of persons with disabilities in decision making on disability matters." At the same time, the Standard Rules showed in their preamble a broad approach to representation: They emphasized that "persons with disabilities, and their parents, guardians, advocates and organizations, must be active partners with States in the planning and implementation of all measures affecting their civil, political, economic, social and cultural rights."[46] This approach, as we shall see in chapter 6, was framed rather differently by the drafters of the CRPD.

DIVERSITY

The participation of disabled people that has been so important and remarkable for both the drafting process and the text of the convention has a long and continuous history since 1981. When we look more closely at who exactly has been participating and who has been mentioned in the UN documents, a complex picture arises. The convention has been praised because of its intersectional approach. It contains for instance separate articles on women, children, and international cooperation.

However, later reflections from minority perspectives such as Deaf self-advocates show that participation and inclusion of minorities within the disability community was not always apparent during the drafting of the convention. The struggle for inclusion of disability minorities is not well documented, but the UN documents and additional sources show that this struggle has a longer history too.

The collaboration between people with different disabilities that was part of the new wave of disability internationalism in the 1980s brought new challenges. One was to include people with cognitive disabilities, as was already indicated in the WPA: "Mentally handicapped people are now beginning to demand a voice of their own and insisting on their right to take part in decision-making and discussion." This will be discussed in more detail in chapter 6, but it is interesting to note that the WPA addressed this group separately and stated that people with cognitive disabilities "have much to learn from the self-advocacy movement of persons with other disabilities."[47] Here we can observe a framing that matches the way disabled people's organizations (DPOs) and the United Nations have dealt with other "special groups" such as women, children, older persons, and refugees: The inclusion of these groups was expected to need attention, and was often also (unconsciously) measured by the yardstick of the vocal, well-off, male person with a physical disability.

At a conference in Nassau in 1985, the same year as the international women's conference of the United Nations in Nairobi, women started to protest against the dominance of men within DPI. They wanted to end the imbalance between the sexes within DPI and organized a separate meeting in which they drafted a resolution that would guarantee better representation of women. After a "fast and furious" debate and "in an atmosphere charged with emotion" the women's resolution was adopted by the assembly. After this intervention Fatima Shah from Pakistan, whose activities were discussed earlier, was "left with no option but to agree to the demand that I become the representative for Asia and be included in the World Council" of DPI.[48]

Some minority groups have always had an ambivalent relationship with the disability movement, most notably the Deaf community. Deafness has not always been seen as a disability by this community, which has understood itself instead as an ethnic group or linguistic minority. Their issues did not always match those of other groups within the disability movement. The history of Deaf internationalism is not well integrated into the dominant narrative of disability internationalism and human rights, and some scholars have written about Deaf internationalism and human rights separately. Based on an analysis of the themes of the world congresses of the World Federation of the Deaf (WFD), Joseph Murray has said that "from 1987 on, themes largely turned away from a view of deaf people versus wider society and toward a rights-based discourse that emphasized diversity, a presumed global unity within deaf communities, and human rights."[49] In 1987 the WFD used the concept of sign language recognition in a legal sense for the first time. According to Maartje de Meulder this change can be traced back to self-advocates from the Northern countries or the United Kingdom or both, who started in the 1980s to see sign language rights as human rights.[50]

Since the late 1980s we can see issues related to Deafness more explicitly addressed in UN disability policies, especially when it comes to education. The disability movement in general has been focused on full inclusion of children with disabilities in education, but the Deaf community has wanted "to allow deaf children to be educated in sign language settings with access to peers who use sign language and teachers who were fluent in sign language."[51] The Standard Rules in 1993 therefore contained a separate article about Deaf education because "equal educational opportunities in integrated settings" had to come with "special classes and units in mainstream schools" in which "their education may be more suitably provided." Nevertheless, as pointed out by Deaf self-advocates Liisa Kauppinen and Markku Jokinen, it was a real struggle to include rights relevant to Deaf people, often sign language related, in the CRPD.[52]

The same is true for self-advocates from the Global South and their issues. Pamela Molina Toledo, a self-advocate from Chile, gave her reflections on the drafting of the convention the telling title "At the United Nations...'The South Also Exists.'" According to her it has been a challenge for self-advocates from the Global South to be included in the decision-making processes of the United Nations and the International Disability Caucus (IDC), the main umbrella organization of self-advocates. "Nothing about us without *all* of us" was the motto of Proyecto Sur, an organization founded to support "leaders with disabilities from developing countries so that they could participate and affect positive change in the different processes of the UN." Such organizations were necessary, stated Toledo, because of the initial overrepresentation of "Northern Hemisphere leaders" in the IDC.[53] This overrepresentation is remarkable because bridging the gap between people with disabilities in the developed and developing worlds was seen by the United Nations and DPI as the most important challenge for disability policies in the early 1980s, both in terms of collaboration and living conditions.

The difference between 1980s ambitions and 2000s realities must be explained by the growing inequality between the Global North and South during the last decades of the twentieth century.[54] Underrepresentation of self-advocates from Latin America in the negotiations had, according to Toledo, at least partly to be explained by the "high costs of airfare and lodging in New York" and the lack of translation from spoken English. Despite the long-lasting development ambitions in disability policies, equal participation of the Global South never became a priority. When in 1993 the Standard Rules wanted to provide "models for the political decision making," they were "bearing in mind the widely differing technical and economical levels" but highlighted in particular that "the process must reflect keen understanding of the cultural context within which it takes place." Taking culture into account is of course relevant but does not solve structural inequalities. The Standard Rules did still mention the "problems of disability in developing countries," but they approached these problems from a human needs perspective that, as explained in chapter 2, accepted inequality up to a certain level and focused on extreme poverty in particular. Moreover, the priority of disability policies and advocacy shifted around the year 2000 toward human rights and gave, in comparison with the early 1980s, less attention to structural inequality between the developed and developing world.

DPI'S HUMAN RIGHTS COMMITTEE

Although human rights were not directly and comprehensively embraced as a leading perspective by policymakers and self-advocates in 1981, in retrospect we cannot ignore the human rights committee established by DPI in 1983, which would become an important hub for disability human rights.[55] This committee aimed to put violations of the human rights of people with disabilities on the agenda of the UN Committee for Human Rights and Subcommittee on the Prevention of Discrimination and the Protection of Minorities, preferably with the appointment of a special rapporteur within that subcommittee.[56] DPI was successful in putting the appointment of a special rapporteur on the agenda of the United Nations in 1984. Although the DPI committee was worried about a possible "weak rapporteur" with the consequence that "our concerns would not be viewed as human rights, but instead solely as social and economic issues," it developed a good relationship with the appointed human rights lawyer Leandro Despouy from Argentina.[57] However, it would take Despouy a long time to publish his report.

DPI was not only active within human rights monitoring at the international level, but was also involved in reports about national cases. In 1982 the North American DPI had already presented to the subcommittee a report on human rights violations under the Reagan administration. The result of this intervention was a resolution in which the human rights of disabled persons were underlined and which requested state and nonstate actors to report violations.[58] This was a limited success, but it reflected an early and limited understanding of disability human rights, influenced by the dominant understanding of general human rights at that time: DPI identified violations in particular in relation to punishment, institutionalization, institutional abuse, forced sterilization, castration and female circumcision, and blinding of detainees.[59] DPI also noted that disability was not part of the International Bill of Human Rights and saw the limitations of the disability human rights declarations from the 1970s: They "limit or compromise the human rights for disabled persons as compared to the rights articulated for everyone."

These declarations were considered by DPI as "ineffective and perhaps have a dangerous potential as a second standard of human rights specifically for disabled persons."[60] It would take until 1987 for the idea of a convention to be born.

The human rights track of DPI will be followed further in chapter 5, but the foundation and early work of this special committee shows that DPI did not simply express human rights as citizen rights or as a concept underlying social policies, as did the United Nations. DPI viewed human rights in the same way as the human rights movement did (e.g., organizations such as Amnesty International), namely as individual freedom rights that needed international protection. The main reason why this perspective remained marginal was the dominance of the development perspective, which will be explained from a new angle in chapter 4.

4

NEW YORK 1987

A Neoliberal Utopia of Development

The Global Meeting of Experts to review the implementation of the World Programme of Action Concerning Disabled Persons (WPA) at the midpoint of the United Nations Decade of Disabled Persons (Stockholm, 1987) is undeniably important in the history of disability human rights because it was one of the first times that the idea of a disability convention was seriously discussed at the international level. It is equally important to investigate how the United Nations responded to the recommendations of the experts, and why. In 1987 a staff member of the secretary-general wrote, probably somewhere in the New York City UN offices, a very short answer to these questions: "As you can see, they [the expert's recommendations] are quite far reaching. The problem is that if all implemented they would have ... financial and adm. implications for the UN."[1] In this chapter I shall discuss the reluctance of the United Nations toward holding a disability human rights convention, and show how another approach to disability took precedence.

INTERNATIONAL LAW AND UTOPIAS

As we have seen, the idea of a separate disability convention did not exist—as far as I can see—in the early 1980s. Human rights were mentioned during the 1981 celebrations and in the WPA but could hardly be seen as a central concept in global disability policies at that time. However, a few figures within or related to the assemblage of UN funds, programs, and specialized agencies did pay serious attention to disability human rights and law in the early 1980s. Most noticeable is the publication by the United Nations Educational, Scientific and Cultural Organization (UNESCO) of *The Protection of the Rights of Handicapped Persons by Different International Instruments*: "A compilation originally undertaken for the International Year of the Child by The Hague Academy of International Law, this is an exhaustive survey covering texts of worldwide applicability as well as regional agreement."[2] The booklet, in English, contained extracts from *Etude juridique de la protection des droits de l'enfant handicapé offerte par les différents instruments internationaux*, a legal study which Maurice Torelli, who worked as international lawyer at the University of Nice Sophia Antipolis, carried out at the request of the UNESCO Human Rights and Peace division. Because texts about the commitment of international organizations to the rights of children with disabilities were "scattered" and had "variable legal value," UNESCO wanted to present an "analytical assessment" in order to "persuade governments to ratify existing conventions and to respond to the need to generalize these rights in a single international convention."[3] The booklet shows that UNESCO did not have a disability convention in mind, but rather the children's rights convention that was in the making during the 1980s. Nevertheless, it indicates that some in the international sphere had started to think about the international protection of disability rights, different from the international exchange of rehabilitation law in which the national framework remained dominant and closer to Disabled Peoples' International's (DPI's) human rights committee.

The emergence of an international framework for disability rights, albeit still marginal and undeveloped, can be seen in the collection *The Disabled Persons and the International Organizations*, published by the Italian international lawyer Maria Rita Saulle in 1981. Saulle's book differs from Torelli's study both in size and content: In almost eight hundred pages Saulle offers an extensive overview of international disability policy initiatives that until then had received little analysis. In hindsight, however, we can see that her study paved the way for an Italian attempt to realize an international disability convention. During the European Regional Meeting on Implementation of the WPA (Ljubljana, March 1987) and the already mentioned Global Meeting of Experts (Stockholm, August 1987) Saulle succeeded in launching the idea: The drafting of a convention became one of the main recommendations of the experts' meeting.[4] After these meetings she took the idea to the UN General Assembly on October 19 in New York. There she proposed as representative of Italy to start the drafting of a convention. Referring to the Convention on the Elimination of All Forms of Discrimination Against Women as adopted by the United Nations in 1979, she explained that a separate convention could address the "specific situation and the particular needs" of people with disabilities and "would bring about radical changes in living conditions for the disabled." The UN General Assembly, however, was not convinced of the need for a separate convention and was afraid of the financial consequences that according to Saulle "should not lead to neglect of the legitimate expectations of particularly vulnerable groups, such as the disabled, who were unable to adequately defend themselves and enjoy equal rights."[5]

Although it is clear that the relative novelty of a human rights approach to disability and the financial situation of the United Nations at the time did not help Italy's proposal nor that of Sweden two years later, it is nevertheless remarkable that the United Nations continued to reject such proposals through the late 1980s and changed its mind only a decade later. Must the decision of the UN General Assembly in 2001 to start drafting a new convention be interpreted as a result of increasing attention to human rights in the 1990s? As Stefan-Ludwig Hoffmann has argued, individual human rights became a "basic concept (*Grundbegriff*), that is, a contested, irreplaceable and consequential concept of global politics, only in the 1990s, after the end of the Cold War."[6] Part of this breakthrough was a new emphasis on bodily suffering: Asylum seekers for instance were "no longer expected to bring up stories of political persecution," but they had to "report their traumatization and literally show their wounds, that is, document their bodily suffering."⁷ Were people with disabilities "discovered" during the 1990s as suffering individuals, like asylum seekers and vulnerable women, who were in need of international protection?

In this chapter I shall argue that global disability policies were less affected by the expansion of human rights during the 1990s as described by Hoffmann than one would expect. The main reason why the 1990s cannot be seen as a breakthrough for disability human rights is that disability was first and foremost seen as an issue of development. My argument is inspired by Antony Anghie, who in response to Samuel Moyn's *Last Utopia* has pointed to the importance of the "utopia of 'development'" that was particularly supported by the Global South.⁸ Although the situation in the 1990s was different, I should like to apply a similar nuance to Hoffmann's statement about the breakthrough of human rights in the 1990s: In the case of disability policies human rights were not omnipresent, but development was. This is evident already in the main argument that Mexico used during its successful lobbying for an international convention: Disability was not well integrated in the Millennium Development Goals and therefore a separate convention was needed.

The social development approach to disability that I shall discuss in this chapter could best be summarized as a global policy that attempts to give people with disabilities "the same opportunities as other citizens" and "an equal share in the improvement of living conditions resulting from economic and social development."⁹ The concept of "social development" has been used by the United Nations to articulate the importance of social welfare in development policy and practice, in particular since the foundation of the UN Research Institute for Social Development in 1963.¹⁰ Global policies concerning people with disabilities were the responsibility of the Centre for Social Development and Humanitarian Affairs, a division of the UN Economic and Social Council (ECOSOC). Within the social development approach human rights could play a role as an underlying concept or moral standard, but preferably not one enshrined in international law. This was partly because human rights law for people with disabilities implies a more radical equality than a policy aimed at "same opportunities" and "equal share." Moreover, human rights law tends to ascribe a central implementational role to nation-states, monitoring international organizations and public funding, whereas the social development approach emphasizes the importance of nonstate actors such as nongovernmental organizations (NGOs) and businesses. In light of the recent literature concerning human rights and neoliberalism, the social development approach to disability could be characterized as a neoliberal approach, not because the approach is explicitly aimed at the free market, but because it supports a neoliberal constellation in which social policies are depoliticized and public spending is limited. At the global level disability was confined to the areas of social development and humanitarian affairs, and therefore put into the voluntary sphere and at a safe distance from state policies and political debate.[11]

Reconstruction of this approach is relevant because it is helpful for understanding the belated integration of disability into international law and the interpretation of the UN Convention on the Rights of Persons with Disabilities (CRPD) since 2006. Moreover, it shows how popularity of the human rights discourse in the 1990s was not always translated into popularity of human rights law. The structural equality for which advocates of international disability law have argued since the 1980s, I shall argue, was not adopted by global disability policymakers in the 1990s. In the case of disability, policymakers often framed human rights as human needs, and therefore they can be seen as a powerless companion or fellow traveler of neoliberalism. The social development approach to disability did not entail a "development utopia" that according to the literature could be seen as an alternative to the "human rights utopia" but served a "neoliberal utopia" in which offering people with disabilities equal opportunities and minimal provision was more urgent than legally ensuring their equal rights. Although the CRPD broke through the dominance of the social development approach in principle, it still plays an important role in the practice of global disability policies. Human rights law does not exclude the market: The women's movement for instance has integrated women's rights into international law but has often, as Samuel Moyn has argued, imagined development "to be available in free market terms."[12]

To understand why the social development approach prevailed, I shall follow a selection of significant figures who were involved in global disability policies during the 1980s and 1990s and ask how and why they used or did not use human rights, and what alternatives they chose. The main figure in this chapter is Alan Reich (1930–2005), an American with a disability who became involved in disability policies in 1981. Reich had served the US government as appointed deputy assistant secretary of commerce for East-West Trade and director of the Bureau of East-West Trade. He also served as member of the US delegation to the World Health Organization (WHO) and adviser of the US Mission to the UN.[13] As a policymaker he developed a diplomatic relationship with the UN secretary-general during the 1980s and 1990s. Although Reich's influence was limited, his interaction with the secretary-general provides an insight into the development of global disability policies that transcends the particular case of his lobbying.

NORTH AMERICAN DISABILITY RIGHTS

In the literature concerning the global disability movement, developments in disability activism and law in North America are generally considered very influential. Activists such as Ed Roberts and Judy Heumann brought their ideas to other parts of the world, and the Americans with Disabilities Act (ADA) passed in 1990 inspired the writing of disability law in other countries and regions.[14] As I argued in the Introduction, the literature sometimes too easily follows a narrative in which the convention is presented as an outcome of a process that started in North America. In this chapter I shall further complicate this narrative by following figures from North America who reveal a framing of disability that has remained almost unnoticed but without which we cannot understand global disability policies and the late inclusion of disability in international law.

An important moment for the development of global disability policies was the International Year of Disabled Persons (IYDP) in 1981. It was preceded by other initiatives such as the Declaration on the Rights of Disabled Persons (1975), but because of the enormous attention given to the IYDP and the development of the WPA, "1981" further established disability as a separate (policy) category at the global level. The United States also joined the IYDP.

During the national celebrations of the IYDP human rights were not a central concept. However, when the WPA was discussed at the United Nations, the human rights perspective was supported by the United States. In a speech to the advisory committee for the year, the US delegate—probably Harold O'Flaherty—mentioned human rights in his commentary on the draft WPA as follows: "The document also calls for a very strong statement in the area of human rights. I was distressed, Sir, to learn that the document is calling for the establishment of separate mechanisms and vehicles to handle the human rights and civil rights of disabled persons. This seems, Sir, to be a paradox, for the rest of the document calls for meaningful integration of disabled persons. I think it is time, Sir, that we establish consistency throughout the entire document. The same societal components, strategies which protect the human rights on a nation-by-nation basis of all persons, should consider human rights of disabled persons—in our judgment Sir, this is the true reflection of the UN theme (i.e., full participation and equality of life)." This statement was accompanied by another statement. In looking back on the year, the US representative mentioned both the work of the national council in collaboration with "the private sector, or business community, and the voluntary" and the coordinating Federal Interagency Committee for the year that had focused on the public sector but had implemented their projects "at no additional cost to the American taxpayer—truly this is a do-it-yourself year in the United States."[15]

The speech shows human rights entangled with issues of public spending and the role of NGOs.[16] This probably had its roots in the neoliberal agenda of the US president since 1981, Ronald Reagan. In another speech the US delegate Harold O'Flaherty briefly discussed "Reaganomics" in the following way: "People say to me with Reagan-economics—Reaganism that we've lost our hope—we don't have a chance. I say to you that—ANYTIME that someone doesn't tell me what I have to do, and I can do it for myself, that I am that much better off. Choose this day whom ye shall serve."[17] O'Flaherty did not consider Reagan a threat. On the contrary, he suggested that the president's neoliberal agenda of lowering public spending and stimulating self-reliance and business served the integration of people with disabilities that he, a blind person who served as director of the Federal Interagency Committee for the IYDP, stood for. Because of his austerity policies, Reagan would not have been liked by every disabled person, but the pursuit of equal rights by self-advocates in the United States during the 1980s was not incompatible with neoliberalism.

GOING TO THE UNITED NATIONS

Alan Reich, director of the national IYDP council, went a bit further than O'Flaherty: He framed the UN policies in neoliberal terminology. When he received the District of Columbia UN Day Award for the council, he said in his speech that "the voluntary response in Washington, D.C., throughout the US and worldwide to the IYDP challenge demonstrates the tremendous moral force of the UN. With almost no special funding, the UN has fostered programs and long-term commitments in all countries, benefiting the world's one-half billion disabled persons."[18] This was the approach that Reich wanted to pursue in the following years, not only for the United States, but for the world.

Like other countries, the United States had conceived the IYDP as an opportunity to support disability policies in the Third World, and Reich wanted this to continue.[19] The International Decade of Disabled Persons (1983–1992) as proclaimed by the United Nations seemed to offer an excellent opportunity for his program. Reich's council wanted to build on the momentum of the IYDP: "Specifically the US Council supports the proposal before the United States congress to designate 1982 as a special national year of disabled persons and urges the United Nations to help capitalize on what has been so well begun by naming the remainder of the 1980s 'The Decade of Disabled Persons.'"[20] An American national year did not happen, but Reich continued trying to win over the United Nations for his approach. To that end he chose the shortest route: trying to influence the secretaries-general, first Kurt Waldheim (in office 1972–1981) and later Javier Pérez de Cuéllar (1982–1991), Boutros Boutros-Ghali (1992–1996), and Kofi Annan (1997–2006).

Having described US disability activism, historians have begun to investigate the transnational exchange between self-advocates and the way in which US activists spread their ideas all over the world.[21] The emphasis, however, has been on politically progressive individuals, and the role of the United States in shaping the UN disability policies is hardly ever investigated—except that the reluctance of the United States to support international (disability) law is well known.[22] From the international history literature we know that the United States since the 1970s disengaged from the United Nations and turned to "the more easily controlled World Bank, GATT, and IMF."[23] The increasing influence of these financial institutions challenged the United Nations to redefine itself and its role in social and development policies.[24] So it was no coincidence that Reich developed a diplomatic relationship with the UN secretary-general. He stressed the importance of nonstate actors, NGOs as well as businesses, which would become increasingly important for the United Nations during the 1980s and 1990s.[25]

Sources in the archives of the UN secretary-general clearly document that Reich had already communicated with the secretary-general during the year about the activities of his council and had tried to arrange regular meetings. However, Secretary-General Waldheim did not have much time for him.[26] In April 1982 new Secretary-General Javier Pérez de Cuéllar was informed by a member of his staff that Reich "was extremely critical of the UN's handling of IYDP." Waldheim had met Reich at a luncheon organized in 1981 by Reich and US Ambassador to the United Nations Jeane Kirkpatrick, "who is apparently a friend of Mr. Reich" and "a fiasco, as neither realistic proposals nor high-level attendance by major media people came forth." Moreover, the "US Government-sponsored organization for IYDP expressed discontent at Mr. Reich's access to the Secretary-General."[27]

Although there does not seem to be a report of the luncheon, the program as developed by Reich shows that he saw the US response to the IYDP as exemplary and that he would use the remaining days of the IYDP for a large awareness campaign.[28] This attempt was unsuccessful, but Reich was not discouraged. He wrote "chiefs of state and heads of international organizations to urge their ongoing commitment."[29] He wanted to follow up the IYDP with a "Bimillennium Project" that would "enhance recognition over time of the UN's significant humanitarian contribution and its great value as a moral force."[30] He wanted to "involve both governments and private sectors in setting goals to assist the disabled and to serve as a clearing house for information in the field of rehabilitation."[31] Throughout the 1980s Reich tried repeatedly to involve the secretary-general in his project.

From 1982 Reich and Javier Pérez de Cuéllar met almost annually, but the secretary-general's staff remained wary.[32] The UN staff possibly feared informal influence on Reich's part, whereas they wanted to shape disability policies through the official channels. The main responsibility for UN disability policies lay with the UN Centre for Social Development and Humanitarian Affairs in Vienna. However, the secretary-general himself did not seem to share his staff's concerns. He was willing to speak at a luncheon in 1984 organized by Reich.[33] The United Nations had limited ability and resources to carry out their disability policies, and the secretary-general was probably interested in Reich's attempt to encourage support for people with disabilities to be delivered with the help of NGOs and private companies instead of public money.[34]

A POTENTIAL TURNING POINT IN GLOBAL DISABILITY POLICIES

Although Reich wanted to improve UN policies, he did not really attempt to change them fundamentally, focused as they were on prevention, rehabilitation, and equalization of opportunities—the keywords of the WPA. Other figures at the international level, however, tried to steer UN disability policies during the late 1980s in the direction of human rights, and to get rid of medical concepts such as prevention and rehabilitation. Human rights were, as mentioned already, part of global disability policies, but were certainly not central to them. During the 1970s and early 1980s human rights had only formed the conceptual basis for social development policies. In the late 1980s, however, several figures attempted to make human rights more central.

The attempt I want to discuss first was undertaken by Norman Acton, a collaboration partner of Reich and secretary of Rehabilitation International (RI). This organization was an important partner of the United Nations in disability policies, especially because "in view of the financial constraints currently facing the United Nations the support of nongovernmental organizations is even more essential." Acton suggested to the secretary-general that the Disabled Persons Unit "might function better in a different administrative and geographic setting" such as Geneva or New York. Perhaps the unit could be associated with the Centre for Human Rights in Geneva instead of the Centre for Social Development and Humanitarian Affairs in Vienna, since "the human response to disability has evolved in recent years, emphasis has shifted toward greater attention to the rights of people who are disabled." However, Acton's suggestion was not followed up. One of the staff members said the UN General Assembly had made this decision because "issues related to disabled persons which are not solely a human rights concern should be considered in a broad development context."[35]

However, the United Nations did not subsequently consider disability in "a broad development context," as we have seen already in chapter 2. The dominance of the social development approach meant that disability was not well integrated in broader development policies, as became clear later when disability was not included in the Millennium Development Goals. The marginalization of disability within the UN system has been challenged repeatedly since the 1980s. In chapter 5 I shall deal in more detail with the human rights agenda of DPI, but I can state here that this organization had the same approach as Acton. In a World Council Meeting in July 1986, DPI had concluded that the "UN lacks financial resources to initiate any major effort to rescue the Decade."[36] In a letter to the secretary-general, DPI Chairman Henry Enns asked for "immediate action" to save the International Decade of Disabled Persons, to focus on "Equalization of Opportunity" instead of rehabilitation and prevention, and to move "the Disabled Persons Unit to New York or the Human Rights Centre in Geneva" because "this would facilitate coordination, as many International Bodies have their administrative base in those places."[37]

The arguments of Acton and Enns had similarities to that of Reich: In their opinion the disability unit at the Centre for Social Development and Humanitarian Affairs in Vienna was doing too little for global disability policies. In 1989 Reich wrote about the way the International Decade of Disabled Persons was being managed by the Vienna office as follows: They "truly are doing everything possible with limited resources" but had "not achieved the visibility or results for which we all had hoped."[38] However, Acton was driven not only by dissatisfaction with the Vienna office. He also pointed to the rise of the human rights perspective. Since the 1970s his organization had been interested in the legislative dimension of rehabilitation, but other organizations and individuals had also argued for a human rights approach to disability, and investigations into human rights violations. Here the increasing popularity of human rights may have been influential: Self-advocates and disability policymakers expected to improve the situation of people with disabilities by operating within the human rights framework.

However, the United Nations, as is clear from the secretary-general's response, was not eager to reframe disability in terms of human rights. Although research into violations began in 1984, we can see that the United Nations wanted to keep disability in the sphere of social development. In March 1985 the secretary-general received a letter from Mr. A. Cielens from Australia, who was wondering how he could use the 1975 declaration in his work to enhance the "welfare and rights of handicapped persons in this country," and "which procedures I should follow in lodging a formal complaint in relation to the exploitation and mistreatment of handicapped persons by non-profit and government organizations?"[39] The special assistant of the secretary-general explained in his reply that the United Nations did not have the "intention of endowing it with a binding quality such as treaties and other international agreements have under international law. However, the General Assembly called for national and international action to ensure that the Declaration will be used as a common basis and frame of reference for the protection of the rights contained in the Declaration."[40]

This policy was contested at The Global Meeting of Experts in 1987 in Stockholm organized by Bengt Lindqvist, Swedish deputy minister for social security, and prominent member of DPI. The Swedish government supported this meeting, aiming to strengthen the UN disability unit in Vienna. At this expert meeting, where self-advocates were well represented, the idea of developing a UN convention was discussed for the first time and became one of the experts' recommendations.[41] As already mentioned, this inspired representatives of Italy and Sweden to propose the drafting of a new UN disability convention, although these attempts were not successful. The reluctance of the UN General Assembly may be explained, as Lindqvist has suggested, by the framing of disability as an issue of social development and by "convention fatigue," because the United Nations at that time had adopted a women's convention and was also working on a children's convention.[42] As already mentioned at the start of this chapter, the staff of the secretary-general was also not keen on the recommendations from Stockholm.[43] Was collaborating with NGOs and companies in social development seen as a more feasible option?

CONSOLIDATION OF THE SOCIAL DEVELOPMENT APPROACH

This reluctance of UN bureaucrats to effect far-reaching changes in UN disability policy was similar to their response during the first years of Reich's diplomatic mission. Before a meeting with Reich in November 1986, for instance, the secretary-general was advised by staff members to make no commitments concerning publicity. The staff of the secretary-general had, in the words of Undersecretary-General for International Economic and Social Affairs Shuaib U. Yolah, "problems" with Reich's ideas because of "their financial and programmatic implications."[44] However, it is striking that the secretary-general remained interested in Reich's ideas whereas the idea of an international convention did not stand a chance in the late 1980s. Why this was the case may be illuminated by the following exchange between Reich and the secretary-general.

Reich arranged a meeting with the Secretary-General Javier Pérez de Cuéllar in 1986 because he was worried about the progress of the International Decade of Disabled Persons. On another occasion that year Reich had given a talk titled "The International Decade of Disabled Persons: Can it be saved?" According to Reich the hope with which the decade had been launched was fading: "So far, the world's attention has not been aroused. There is little political will." In this talk Reich quoted Pérez de Cuéllar, who had said that "outside the disability community, I have noted only minimal public awareness." The limited impact of the decade was not only to the disadvantage of the global "disability family" as Reich stated, but it would also damage the image of the United Nations: "If people were made aware that the UN successfully conducts and promotes important social and humanitarian programs, such as its Decade of Disabled Persons initiative, confidence in the UN itself would be enhanced."[45] It was probably this rhetoric to which the secretary-general was sensitive, although he would not always directly adopt Reich's solutions.

During the meeting Reich suggested the appointment of a special representative of the decade who could "save" it. To that suggestion he received the following response: "The Secretary-General does not deem it advisable to designate a special representative solely on his own initiative in relation to one of them."[46] The secretary-general did not leave it at that. In 1988 he appointed a special representative for the promotion of the decade, businessman and humanitarian Hans Hoegh from Denmark, and established a supporting "Committee of Wisemen." It appeared, as legal officer Sinha Basnayake wrote, "that the 'Wisemen' in question are commercial organizations ... the Note for the Secretary-General describing the proposal states that the involvement of the commercial organizations would be pro bono publico. We understand this to mean, inter alia, that these organizations would not use their association with the UN for commercial purposes." Hoegh felt that his efforts "particularly in the area of fund-raising, could greatly benefit from professional advice" from a committee for which he had identified organizations such as McKinsey & Company consultancy, known today as an influential neoliberal hub.[47]

Although UN staff remained cool toward Reich personally, it is evident that his business approach to disability policies was seen as promising. In retrospect we can even say that this approach foreshadowed "inclusive capitalism" as developed under the leadership of Kofi Annan.[48] Efforts to move disability policies in the direction of human rights (law) were, by contrast, simply blocked. Reich's approach remained in line with UN policies by keeping disability in the social development box and using human rights only as an underlying concept. It is plausible that many countries also favored this approach over a more radical human rights law perspective. Reich had good relationships with several important players at the global level. In a letter of the World Committee for the UN Decade of Disabled Persons, chaired by Reich, China for instance was mentioned as exemplary in disability policies: "We exchanged ideas with committee member Hon. Deng Pufang [son of Deng Xiaoping] during his recent visit to the United States, on the approach to national goal setting in China. China, almost uniquely among the nations of the world, has set forth a statement of national goals to be met by the end of the Decade. It is a model for possible use by other nations."[49]

Because of the reluctance of the United Nations to turn disability into an issue of human rights law, Lindqvist developed an alternative: a nonbinding document on disability policies. At a series of conferences, he and other participants from all over the world wrote a draft that was proposed by Swedish diplomats to the United Nations and became the Standard Rules on the Equalization of Opportunities for Disabled Persons (1993). Lindqvist was asked by Secretary-General Boutros Boutros-Ghali to become the special rapporteur responsible for monitoring implementation of the Standard Rules—although this position would not have been possible without financial support from Sweden.[50]

STEPS TOWARD A HUMAN RIGHTS CONVENTION?

The Standard Rules have often been seen as an important step toward the convention. In a tribute to Lindqvist, Alexis Buettgen and Ezra Zubrow present excerpts from his writings in which Lindqvist places the United Nations' adoption of the Standard Rules beside "two other important steps forward": the publication of Despouy's report *Human Rights and Disabled Persons* and the moment "when, in 1994, the Committee on Economic, Social and Cultural Rights (CESCR) issued General Comment No. 5, which deals with disability from a human rights perspective."[51] According to Lindqvist, this committee decided in the course of the 1990s that "disability should be fully recognized as a human rights concern for the UN and all its human rights bodies." He also suggests that he, during one of his sessions as rapporteur, inspired Maria Eugenia Antunez of Mexico with the idea of a disability convention.[52]

Lindqvist's priority during the 1990s, however, was clearly not the creation of a new convention. What he, human rights scholar Marcia Rioux, and others did was very much in line with CESCR General Comment No. 5: using existing international law and instruments to improve the national situations of disabled people. In 1995 Lindqvist contributed to a volume edited by Theresia Degener and Yolan Koster-Dreese in which several human rights instruments were evaluated from a disability perspective. The volume was the outcome of a project on disability and human rights led by the Dutch self-advocate Koster-Dreese and paid for by a Dutch foundation. The project was inspired by an international conference for and by people with disabilities in Maastricht in 1993 where international lawyer and self-advocate Degener had given a lecture on disability and human rights. According to the editors, this "paper work ... can become a strong weapon in the hands, minds and feet of those who are willing to fight repression and discrimination." In addition to the scholarly publication they also made a popular edition: "In order to assist Dutch organisations of disabled persons in improving this role, the Gehandicaptenraad has published a Hand- Nose- and Foot-Book as a supplement to this volume. Other countries are encouraged to follow this path."[53] This volume makes clear that disabled self-advocates at that time prioritized the use of existing human rights instruments to improve the national situations of disabled people.

Internationalists such as Lindqvist and Rioux continued to follow that trail. When they organized an international seminar on disability and human rights in 2000 titled "Let the World Know," they focused on the development of "mechanisms for using current International instruments and mechanisms for bringing disability in the mainstream of right concerns" and the option "to pursue a specific convention on disability" was not addressed.[54] The choice to work with the existing instruments also explains why Lindqvist was positive about the way in which the CESCR dealt with disability. This evaluation, however, was not shared by everyone.

During the late 1990s other self-advocates, including Theresia Degener, had become increasingly dissatisfied with the social development approach, because the UN Commission for Social Development, to which the special rapporteur had to report, turned out to be "a poor cousin" of the Commission on Human Rights: Meetings of the latter "were crowded and often standing room only," whereas the former "barely attracted attention in capitals, was attended mainly by junior delegations from New York Missions, and numerous empty seats signified that many delegations simply did not bother to turn up."[55] Therefore the International Disability Alliance, in which the main international disability organizations worked together, began in around 2000 to strive for a separate convention. Their lobbying was accompanied early in 2002 by publication by the Office of High Commissioner for Human Rights of an evaluative study on human rights instruments in the context of disability. This study showed clearly how the human rights of people with disabilities were not fully protected under existing human rights law, and recommended drafting a new human rights convention.[56]

The emergence of this new approach explains why I am reluctant to see the Standard Rules as a step toward the convention. According to the participants of "Let the World Know" these two trails or approaches did "not preclude each other," but the existence of different approaches shows at least that the convention cannot be explained as a logical or necessary outcome of the Standard Rules.[57] That is—as I argued in chapter 2—already clear from their content: The emphasis of the Standard Rules was more on equal needs and social development than on equal rights. The Standard Rules would set the tone for the 1990s: Although it was very difficult to include disability in general development programs, the Standard Rules further strengthened disability as a relevant category in global policies and stimulated national action plans and self-advocacy.[58] The inclusion of disability in international human rights law, however, was blocked in the late 1980s, and a social development approach gained ground.

This approach continued during the 1990s, owing partly to Reich's diplomatic relationship with the secretary-general. For instance, at a meeting of the secretary-general with DPI in 1992, Joshua Teke Malinga stated that "one frustration that NGOs had was the layers of hierarchy in the United Nations. That day was the first time that they were in direct contact with the Secretary-General."[59] Reich by contrast, in collaboration with the secretary-general's secretariat, launched in 1995 the Franklin D. Roosevelt International Disability Award (see figure 4.1) that "will be presented each year, beginning in 1996, to a nation that has made noteworthy progress toward the goal of the UN World Programme of Action Concerning Disabled Persons."[60] Reference to this program, designed in 1981, shows that Reich considered the social development approach to disability as relevant as ever, and saw no need to refer to a human rights (law) approach that was increasingly being championed by others. Reich was not an opponent, but human rights were simply not a central concept for him.

In 2002 he wrote to Secretary-General Kofi Annan with great enthusiasm that disability was being embraced as a relevant policy category by the president of the World Bank.[61] Disability activist and policymaker Judy Heumann was appointed that year as advisor on Disability and

FIGURE 4.1 Alan A. Reich at the UN Headquarters in 2003 when Italy received the Franklin Delano Roosevelt International Disability Award. Left to right: Marcello Spatafora, Permanent Representative of Italy to the United Nations; Alan A. Reich, Chairman of the World Committee on Disability; Julian Robert Hunte (Saint Lucia), President of the fifty-eighth session of the UN General Assembly; Roberto Maroni, Minister for Social Welfare and Labour of Italy; Mrs. Nane Annan; William J. vanden Heuvel, Co-Chair of the Roosevelt Institute; David A. Roosevelt, great-grandson of Franklin Delano Roosevelt and Trustee of the Roosevelt Institute; and Christopher Breiseth, President of the Roosevelt Institute. (UN Photo/Eskinder Debebe)

Development in order to "integrate a disability lens across the institution" in its focus on the "development for the poorest of the poor."[62] A year earlier Reich had written to the secretariat that he had started to challenge "our good friend" Jim Wolfensohn to make disability more central in the bank's policies. This seems to fit the UN "inclusive capitalism" strategy as developed under the leadership of Annan: Gillian Martin Sorensen, the assistant to the secretary-general for external relations, wrote to Reich that she was happy to hear about the attempt to involve the World Bank: "You are doing wonderful work!"[63]

Interestingly, negotiations about the convention had started at the same time. One of the reasons why in 2001 the United Nations adopted Mexico's proposal to create an Ad Hoc Committee of the General

Assembly to "consider proposals for a comprehensive and integral convention to promote and protect the rights and dignity of persons with disabilities" was, as mentioned, the omission of disability from the Millennium Development Goals.[64] It was therefore unclear if the convention would become a human rights or a social development treaty. According to Theresia Degener, it was clear "from day one" during the first meeting of the Ad Hoc Committee in July 2002 that there was "no agreement on the need for a convention." Apart from the divide between opponents and supporters of a human rights convention, some delegations were cautious because they feared "a convention could end up focusing on social development," and others suggested a social development treaty.[65]

However, the second meeting, in June 2003, was no longer focused on the need for a convention, but on the appropriate scope for a holistic convention covering a broad range of rights.[66] During this meeting and its year of preparation disability was finally moved into the sphere of human rights, mainly due to the influence of a coalition of international lawyers and disability self-advocates who had been working from an international law perspective on disability since the late 1990s.[67] The turn from social development to human rights during the convention negotiations did not mean that social development was no longer important: In 2008 the secretary-general characterized the convention as "a human rights instrument with an explicit social development dimension."[68] Yet human rights were to come first. The story of Reich's efforts shows that this was by no means the logical outcome of the previous decades.

This chapter has shown that global disability policies were hardly affected by the "breakthrough" of human rights during the 1990s as described by Hoffmann. Inspired by Anghie's review of Moyn's work, I have argued that disability was first and foremost seen as an issue of (social) development. However, the development approach to disability that hindered its integration in international law was not the "utopia of development" characterized by a "structural" approach to (in)equality as described by

Anghie and others.⁶⁹ The development approach I have traced in this chapter followed a different idea, one that may be characterized as neoliberal imagination. In a slight departure from the existing literature, this chapter has shown that global disability policies were not so much determined by a coalition between neoliberalism and human rights, but by a coalition of neoliberalism and development that thought no benefit could be gained from applying human rights law. This does not mean that the "suffering" of people with disabilities did not receive attention from a human rights perspective during the 1990s, or that the human rights approach was not worked out further by international lawyers.⁷⁰ But it was not until negotiations about the convention began that the United Nations started to move away from a social development to a human rights approach. Remarkably, this latter approach was not a variation on the nonutopian interpretation of human rights, namely as the "bare minimum" that Hoffmann sees as becoming dominant after the Cold War.⁷¹ Compared with other international law, the international disability convention of 2006 was sensitive to "issues of structural power and oppression." It seems therefore to have stimulated the "social imaginary of a different, more perfect society."⁷²

The use of human rights by global disability policymakers thus seems somewhat atypical when considering the broader developments in post–Cold War human rights history. However, in historiography the emphasis has mainly been on the use of human rights in relation to "high" international politics, whereas attention to the use of human rights by and for marginalized groups such as disabled people may suggest other trajectories.⁷³ It is interesting in this regard that a "more perfect society" for people with disabilities has often been imagined as a national society. Disability human rights were not only influenced by the understanding of human rights as individual rights which enjoy international protection that has dominated recent decades, according to Moyn and Hoffmann. The convention shows human rights being aimed at domestic policies, parallel to the use of human rights in foreign policy and by NGOs such as Amnesty International in recent decades. Has the national framework remained more important than the literature suggests, and is it perhaps again one of the dominant framings of human rights today? China for instance is known for its resistance to international intervention but has not considered the convention as a threat.[74] Does the case of China indicate that we are currently moving away from using human rights as an international yardstick by which to judge the bad behavior of others, and toward understanding them as an instrument to show one's own good behavior to vulnerable others within the nation? Before I discuss these questions in the Epilogue of this book, I shall first continue the story of self-advocates and how they cocreated the convention.

5

VIENNA 1993

"Adopt or Adjust Legislation to Assure Access"

Before negotiations concerning the convention, social development was unmistakably the dominant international approach to disability. The human rights of people with disabilities were regularly mentioned in global policies but attempts to recognize and protect them internationally were unsuccessful. The World Conference on Human Rights in 1993 in Vienna, Austria, was important for human rights more broadly and for the rights of "vulnerable" groups in particular. According to Roland Burke a narrow understanding of human rights as internationally protected, individual freedom rights dominated the conference. But the rights of groups such as women and Indigenous people also "found prominent expression."[1] The Vienna Declaration and Programme of Action also "unreservedly" included the human rights of disabled people and called on "Governments, where necessary, to adopt or adjust legislation to assure access to these and other rights for disabled persons."[2] Although this recognition in Vienna did not directly contribute to the making of a new international disability law, it nevertheless indicates that it had become acceptable at the international level to refer to disability as a human rights issue. This is mainly to the credit of the human rights committee of Disabled Peoples' International (DPI). In this chapter I shall discuss how the human rights agenda of self-advocates developed from the late 1980s and how it took a surprising turn in the European context.

FROM TRIBUNAL TO STANDARD RULES

The inclusion of disabled people at the Vienna conference was not straightforward. "Disabled Pushed Aside at Conference" was the headline of a short article in a nongovernmental organization (NGO) bulletin published on June 15, 1993. In this article self-advocate Rachel Hurst reported restrictions in the use of elevators in the conference building, the steep ramp at the Metro station near the conference venue, and the absence of braille materials and sign language, all of which made the conference less accessible to people with disabilities. Another self-advocate, Anthony Sivabalan Thanasayan from Malaysia, had to leave the conference earlier than planned: "disappointed" because he "has hit many problems with his wheelchair since arriving. His hotel had three steps up to the elevator and one up to the bed." DPI organized a protest to address the inaccessibility of the conference venue and meetings for people with disabilities, but it was of course too late to realize full accessibility during the conference.[3]

It was not the first time that DPI had confronted the United Nations concerning inaccessibility. In 1987 self-advocates had entered the UN Headquarters in New York City. Henry Enns wrote in a short report that:

> the Clerk of the Third Committee of the United Nations General Assembly jumped to his feet as a dozen disabled people, some blind, in wheelchairs, or using crutches, entered the main floor of the UN buildings. Quickly he approached Irene Feika, the Chairperson of COPOH from Canada, who displayed no obvious disability, with the question "Are you in charge of these disabled persons?" The implication being clearly: "Get these disabled people out of there." Her response was quite innocently, "No, I'm not in charge." When asked who she was, she

pointed to the Chairperson of DPI who was in a wheelchair. Where upon he turned white as a sheet and was speechless.

When representatives of governments started to talk with the self-advocates, the clerk had to accept "disabled people occupied the main floor of the Human Rights Committee meeting room" because the balconies for observers were not accessible. As Enns stated, "the 'storm' was symbolic, not only of the attitudes and barriers that disabled people still face within the UN system, but the efforts of disabled persons to break down those barriers."[4]

DPI followed different strategies to break down barriers and to put disability on the agenda. The full paragraph on "the rights of the disabled person" in the Vienna Declaration and Programme of Action has not only been attributed to the above-mentioned protest but was mainly due to DPI's preparation for the conference. The DPI Human Rights Committee did everything in order "to try to make the Human Rights of persons with disabilities a major part of the Conference agenda." In their newsletter they provided DPI members with the contact details of people who could be helpful during the organizing of the conference. Among them was human rights lawyer Manfred Nowak, who was designated by the Austrian government to work with NGOs on accommodation and other facilities such as accessible transportation, and the German self-advocate and lawyer Theresia Degener, who at that time had an internship at the UN Committee on Economic, Social and Cultural Rights (CESCR) in Geneva.[5] From 1993 Degener would become one of the main advocates of the human rights perspective at the international level, building on what DPI had done since the early 1980s. During 1981 Degener had already been involved in one of the most striking initiatives of people with disabilities, the so-called cripple tribunal in Germany. As an alternative to the self-congratulating official German celebration of the International Year of Disabled Persons (IYDP), self-advocates organized a tribunal where people with disabilities could report human rights violations.[6]

The understanding of human rights by the German self-advocates as an (international) yardstick for the maltreatment of people with disabilities was carried forward in the Human Rights Committee of DPI. As we saw at the end of chapter 3, DPI soon developed a critical understanding of the disability human rights declarations of the 1970s. During the 1980s they preferred an understanding of human rights that was, as was common at the time, focused on freedom. They worked closely with the special rapporteur, Leandro Despouy, who collected stories about human rights violations, often in an institutional setting. In the case of Japan, DPI brought out a report about the maltreatment of the "institutionalized mentally ill" to the UN Sub-Commission on Prevention of Discrimination and Protection of Minorities in 1985. This was a success: Japan changed its law.[7]

In its attempts to put disability on the UN human rights agenda in the 1980s and early 1990s, the drafting of a convention was not the main aim of DPI. This does not mean that it was against a convention. At a DPI meeting in Stockholm in 1987 related to the Global Meeting of Experts that would recommend the drafting of a convention, Henry Enns emphasized that collaboration between international organizations of people with disabilities was important for the World Programme of Action (WPA) and for "an international convention to eliminate all forms of discrimination against disabled persons."[8] The organizer of the Global Meeting of Experts, the UN Centre for Social Development and Humanitarian Affairs, had written in a Preliminary Information Note that the WPA "explicitly promotes the right of all human beings to equal opportunities and is an important extension of the concept of human rights," but the idea of a convention seems not yet to have been fully formed and was probably the individual initiative of one of the participants, the Italian international lawyer Maria Saulle.[9]

Although DPI supported Saulle's initiative and expressed the hope that the United Nations would begin drafting an "international convention on the elimination of all forms of discrimination against disabled persons, to be available for ratification before the end of the Decade of Disabled Persons in 1992," the self-advocates did not seem entirely sure of the relevance of a convention.[10] In his capacity as representative of the Nordic countries, Bengt Lindqvist said in the UN discussion about Saulle's proposal that these countries "were not convinced of the need for another convention because the human rights of all persons were already set forth in the Universal Declaration of Human Rights and the International Covenants on Economic, Social and Cultural Rights and on Civil and Political Rights."[11] This doubt was not unknown to DPI either. In 1988 their Human Rights Committee wrote that the organization:

> needs to seriously consider whether a convention on the Rights of Disabled is a useful initiative at this time. Some talk is circulating about such a Convention. We are concerned that we cannot even get countries to ratify our existing Convention under the ILO. As far as substantive rights go, we have the General Assembly, Declarations, the resolutions, DPI has gotten passed by the Commission and Sub-Commission, the World Programme of Action, and the up-coming report of the Special Rapporteur [Despouy]. We think these rights are clear in themselves and our efforts should be in using the Rapporteur's mandate to indicate violations, in urging ratifications of the ILO Convention, and in assisting national chapters in implementation by way of direct work with governments, or by way of the denunciation/negotiation process at the UN forums.[12]

Despite this reluctance toward a convention, Bengt Lindqvist put forward the idea again in 1989 to the United Nations as representative of Sweden. During the forty-fourth session of the UN General Assembly, he "expressed disappointment at the inadequate implementation of the World Programme of Action concerning Disabled Persons" and stated that "legally binding international regulations must be laid down to guarantee the full implementation of existing international instruments on the rights of disabled persons." There was, according to Lindqvist, "little use in asserting that all individuals had the right to use public transport, if the need for special services and arrangements for disabled persons was not recognized." In order to improve the situation, Sweden would request "at the appropriate time . . . to prepare a draft international convention on the rights of disabled persons."[13] It soon became clear that the "appropriate time" had not come yet: As I mentioned in previous chapters, the United Nations did not start drafting a new convention.

The response of DPI was ambivalent. On the one hand, in the early 1990s the organization expressed the ambition to develop an international monitory mechanism for human rights violations against disabled persons similar to that of Amnesty International.[14] On the other hand, DPI wrote in 1990 that "our committee's position is to discourage such a convention at this time and to focus on developing a stronger General Assembly declaration." They referred again to the International Labour Organization (ILO) convention and its low number of ratifications. Moreover, the committee thought "the cost in time and money in pursuing a convention are enormous, and well beyond the present capability of DPI."[15] The reluctance of DPI is maybe surprising from a contemporary perspective, but it is understandable given the international experiences of disability self-advocacy at that time. Year in, year out the DPI human rights commission was trying to draw attention to the delay of Human Rights Rapporteur Leandro Despouy's report owing to financial constraints and its low priority.[16] Despite everything, DPI kept looking for the "possible creation of an international structure to address the human rights violations of disabled people."[17]

Thanks to the efforts of Bengt Lindqvist the United Nations decided in 1990 to start the drafting of a nonbinding instrument that in 1993 became the Standard Rules.[18] Compared with his attempt in 1989 this was a compromise: The Standard Rules were not binding international law, and disability rights did not become part of the human rights machinery of the United Nations. In the Standard Rules the human rights of people with disabilities were kept in the social development sphere of the United Nations and were mainly understood within a national framework. When DPI board member Joshua Malinga gave a speech to the UN General Assembly in 1992, he stated that disability was a human rights issue and that "each nation should enact human rights legislation to protect and promote the rights of disabled people."[19] This was the same understanding of disability human rights as formulated in the Vienna Declaration and Programme of Action. The World Conference and the Standard Rules thus did not mark the inclusion of people with disabilities into the UN human rights policies and into international law, but they did embrace human rights as human needs in global disability policies. The Standard Rules did not approach the "legal disadvantage" of people with disabilities "in relation to other vulnerable groups" by launching "an international body to provide them with particular and specific protection" as proposed by Despouy and others, but by encouraging states to improve their legislation. In fact, many countries introduced disability into their anti-discrimination law during the 1990s. Therefore, one would expect the Convention on the Rights of Persons with Disabilities (CRPD) to be focused on discrimination in the same way as the women's convention was, but it had a much broader scope. This can be better understood if we take into account historical developments at the European level.

THE EUROPEAN SOCIAL MODEL

Europe is famous for its social model. Even "people who blame 'Europe' for threatening their national welfare state" often, as historian Sandrine Kott recently pointed out, "would agree that a special 'European social model' exists and that it provides a level of protection and redistribution unmatched anywhere else in the world." According to Kott, the ILO was "instrumental in first defining what could be called a 'European social model,'" developed during the interwar period against the competing models of communism and fascism. After the Second World War this model was not initially institutionalized at the European level, but at the national level: European institutions were usually aimed at an open economic market and left social policies to national governments. During the Cold War the European model fostered social dialogue, self-administered insurance schemes and social rights, and was seen as a "middle way taken by Western Europe, between the US attitude of 'laissez-faire' and the Eastern European welfare dictatorships." From the 1980s onward the "social pact" which lay "at the heart of the European social model" was undermined, according to Kott, by conservative

European political leaders, a development which appeared to be further strengthened by the fall of communist regimes after 1989.[20]

As already explained in the Introduction, the assumption that (European) welfare states have improved the lives of people with disabilities has been increasingly questioned by disability self-advocates since the 1980s. Their critique is often framed in the literature as part of a paradigm shift from disability as a social-welfare issue to disability as a human rights and discrimination issue. However, this shift appears less clear than sometimes suggested, and social-welfare issues became relatively well integrated in the CRPD. In order to explain this, I shall use the remaining part of this chapter to discuss the way in which disability rights were approached by European institutions and self-advocates. I shall do this from an entangled perspective, approaching developments at the European level in relation to what happened at other levels and as entangled with institutions and self-advocates elsewhere.[21] In approaching European disability policies in a non-internalist way, I shall show that the support of disability self-advocates for the European social model was less complete than one would expect from this group: Despite their critical perspective, however, they kept this model on board after 1989 when general support for it was declining, as Kott pointed out.

A "CONSIDERABLE BURDEN"

Considering the fact that what is now the European Union (EU) started out as the European Coal and Steel Community and European Atomic Energy Community, and that one of the fundamental aims of this community was to foster the free movement of labor, it is not surprising that the initial concern of the community regarding disabled (or—as they were then still called—handicapped) people was integrating them into the labor market, which was not at all simple in the free-market economy and particularly in times of crisis.[22] In 1973 a document called "Proposal for a Decision on Action by the European Social Fund to Assist the Social and Occupational Integration of the Handicapped" declared that "In the countries of the European Community responsible circles are becoming increasingly aware of the problems of handicapped persons." It established that the number of those persons whose working capacity was reduced because of handicap was increasing, and that although no precise statistics existed, it was estimated that several millions of people were affected in this way. It then went on to state that:

> In economic terms the existence of such a large number is a *considerable burden*. Non-rehabilitated handicapped persons do not contribute to the production process, they are below average consumers, they do not pay taxes and they account for a considerable share of the social budget. The integration of handicapped persons into active life makes it possible to reduce these disadvantages and provides a considerable contribution to the labour force.... Vocational and social integration, by giving handicapped persons fresh motivation and new dynamism, helps to make them *more independent and responsible*. This is one of the major factors in a social policy to help these people.[23]

Aiming to relieve this "burden," a great deal of policymaking in the 1970s revolved around health and safety regulations intended to help to avoid industrial accidents. Rehabilitation of injured people to enable them to reenter the labor market was another important goal. In European institutions disability was thus primarily seen as an issue related to a labor-based welfare state which was mainly organized at the national level but embedded in Europe. The framing of disability at the European level thus reflected the way in which the concept and the group were often approached in European welfare states.[24] As I shall show below, the International Year of Disabled Persons as it was given shape by the United Nations in 1981 did not really contest this framing, but nevertheless did add new layers and strengthened certain tendencies.

NEW AWARENESS

The main aim of the IYDP was to integrate disabled people into the mainstream of life. In addition to the United Nations and its member states, the IYDP was also observed at the regional level.[25] The European Parliament passed a resolution on March 11, 1981 which affirmed a commitment to promote social and economic integration for disabled people, in addition to their vocational integration.[26] During the IYDP the development of a European community action program concerning disabled people was considered, but mainly because of the economic crisis at that time this remained only an idea.[27] Nevertheless, the IYDP marks a change in European policies: Up to this time integration was first and foremost understood in terms of vocational rehabilitation. The broad focus of the IYDP stimulated the commission to expand its efforts in rehabilitation for work with attention to the social integration of the disabled. For the first time European institutions were challenged to set up a coherent and overall policy on all matters concerning the disabled, with the aim to promote social and economic integration and an independent life.[28] In this way the IYDP stimulated an integrated approach to disability that would become increasingly common in Europe and elsewhere.

It took until 1986 for the European Council to approve a new disability recommendation. The recommendation itself was meant "to promote fair opportunities for disabled people in the field of employment and vocational training." It also called for realistic targets for the employment of disabled people in firms and the preparation of a code of good practice. It was expected that the commission would coordinate the exchange of information and experience on the rehabilitation and employment of disabled people between national authorities. Moreover, the recommendation called for "giving particular priority to the active involvement of disabled people, whether in a representative or personal capacity, in the taking and implementation of decisions concerning them."[29]

The recommendation shows in the first place that employment remained the focal point of European disability policies. Second, it makes clear how the "European social model" functioned: Nation-states were responsible for welfare, and Europe facilitated the exchange between nations. Third, it acknowledged in line with the IYDP the need to grant more autonomy to disabled people and to foster their initiatives. Within

European institutions this acknowledgment was already marked by the foundation of the "Disability Intergroup" in 1980, in which parliamentarians and self-advocates could informally meet.[30] Partly due to the informal character of the intergroup, however, the voice of disabled persons was hardly heard in the European institutions, let alone their opinion about the European social model. That would change a little in the 1990s.

THE INSTITUTIONALIZATION OF SELF-ADVOCATES

In the 1980s the possibilities to use European institutions for improving the situation of disabled persons were limited, certainly when compared with those offered by the United Nations and several individual countries. The IYDP, as the current literature indicates, initially had the greatest impact in Europe at the national level, bringing together disability activists in several countries and challenging governments to deal with disability as an umbrella concept for groups previously approached separately.[31] The transnational exchange between disability activists as invoked by the IYDP, most notably DPI, proved crucial. As discussed in chapter 3, this cross-disability organization was founded during the IYDP as a result of disabled self-advocates' dissatisfaction with the dominance of nondisabled experts in the international sphere. With the IYDP the United Nations became an important venue for disability activists to raise their concerns, but it took a while before their ideas, such as a (human) rights-based approach to disability, were really picked up. One of the reasons why their new approach to disability made slow progress was the fact that disability was already institutionalized in other ways—a phenomenon that could be seen as "path dependency." Rehabilitation was, as I argued in chapter 2, for a long time a much more important concept in UN disability policies than were human rights.

When disability activists intensified their attempts to influence European institutions in the 1990s, they ran into this "path dependency" of disability. It will not be a surprise that the path of European disability policies in the 1990s was still focused on labor. One of the main aims of the Community Action Programmes for Disabled People HELIOS I (1988–1991) and II (1993–6) was to improve employment opportunities by stimulating the vocational training and rehabilitation of people with disabilities.[32] Europe was not alone in following this path as before. In the Asia-Pacific region for instance the United Nations Economic and Social Commission for Asia and the Pacific (UNESCAP) declared an Asian and Pacific Decade of Disabled Persons (1993–2002) that, in line with the IYDP, focused on "the expansion of opportunities for the full participation of people with disabilities in society and their equality in the development process."[33] In Europe the welfare state remained the dominant lens through which disability was viewed.

However, continuity in policies should not disguise the increasing role of disabled self-advocates. The previously mentioned development of self-advocacy in the international sphere in the 1980s was not directly visible in Europe. Within DPI, besides national councils, five regional councils were formed, including one for Europe. Resources within DPI were mainly used for developing countries, which meant that there was no money available for Europe. Regional work was therefore for a long time dependent on the resources of individual members. DPI Europe was concerned with European initiatives like the computerized database Handynet, but this self-advocacy organization was only one of a myriad of NGOs, many run by nondisabled people.[34] The influence of disabled people was, according to disability self-advocate Rachel Hurst, also limited during the HELIOS programs.[35]

A closer look at these programs and in particular HELIOS II shows that Hurst's observation is only partly true. In practice the HELIOS programs facilitated mainly the exchange of information, and in this exchange the voice of disability self-advocates was probably not always heard. The HELIOS II program, however, was seen as a way to realize a more "comprehensive, consistent policy." Moreover, the "dialogue group" that was already part of HELIOS I was formalized under HELIOS II: "This group comprises only representatives of the representative European non-governmental organizations, the aim being to exchange views on HELIOS II activities."[36] In the program disabled self-advocates were officially acknowledged as advisers of the European commission. In this way the first European cross-disability self-advocacy organization, the European Disability Forum (EDF), was formed as a working group and explicitly integrated into the HELIOS II program.[37] With HELIOS II the European commission took a step beyond general statements about the importance of self-advocacy: How could this official recognition come about?

Meanwhile, from the early 1990s the World Council of Disabled People International offered money and "lobbying skills learnt at the international level" with which DPI Europe could strengthen its influence in Europe. When the European Parliament decided not to renew Helios I in 1991, DPI Europe used this decision to ask together with other self-advocacy organizations for a "more democratic consultative mechanism." Moreover, DPI succeeded in the 1990s together with the European Network on Independent Living in obtaining funding from the European commission for several independent living programs.[38] An important symbolic moment was the first European celebration of the International Day of Disabled Persons, December 3, 1992. DPI wanted to use this day, as announced by the United Nations, to raise awareness with "its message of human rights (not rattling charity cans at street corners!)."[39] After several requests and a threat of action they received permission to use the official Parliament chamber of the EU in Brussels to have a so-called "parliament of disabled people": 440 disabled people from all over Europe came to the Parliament to talk with the commissioner for Social Affairs, members of the European Parliament, and commission officials. The attendees were impressed by the stories told by disabled people, and the European Parliament decided to support the "Disabled People's Parliament Resolution to Support the UN Standard Rules" and "to research the real situation of disabled people in Europe and to find out what was happening with the rise of violence and fascism." According to Rachel Hurst this day was a watershed moment and since then the voice of disabled people at the European level has been strengthened.[40] The result of these actions was that self-advocates gained the opportunity in 1993 to start a working group with self-advocacy organizations that became in 1997 the EDF and continues to play an important role on the European scene.

BEYOND A WELFARE STATE PERSPECTIVE?

HELIOS II shows that a stronger voice for disabled people went along with a new critique that challenged the welfare state. In an interim evaluation report from January 1996 the commission mentioned the innovative results of the program, most notably the "active participation by the disabled people" and an "approach recognizing the equal rights of disabled people as opposed to being based on assistance." According to the commission this was part of "an approach to policy on the disabled in terms of human rights as opposed to a 'social welfare' approach." At the same time the commission noted "differing and sometimes contradictory views" in the program "reflecting the contradictions inherent in all policies concerning the disabled as implemented in the Member States, and in particular the tensions between the 'medical' and 'social' concepts of disability."[41] In the final report published in 1998 the program was seen as a laboratory from which lessons had to be drawn. The focus on exchange was seen as the main limitation because "with limited resources" it remained dependent on participants at national and local levels for its capacity to bring about "real" change (in services and policy for disabled people). Moreover, it remained "very dependent on local and national participants for its capacity to bring about real participation and consultation for disabled people." Therefore, the program, according to the commission, had to be followed up by "steps to promote a rights-based approach in the field of disability."[42]

The 1998 report shows that Helios II contributed to the slow integration of a new rights-based perspective on disability. Before I discuss the further institutionalization of this approach, I shall discuss the context in which European institutions became a venue for disability rights. Important developments in the process of European integration such as the Maastricht Treaty (1992) probably encouraged disability self-advocates to aim at Europe. Moreover, two developments outside the direct influence of the European institutions played a role in the rise of a rights-based approach to disability at the European level.

First, the reluctance of international organizations to make disability part of their human rights work seems to have encouraged the development of human rights (law) expertise within and related to self-advocacy organizations in Europe.[43] Already in the late 1980s, DPI Europe organized an international seminar on human rights with Maria Saulle as one of the main speakers.[44] In 1993, at the international conference for and by people with disabilities in Maastricht titled Eur'able, Theresia Degener mentioned the UN Report on Human Rights and Disability (1993) as the "first official study of the causal connection between serious violations of human rights and fundamental freedoms and disability." Although this study did not result in a direct change at the UN level, we can observe during the 1990s the increasing attention of European self-advocates to anti-discrimination law and disability, and exploratory investigations of human rights violations. The Dutch council of disabled people initiated, as already mentioned, a book project about human rights and disability, which was published in 1995 and contained several chapters written by lawyers.[45] The views developed from this (human) rights perspective had already gained influence during Helios II and continued to do so afterward. Contrary to what was suggested in the program evaluations, however, I shall argue below that the adoption of a rights-based approach did not necessarily come at the expense of the welfare perspective.[46]

Second, emancipation of people with disabilities in the United States came to be seen as exemplary. The understanding of disability as a (civil) rights issue inspired activists in the United States to aim for anti-discrimination laws in the 1980s, resulting in the Americans with Disabilities Act (ADA) in 1990. This law related to the welfare state in an interesting way. As research on the realization of the ADA shows, this anti-discrimination law and the welfare state were framed as almost mutually exclusive. The law was promoted on the grounds that discrimination not only "denies people with disabilities the opportunity to compete on an equal basis," but also costs the United States "billions of dollars." This framing was crucial for the passage of this law: It was, according to Katharina Heyer, "good economic policy to turn people with disabilities from welfare dependents into productive taxpayers." In lobbying for the law this "welfare argument" was frequently used. The Republicans and the disability community were even called "strange bedfellows," united in the conviction that "only the truly needy should receive welfare and that others should be given the opportunity to work and to become self-reliant and responsible citizens."[47] During the 1990s the ADA would be seen internationally as a model of disability law. In the next section I shall discuss the way in which this law was followed up by European self-advocates, and the consequences for the European social model.

A EUROPEANS WITH DISABILITIES ACT?

Without these developments we cannot really understand the institutionalization of disability self-advocacy and the change in policies in Europe during the 1990s, most noticeably the inclusion of disability in Article 13 of the Treaty of Amsterdam (1997). Legal experts were heavily involved in lobbying the EDF to include disability in this treaty, an addition to the Maastricht Treaty, the founding treaty of the EU. The inclusion of disability in the Treaty of Amsterdam had not been intended by the European institutions.[48] However, the EDF had developed an argument on how disability could be part of the broadening and deepening of existing anti-discrimination measures, and received support from the Intergovernmental Conference Reflection Group that prepared the negotiations—with only one dissenting voice ("widely presumed to be the U.K. Conservative Government of the time").[49] The desire of the European disability NGOs for a general nondiscrimination provision was not granted, but the inclusion of disability in the Amsterdam Treaty was seen as a breakthrough because European governments acknowledged for the first time the reality of the discrimination experienced by people with disabilities.[50] According to Mark Priestley, the

Amsterdam Treaty gave momentum to the "disability rights" agenda and made possible the Framework Directive on Non-discrimination in Occupation and Employment in the year 2000 as the "first legislative intervention on disabled people's rights."[51] Disability was also included in the Charter of Fundamental Rights, a nonbinding document adopted by the EU in the same year.[52]

Because of this the impression could be given that European disability policymakers shifted from a welfare state and "social Europe" approach to one based on equal rights. This impression seems to be underlined by the role played by British self-advocates at the European level. British activists were one of the driving forces behind European disability self-advocacy, in contrast to the UK government, which played an obstructing role during the negotiations about Article 13 and the subsequent Framework Equal Treatment Directive (2000).[53] The British activists not only brought the social model of disability, as coined by Mike Oliver, to Europe, but in their own country and in Europe they fought for anti-discrimination laws.[54] These British perspectives included critical evaluations of the welfare state, although less critical and less legalistic than in the American context.[55] Can we therefore say that Europe in the late 1990s followed the Anglo-American shift to equal rights that would "replace and not complement measures of social security?"[56]

A closer look at the European discussions reveals that the ADA and the British Disability Discrimination Act (1995) could not be translated easily into a "Europeans with Disabilities Act" because of the tension "between the solidarity-based social welfare model, traditionally associated with Europe, and the more individualistic civil rights approach, traditionally associated with countries such as the United States."[57] In the literature on disability policies and movements this tension is often framed in a negative way, opposing the welfare approach to the equal rights approach. However, that seems not to have been intended by the European institutions. In the post-Amsterdam disability policies, we still find much attention to employment, as for instance in the case of the 2000 directive. Moreover, equal rights were often not seen to be in opposition to a welfare approach. Deborah Mabbett has pointed to a Comité des Sages, established by the European commission in 1994 to reflect on the future of the community chapter, that argued "that the crisis of the welfare state called for a new unified approach to rights" beyond the separation of civil and social rights. She also mentions the development of the concept "social exclusion" that "widened the traditional focus of poverty policy beyond concern with income adequacy and towards issues of access to employment, housing, health care and education." Therefore the "inclusion of disability, age and sexual orientation" in Article 13, according to Mabbett, must be seen as part of the "modernizing and restructuring" of the way "European welfare states regulate the life courses and family arrangements of their citizens."[58]

Moreover, the scholars who worked alongside European self-advocates were explicitly aiming at a fusion of the Anglo-American civil rights model with the European social-welfare approach. The desire for a "Europeans with Disabilities Act" did not prevent scholars such as Lisa Waddington, who has worked with the EDF, from arguing for a new synthesis between the two approaches, and "a system based on a broader notion of social justice that stressed the right of each individual to a basic income and the opportunity for economic success" and a "set of economic and social rights that are grounded on principles of respect for human dignity."[59]

We can observe in both these European policies and in the literature of activist scholars an attempt to combine the European social model with a civil rights- and anti-discrimination-oriented model. Therefore we have to be careful about claiming a paradigm shift, as has been recognized in the formulation of Anne Waldschmidt that European disability policies changed during the 1990s from "a formerly disregarded branch of traditional social policy into a modern formation which comprises *not only* social protection and labor market integration, *but also* equal rights and non-discrimination."[60] The same is true for the CRPD, which includes rights that could be related to both an anti-discrimination and a welfare perspective. The inclusion of social rights seems not so much an effort of European diplomats but in my view the result of efforts by European international lawyers and self-advocates such as Theresia Degener.[61] In the historiography of disability self-advocacy this relatively recent and positive engagement with the welfare state and the European social model is often overlooked.

Moreover, European developments show how much self-advocates encouraged research into relevant (international) law. The idea of a convention was introduced in the 1980s by Maria Saulle who was not part of the disability movement. During the 1990s self-advocates took the lead: They worked closely with international lawyers or became lawyers themselves and put disability on the agenda of scholars of international law. Although global policies during this decade were not focused on the making of international law, engagement with international disability law took off nevertheless. Expert meetings in Berkeley and Hong Kong in the late 1990s stimulated the mainstreaming of disability in the "human rights regime" and "helped to create networks between human rights scholars and disability rights advocates," although traditional human rights organizations such as Amnesty International did not really include disability in their policies. The meetings resulted in "elaborated recommendations for a new thematic convention."[62]

Research into issues of international disability human rights was mainly carried out by academics from the Global North, who after successful lobbying of diplomats from the Global South would leave their mark on the convention. With their Office of the High Commissioner for Human Rights (OHCHR) report disability law scholars Gerard Quinn and Theresia Degener for instance had a decisive influence on the prenegotiation process.[63] During the negotiations about the convention self-advocates also benefited from advice from experienced international lawyers such as Janet E. Lord, who had been involved in other international negotiations on behalf of the Landmine Survivors Network.[64] The fact that Degener, who was a relatively uninfluential UN intern during the Vienna conference in 1993, saw her advice often accepted ten years later illustrates how important the work of the 1990s turned out to be.[65]

What does this history of disability human rights self-advocacy at the global and European level add to existing historiography? First, it shows the nonlinear trajectory from the Global Meeting of Experts in 1987 to the Vienna Conference in 1993 and to the negotiations about the convention in the early 2000s. After failed attempts to include disability in international law, disability human rights were added as human needs to the United Nations' social development approach to disability. While self-advocates did not seem to make much progress in terms of pushing a human rights approach at the global level, their persistence bore fruit during the negotiations about the convention.

Second, a closer look at self-advocacy's work on international law in the European context shows that, although during the 1990s disability was no longer seen exclusively through the lens of welfare, the idea of "social Europe" and the welfare state did not disappear. This chapter reminds us that disability self-advocates did not say farewell to social Europe, a position that can be understood if we look not only at interaction between the European arena and national arenas, but also at the influence of institutions like the United Nations and independent disability activists from the United States and Europe.

Third, this chapter reveals the influence of the (human) rights model of disability in the European context, which has hardly been addressed in the general historical literature until now. This model is often associated with a shift from a welfare perspective on disability to one based on civil rights and anti-discrimination. In Europe we see that this model was introduced mainly by British activists inspired by developments in the United States. During the 1990s the EDF was successful in bringing the anti-discrimination perspective into the spotlight. However, in contrast to the US context and what is suggested in the literature, this does not mean that the welfare perspective was put aside. This becomes clear when we consider that the entry of disabled citizens into the European arena went along with an increasing influence of legal scholarship. Legal scholars tried to combine the anti-discrimination approach with the tradition of social Europe. The increasing attention devoted to equal rights since the 1990s must therefore be understood as an extra layer added to the welfare state model and "social Europe," and not as a paradigm change.

6

MEXICO CITY 2002

Taken by Surprise

Deprivation of legal status and civil rights such as the right to vote exemplifies discriminatory treatment of people labeled with psychiatric disability as outside the human family. Where this is practiced, it hinders the ability of people labeled with psychiatric disability to organize and advocate in their own interest, as well as violating our basic human rights to be recognized as persons before the law, and to participate equally in the societies we live in.

This statement was made by Tina Minkowitz, representing the World Network of Users and Survivors of Psychiatry (WNUSP), during the Global Meeting of Experts at the International Convention to Promote and Protect the Rights and Dignity of Persons with Disabilities in Mexico City, June 11–14, 2002.[1] This meeting was organized in preparation for the first gathering of the Ad Hoc Committee of the General Assembly in July 2002 after the UN General Assembly in 2001 had agreed with Mexico's proposal to draft an international convention. In this expert meeting the Mexican government gave disabled people's organizations such as the WNUSP the opportunity to express their views about the convention.² It would not stop there: Self-advocates such as Minkowitz would also sit at the UN negotiation table, and they took the convention in surprising directions. This chapter discusses the unexpected start of the negotiations and the history of the right to live independently in the community, and the right to support that disabled people may require in exercising their legal capacity, one of the most remarkable outcomes. One of the negotiators, human rights scholar Gerard Quinn, wrote about this outcome: "Few . . . saw at the time how the evolving text of Article 12 had the potential to zip open some deep contradictions in human rights-talk about personhood and what its implications for human rights might be more generally."³

NEW HUMAN RIGHTS DIPLOMACY

The late 1990s experienced, as already mentioned in previous chapters, an increasing attention to the human rights approach to disability.⁴ Nevertheless, the social development approach was still influential, and only a few self-advocacy organizations worked from an exclusively human rights angle. For instance, the nongovernmental organization (NGO) Mental Disability Rights International, founded in 1993, followed the methodology of mainstream human rights organizations such as Amnesty International with "lengthy investigations, public reports meticulously detailing abuses, and campaigns to shame authorities into improving treatment of psychiatric patients around the world." This was because one of the founders, Eric Rosenthal, was a staff person at Human Rights Watch. Such intersections between self-advocacy organizations and the human rights movement were rare: Disability was not really on the agenda of mainstream human rights organizations such as Amnesty International and Human Rights Watch. During the Cold War, they only protested against the internment of political dissidents in psychiatric institutions.⁵ Self-advocates such as Disabled Peoples' International (DPI) on the other hand were not only focused on human rights but also often had a broader scope.

It was not until the year 2000 that a broad international coalition of disability organizations asked for an international convention, building on the knowledge mentioned at the end of chapter 5. This request was the main outcome of the World NGO Summit on Disability, convened in Beijing by the International Disability Alliance (IDA). This alliance was founded in 1999 by seven international disability organizations: DPI, Rehabilitation International (RI), the World Federation of the Deaf (WFD), the World Blind Union, Inclusion International, the World Federation of the Deafblind, and the European Disability Forum (EDF). These organizations had learned to work together in the expert panel that had monitored the Standard Rules since 1992.[6] The inclusion of RI and Inclusion International was remarkable since they did not have the status of disabled people's organizations, although self-advocates played a far more important role in these organizations than in the past. The IDA organizations all had UN Economic and Social Council (ECOSOC) consultative status and had for a long time been active in global disability policies.[7]

Nevertheless, Mexico "took the international disability movement by surprise," as human rights lawyer Janet E. Lord has put it.[8] After attempts by Ireland and the IDA in 2000 and 2001 to persuade the United Nations to start drafting a convention, Mexico was all of a sudden successful in introducing a resolution to the UN General Assembly. Encouraged by his disability office and probably in particular by DPI representative Maria Eugenia Antunez, Mexican President Vincente Fox gave "a high-level political commitment" to this resolution.[9] Self-advocates were surprised because Mexico had "no prior record of supporting disability advocacy internationally."[10] Moreover, there had been "a lack of respect for human rights in their country and elsewhere" in the past. Since the late 1990s the Mexican government had changed its approach to human rights: "Championing the CRPD as part of Mexico's foreign policy agenda was one way to sure-up its liberal democratic identity."[11] However, if we take into account the fact that Mexico's main argument for the convention was that "persons with disabilities were not identified as a specific target group in the recently-adopted Millennium Development Goals" and that the resolution was cosponsored by nineteen other countries from the Global South, the role of Mexico could be seen partly as an offshoot of the Mexican tradition of international diplomacy aimed at reforming the global agenda of development and redistribution.[12]

The arguments presented by Mexico did not mean that Mexican diplomats were in favor of a limited convention focused on social development. On the contrary, the Mexicans quickly involved people with disabilities in the negotiation process by organizing the above-mentioned specialist meeting of experts in Mexico City, which enabled them to produce before the first meeting of the Ad Hoc Committee of the General Assembly a draft treaty that followed the model of a comprehensive convention.[13] The Mexican draft, however, did not make it into the leading text of the committee, which was not agreed quickly. Thanks to a proposal by New Zealand during the second meeting of the Ad Hoc Committee of the General Assembly in 2003, self-advocates nevertheless became very much involved in the drafting process. In addition to the IDA organizations some younger self-advocacy organizations such as WNUSP (founded in 1991) and Landmine Survivors Network (founded in 1997) joined the negotiations and played an important role in the drafting of the convention (see figure 6.1).[14] This involvement of NGOs was a new type of human rights diplomacy: Disabled persons moved from being objects of human rights to being subjects of human rights and even "actors in shaping those rights."[15]

EQUAL RECOGNITION BEFORE THE LAW

The shift from object to subject not only characterized the process of drafting the convention, but also informed its content. This is particularly clear in the passages of the convention that deal with the equal recognition of all disabled persons before the law (Article 12) and with living independently in the community (Article 19), because these articles deal with disabled persons and their relations with others, the family, and with professionals in particular. Ever since people with disabilities have organized themselves in cross-disability organizations that

FIGURE 6.1 Tina Minkowitz (seated, second left) at a meeting with journalists after the UN General Assembly's adoption of the Convention on the Rights of Persons with Disabilities in 2006. She is joined by Don MacKay (seated, second from right), Permanent Representative of New Zealand to the United Nations and Chairman of the UN General Assembly committee that negotiated the convention, and Pamela Molina Toledo (seated, left), who together with Minkowitz represented an international collective of self-advocates. (UN Photo/Devra Berkowitz)

claim equal rights, they have encountered the family and the professional as challenging concepts. The family and the professional could be seen as a challenge for disability rights because family members and professionals have traditionally been seen as responsible for the care of people with disabilities, and even as their representatives. This caring and representative role of the family and the professional is often based on the assumption that disabled people might need help because they are not cognitively or physically able to do things on their own. Because of this assumption families and professionals have often been, or been seen as, obstacles rather than allies of the emancipation of people with disabilities.[16] Critical self-advocates have considered the family and the professional as threats to the right to independent living that has been central in the struggle for disability rights. In the remaining part of this chapter, I shall examine the discussions about the caring and representative role of the family and the professional in the United Nations' disability policies since the 1970s.

Why is this particular history so relevant? In the case of the right to found a family, as I argued in chapter 1, the UN Convention on the Rights of Persons with Disabilities (CRPD) is unique in international law in granting equal rights to people with disabilities. At the time, the emphasis in the convention was on protecting individual rights, and it did not explain in a positive and more structural way what had to be done to guarantee the reproductive rights of people with disabilities.[17] Here the convention adopts the common understanding of the human rights subject as a rational and autonomous agent, without giving much attention to the environment in which the subject lives, an understanding that has been increasingly criticized in human rights scholarship.[18] Interestingly, if we focus on the caring and representative role of families and professionals, we also find a different understanding of the human rights subject.

This understanding is addressed in the literature about the (legal) capacity of people with disabilities, one of the recurrent topics of debate since disability was framed as a human rights issue at the international level. Capacity was not self-evident, especially in the case of mental or cognitive disabilities, and it was seen differently by stakeholders across the world. Article 12 of the CRPD about equal recognition before the law deals with legal capacity, and it continues to be discussed extensively by policymakers and scholars. It is seen as an important innovation in international disability law: It "implies a shift from the substitute decision-making paradigm to one that is based on supported decision-making."[19] Moreover, this passage of the convention moves away from a "deficits-oriented" approach to "one that views fragility as a universal aspect of the human condition and remediable with sufficient supports," as Gerard Quinn puts it.[20] Article 12 challenges us, according to Quinn, to think of the human person beyond the rational autonomous subject and to acknowledge "shared personhood" and "the myriad of supports—formal and informal—that we all rely on."[21] As such, Article 12 is a challenge for professionals and for families of people with mental disabilities: In history they have often been seen as the obvious representatives and support providers of people with mental disabilities, but the convention does not address whether they must provide some of the support that people with mental disabilities "may require in exercising their legal capacity."[22]

In this chapter, I shall try to historicize this different understanding of the human rights subject that acknowledges "myriads of support." By following how and by whom families and professionals were conceptualized in UN disability policies and how and why this changed (or did not change) over time, this chapter provides a historical context for debates about legal capacity among scholars of international law. This chapter is also situated in the historiography about human rights and international law. Historians pay increasing attention to "new legal subjects" and marginalized groups in international (human rights) law.[23] Moreover, recent historical studies concerning neoliberalism and human rights show that human rights were often based on a concept of the individual that tended to ignore the relevance of structural support.[24]

By addressing the conceptualization of families and professionals, this chapter provides a fresh contribution to this historiography. It will argue that the CRPD may be seen as an attempt to include a new marginalized group within international human rights law, thus missing—like other human rights law—a structural approach that could have improved the situation of the group.[25] The history of disability human rights law has a dynamic that we can observe also for other groups, namely that marginalized groups since the 1970s have used international law and policies to strengthen their position in the struggle for emancipation. However, the lens of families and professionals enables us also to see that the convention contains elements that have the potential to overcome the dominant minimalist human rights approach.[26] With Article 12 the convention contains a notion of "shared personhood" that goes beyond the independent subject of human rights and highlights the indispensability of structural support. In the following paragraphs, I shall investigate whether this notion was long in the making or has to be seen as an unforeseen outcome of the negotiations about the convention. In examining the concept of the family and the professional in disability policies, my focus will not only be on the history of Article 12, but also on historicizing Article 19 of the convention. The ideal of living independently (in the community) has been important for many self-advocates since at least the 1960s, but how has the international discussion developed over time? I shall go into some detail about Community Based Rehabilitation (CBR) because this approach has given local communities, instead of (medical) professionals, a key role in the support of disabled people. Did this approach contain a new way to acknowledge "myriads of support," and how was it integrated (or not) into international disability policies?

THE EMERGENCE OF THE COMMUNITY

As mentioned previously, Dagmar Herzog has begun to historicize the framing of disability in terms of human rights. She interprets the convention and in particular Article 12 as part of a wider trend to rethink the human subject.[27] Although the convention highlights the independence of people with disabilities, it also takes into account the interdependence of people and institutions. In the case of Article 12 this is captured in a sentence that underlines the state's obligation to provide "support they may require in exercising their legal capacity." Herzog relates the idea of "support" to the idea of "assisted freedom" as recently developed by the German philosopher Sigrid Graumann, but it could also be related to the older idea of assistance or support that has for a long time been part of the global Independent Living Movement.[28] In both cases people have tried to think beyond a deficit-oriented or paternalistic care approach without at the same time ignoring the need to support people with disabilities to exercise their rights. In this context the role of the family and the professional in relation to the individual with a disability has been conceptualized in different ways, varying from being a thread for individual freedom to being an ally of people with disabilities.

When disability human rights were discussed for one of the first times in the international sphere, the idea of "supported freedom" did not appear. As I have shown elsewhere, the participants of the International League of Societies for Persons with Mental Handicaps (ILSMH) conference in Stockholm in 1967 agreed on the importance of individual basic rights of "retarded persons," but also saw the family as a self-evident representative of people with mental disabilities, and did not rule out the appointment of a guardian "who will have the legal and moral obligation to make necessary decisions on behalf of the retarded person who cannot act for himself."[29] The 1971 UN declaration mentioned services with the aim to "enable him [the person with a mental disability] to develop his ability and maximum potential" and not, as in the Stockholm conclusions, to exercise his right. Moreover, the ILSMH addition that "no person should be appointed [as guardian] who is responsible for rendering a direct service to the retarded person" was dropped by the United Nations, who did not worry about the "possibility of conflicts of interest on the part of service personnel."[30]

In general, the 1971 declaration seemed to be more in favor of (medical) professionals, probably due to the contribution of the World Health Organization (WHO) representatives.[31] The declaration prioritized the "right to proper medical care" and did not rule out "care in an institution." Article 7 stated that the "evaluation of the social capability of the mentally retarded person" was the responsibility of "qualified experts."[32] However, the differences between the ILSMH and UN declaration should not be exaggerated. The ILSMH asked the United Nations for extra copies of the WHO memorandum "Health Aspects of Mental Retardation" to distribute among its members in the early 1970s.[33] This is no surprise if we look more closely at ILSMH policies in the previous years. Although community care was mentioned in the conclusions of its 1967 Stockholm conference, the ILSMH recognized the important role of specialist staff and followed the medical WHO terminology on mental retardation.[34]

The Declaration on the Rights of Disabled Persons (1975), inspired by the 1971 declaration but proposed by others such as the Belgian government, did not change the way in which the disabled individual, the professional, and the family were framed.[35] It defined the disabled person as a "person unable to ensure by himself or herself, wholly or partly, the necessities of a normal individual and/or social life, as a result of deficiency," although it listed the "right to medical, psychological and functional treatment" a bit lower than the 1971 declaration.[36] As Gildas Brégain has shown in his comparison of the 1971 and 1975 declarations, the diplomats added the concept of the community alongside the family in the last article of the 1975 declaration: "Disabled persons, their families and communities shall be fully informed, by all appropriate means, of the rights contained in this Declaration."[37] Since then, the concepts of families and communities have often appeared side by side in the UN policy documents. The addition of the family could be explained, as Brégain does, by the wish to recognize the "prevalence of the community on the family in some African or Asian societies."[38] But could it also be related to the increasing popularity of the concept in international social policies during the 1970s, and in particular to the WHO's new policy to give priority to communities rather than (medical) professionals?

For several decades the WHO had focused on enormous global campaigns to end diseases such as smallpox and malaria, but under the new leadership of Halfdan Mahler its attention turned to the development of primary health care for every world citizen. This went along with highlighting the importance of laypeople from (local) communities in providing health care, and underplaying the role of specialized medical knowledge. Mahler, who in 1973 became director-general of the WHO, once stated that it would be a good idea to "close the medical schools for two years."[39] There is a striking parallel here with what disabled people began to argue around the same time: They contested the medical model of disability and the dominance of medical experts, and advocated the social model and the importance of their own expertise based on experience.[40] Did the addition of the community to the 1975 declaration encourage such relativization of professional knowledge?

Community and community involvement had already been popular concepts in international development policies since the 1950s.[41] These concepts received renewed interest in the 1970s as part of a broader move to acknowledging the nonmedical determinants of health and to taking the role of lay actors in global health more seriously. The so-called Alma-Ata conference, which took place in the USSR in 1978, is often seen as a key moment in this development. The conference's concluding declaration stated that "health, which is a state of complete physical, mental and social wellbeing, and not merely the absence of disease or infirmity, is a fundamental human right and that the attainment of the highest possible level of health is a most important world-wide social goal whose realization requires the action of many other social and economic sectors in addition to the health sector." Furthermore, the declaration related health and health inequalities to social and economic development as envisioned in the New International Economic Order (NIEO, 1974), a UN treaty that aimed for a more materially equal world. In addition to the social determinants of health, the declaration addressed the importance of primary health care, promoting "maximum community and individual self-reliance and participation in the planning, organization, operation and control of primary health care, making fullest use of local, national and other available resources."[42]

This was the context in which in the late 1970s the WHO developed a new approach to disability: CBR, which has the aim that "rehabilitation can safely and effectively be carried out by lay persons, such as a family member or a friend of the disabled persons, or by the disabled people themselves."[43] Key to this approach was the active involvement of local communities. The WHO had detected many practices of "indigenous, spontaneous rehabilitation," and developed a manual based on a collection of these practices.[44] The CBR approach was not entirely new or unique. Already in the early 1970s David Werner had published a "village health care handbook" in Spanish. This was translated in 1977 into English under the title *Where There Is No Doctor*, and in the following decades over three million copies were sold. Werner wrote in particular from his experience with the project Piaxtla, a village in San Ignacio, Mexico, where the community had arranged rehabilitation practices for disabled children. The WHO never became as radical as Werner, who opened his book with statements such as "ordinary people provided with clear, simple information can prevent and treat most common health problems in their own homes—earlier, cheaper, and often better than can doctors"; "medical knowledge should not be the guarded secret of a select few, but should be freely shared by everyone"; and "basic health care should not be delivered, but encouraged."⁴⁵ That is why the addition of community to the 1975 declaration probably did not reflect a strong preference for community knowledge above professional knowledge, but did this change in the following years?

UN OBSERVANCES DURING THE 1980s

If we follow the way in which the family, the professional, and the community were framed during the UN International Year of Disabled Persons (IYDP, 1981) and Decade of Disabled Persons (1983–1992), we find mixed messages. The role of the family did not change. The role of professionals, however, although still acknowledged, lost the unquestioned priority it had received in the 1971 and 1975 declarations. In discussion about the World Programme of Action (WPA, 1982) at the United Nations, one diplomat proposed that "the document should include a recommendation to the World Health Organization to change and elaborate its definition of disability, with stronger emphasis on structural changes in society."⁴⁶ However, the WPA followed the WHO definitions, which only in the description of the concept of handicap addressed societal structures: "handicap is therefore a function of the relationship between disabled persons and their environment . . . thus, handicap is the loss or limitation of opportunities to take part in the life of the community on an equal level with others."⁴⁷

Moreover, the WPA did not approach rehabilitation as a practice for professionals only: "Important resources for rehabilitation exist in the families of disabled persons and in their communities."⁴⁸ In general the WPA emphasized that people with disabilities had to live "in their own communities" and that "the customs and structures of family and community" had to be taken into account. We can hear an echo of anti-institutionalism here, which argued that people should not be taken out of their families and communities because of their disability. Thanks to "an evolution in both the content and the spirit of the activities described as rehabilitation," communities were not only seen as a "natural environment," but also as a resource for "the efforts of their disabled members to overcome the disabling effects of impairment within a normal social environment." The movement "from institutions to community-based living" had, according to the WPA, made clear that "even severely disabled persons can, to a great extent, live independently if the necessary support services are provided." Communities should play an important role here, for instance by the provision of "simpler, less expensive" technical aids "with local methods of production." The WPA did not seem to expect the disappearance of specialized institutions, but "the number [of disabled persons] requiring care in institutions is much smaller than had previously been assumed."[49]

When it came to the support for people with mental disabilities, the WPA was following the approach of the declarations: "When people such as the severely mentally disabled may not be able to represent themselves adequately in decisions affecting their lives, family members or legally-designated agents should take part in planning and decision-making." The rights of people with mental disabilities also received attention from other bodies within the United Nations than the ECOSOC that was responsible for the WPA. In 1983, Erica-Irene A. Daes, special rapporteur of the subcommission on prevention of discrimination and protection of minorities, published a report titled *Principles, Guidelines and Guarantees for the Protection of Persons Detained on Grounds of Mental Ill-Health or Suffering from Mental Disorder*. Daes stated that "both law and medical practice shall be, wherever possible, the individual's right to self-determination and freedom from coercion in treatment."[50] The focus of the report was on the protection of patients, and it did not deal with the legal capacity of people with mental disabilities and the (supportive) role of families and professionals. Moreover, these principles seem to have focused more on the human rights of patients with a "mental illness" than those of "mentally retarded persons."[51] This was also true for the Principles for the Protection of Persons with Mental Illness and the Improvement of Mental Health Care, adopted by the UN General Assembly in 1991.[52] The further development of human rights (law) concerning people with mental disabilities was not an aim at the United

Nations—and this was also the case at other international institutions such as the European Court on Human Rights.[53]

Although human rights were mentioned in the WPA, we do not see them used to protect disabled people from the undesirable interventions of families, communities and/or professionals—as was the case during negotiations about the CRPD (2006).[54] In that sense, UN and WHO policies during the 1980s did not reflect the understanding of human rights as individual rights in need of international protection, which became popular at the same time due to organizations such as Amnesty International. At that time international disability policies did not prioritize the independence of disabled people and their dependence on support was automatically assumed. UN policies were rather health or social policies that gave (local) communities a key role in addition to the usual suspects such as families, (medical) professionals, and national governments. These policies were not seen as conflicting with human rights, because, in the context of Alma-Ata and the NIEO, human rights were not seen as strictly individual, but as part of a global vision for equality. This vision would lose traction during the 1980s: That is what we have seen in chapter 2, and it becomes clearer when we follow global disability policies into the 1990s.

(UN)POPULARITY OF COMMUNITY BASED REHABILITATION

While the WHO was working on further development of the CBR approach during the 1980s, it seems not to have resonated with self-advocates and policymakers at the UN level. Only one of the many recommendations of the Global Meeting of Experts in 1987, midway through the International Decade of Disabled Persons, dealt implicitly with CBR by stating that "Programmes for disability prevention and rehabilitation should make maximum use of existing facilities and services. Indigenous raw material, scientific expertise and production should be used for the manufacture of aids and appliances to ensure their appropriateness to the consumer and to allow for local repair to be effected." National governments were asked by the experts, among whom were many self-advocates, to stimulate "the duty-free international movement of equipment and material needed to assist in daily living of disabled people," but nothing was said about the role of local communities.[55] On the contrary, the experts underlined the emergence of "the concept of independent living for severely disabled people and the consumer-directed services necessary for achieving that."[56] This was stated without referring to living in and with the community, as was so prominent in the WPA.

The Standard Rules on the Equalization of Opportunities for Persons with Disabilities, as adopted by the United Nations in 1993, did mention the community. They stated that people with disabilities had "the right to remain within their local communities," although in general they preferred to frame people with disabilities as citizens or members of society. In that capacity "they should receive the support they need within the ordinary structures of education, health, employment and social services."[57] These structures were seen as mainly to be provided by the state, and delivered by professionals, although the Standard Rules stated that the "rehabilitation process does not involve initial medical care."[58] Rule 19 about personnel training first mentioned the training of "professionals in the disability field" before highlighting the involvement of disabled people and the importance of community workers. The training of the group last mentioned was seen as particularly relevant in developing countries, and "should involve persons with disabilities and include the development of appropriate values, competence and technologies as well as skills which can be practised by persons with disabilities, their parents, families and members of the community."[59] This shows that the Standard Rules, in particular in comparison to the WPA, valued the involvement of disabled people more than the involvement of the community, and cared more about professional knowledge than about local knowledge.

Compared with earlier policies, the Standard Rules were more strongly opposed to the interference of others, and in that sense they reflect a human rights perspective that assumes an autonomous individual. States for instance had to "ensure that laws do not discriminate against persons with disabilities with respect to sexual relationships, marriage and parenthood."[60] Moreover, the Standard Rules stated that "persons with disabilities are particularly vulnerable to abuse in the family, community or institutions." Despite this remark, the Standard Rules were in general positive toward families, professionals, and communities, and did not consider them a significant threat to the disabled individual. Throughout the Standard Rules the family was seen unquestioningly as an obvious support for people with disabilities: The United Nations often added "and their families" when writing about disabled persons.[61]

The Standard Rules did little in particular to protect and support people with mental disabilities, who had become more vocal at the international level. For example, an international conference of the ILSMH in Nairobi in 1982 was attended by three hundred self-advocates who organized a closing panel. According to social scientist Peter Mittler, it was an "unforgettable experience": "Each panelist came from a different country and not all spoke English.... All of them spoke about their rights: the right to go to school and work in the community, the right to choose how and where to live and the right to choose friends." A couple of years later, self-advocates organized a demonstration during a European ILSMH event, asking why they were excluded from the conference. Mittler remembers, "For the first time to my knowledge, they were not only speaking for themselves but were doing so without parents or professionals and without the League." Thereafter people with mental disabilities became members of the board of the ILSMH and started to participate in UN events and contribute to policies.[62] This involvement, however, did not translate into new conceptualizations of the disabled individual in relation to families, communities, and professionals in UN international documents and debates. There was a search in several European countries for alternatives to guardianship that could guarantee self-determination and autonomy, but this also seems not to have been prioritized at the international level.[63]

Support for disabled people more broadly during the 1990s was often not framed in terms of human rights. This is shown in a position paper about CBR, published by the WHO, International Labour Organization (ILO), and the United Nations Educational, Scientific and Cultural Organization (UNESCO) in 1994. The three specialized agencies, all based in Geneva, wanted to use the CBR approach to stimulate the involvement of local stakeholders such as "the teacher who has a blind child in the class; the primary health worker who is expected to help a child with paralysed legs to walk; the mechanic who wonders whether the young man who cannot hear can be trained in mechanics; the traditional healer who cannot treat the strange behaviour of a child; the mayor who want to plan an accessible community hall."[64] According to the position paper of the UN specialized agencies, CBR "promotes the right of people with disabilities to live within their communities" and "requires upon governments to transfer responsibility and necessary resources to communities so that they can provide the base for rehabilitation." Although the position paper considered CBR "appropriate for both industrialized and developing countries," the approach was set up for and applied most commonly in the latter.[65] The attention of the UN specialized agencies to CBR indicates how much disability was still seen as an issue of social development and not as an issue of human rights.

The situation of people with disabilities in developing countries was perhaps not the focus of the Standard Rules, but it was still seen as an urgent issue by the special agencies, and that is why they brought CBR again to the fore. It is understandable that the UN specialized agencies wanted to give new impetus to the CBR approach: In a time when public institutions were trying to reduce expenditure, an approach that would "transfer responsibility and necessary resources to communities" was attractive. But the choice is also remarkable since development practitioners and scholars had started to question CBR from the mid-1980s onward. CBR seemed to overlook "resources that have not been centrally planned or authorized" and, in the case of education, "already casually integrated disabled pupils." That is why Mike Miles in a 1994 article critically asked if the WHO and other agencies had exaggerated with their slogan "1 in 10 is disabled." According to Miles, "one important way in which people in developing countries assist and integrate their disabled members is by not labelling and counting people as 'disabled' when they are mildly impaired."⁶⁶ One of the main critiques concerned the "Community Base." In the year 2000 Raymond Lang observed that "in fact many CBR programmes remain largely dominated by the medical profession, and hence strongly influenced by the medical model of disability."⁶⁷ In the same vein, Geert Vanneste stated that "Most 'CBR programmes' implemented till now in Africa have not resulted from the inventiveness, creativity and hard work of the local people themselves. They are product of foreign policy and interest, with inputs of foreign manpower and money."⁶⁸

The history of CBR thus reflects the history of primary health care more broadly. In the 1990s the WHO gave primary health and the structural determinants of health less priority, and under new leadership the organization remedicalized.⁶⁹ Primary health remained popular only in a slimmed-down version: so-called selective primary health care with a focus on children's health. Due to economic crises and neoliberal policies in the 1980s and 1990s, international organizations and countries preferred strategies "that would require less investment in people-centered health care while still saving the lives of millions of children."⁷⁰ It is no accident therefore that CBR scholars observed that much of the "attention of CBR programming worldwide has been in concern for children, (this is distinguished from disability self-help and advocacy groups that have been concerned with adults)."⁷¹ The parenthetical addition to this statement shows, moreover, that the representation of self-advocates was seen as something different, whereas the WPA tended to keep self-advocates and their communities close together.

As already shown by the Global Meeting of Experts in 1987, CBR was never embraced by self-advocates as a fully-fledged alternative to support from professionals. In response to the specialized agencies' position paper, DPI stated critically that they believed that CBR "if it is to continue in its present form must be revitalized and disabled persons must direct this revitalization."⁷² Nevertheless, some self-advocates saw possibilities to use the CBR approach, in particular in Asia and the Pacific. Shoji Nakanishi, a Japanese self-advocate, stated in an interview with the DPI newsletter for Singapore that Independent Living (IL) and CBR were "the same in concept, although the IL movement has been developed in industrialized countries": The approaches had in common "that a disabled person has a crucial role in motivating a community for the implementation of community-based activities."[73]

The history of CBR also highlights another important dimension for understanding the development of global disability policies: The United Nations cannot be seen as a single actor. Agencies such as the WHO were always involved in UN policies, but they also had their own agenda and their own collaborative partners. This meant in the case of disability that other approaches became popular alongside the UN policies as laid down in the WPA and the Standard Rules. In addition to CBR, one could think of the introduction of DALY by the WHO and the World Bank in 1993. DALY means disability-adjusted life years and was used by policymakers to calculate the "global burden of disability, impairment and disease, and the effectiveness of health care interventions."[74] The complexity of the international sphere has made it difficult for self-advocates, who during the 1990s increasingly embraced a human rights perspective on disability, to challenge negative and paternalistic approaches to disabled people. It was not only hard, as mentioned in earlier chapters, for them to bring disability to the attention of the UN Human Rights Commission, but also to have an impact on the WHO. Although the DPI rejected the WHO definition of disability and related concepts, the WHO did not revise its position until 2001, and even then self-advocates did not see all their concerns addressed.[75]

LIVING INDEPENDENTLY IN THE COMMUNITY?

How did the CRPD in the end deal with families, professionals, and communities? First, the role that the community could play in the provision of health care including rehabilitation is poorly addressed in the convention. Compared to the earlier policy documents, the convention has health listed relatively low (Article 25 of fifty in total). The convention asks states to "recognize that persons with disabilities have the right to the enjoyment of the highest attainable standard of health without discrimination on the basis of disability," but does not expect anything that comes close to the primary health movement. The same can be seen in the article about "Habilitation and rehabilitation," which does not refer to CBR and only in a general way asks member states to "take effective and appropriate measures, including through peer support, to enable persons with disabilities to attain and maintain maximum independence, full physical, mental, social and vocational ability, and full inclusion and participation in all aspects of life," and to "organize, strengthen and extend comprehensive habilitation and rehabilitation services and programmes."[76] This does not mean that CBR no longer matters: The *World Report on Disability* (2011) for instance presents it as a still useful strategy to improve disabled peoples' lives.[77] However, the convention tends in the end to prefer professionals over communities in the provision of health care—which is remarkable given the antimedical stance of self-advocates.

Second, Article 19 concerning the right of "living independently and being included in the community" does mention the community often and explicitly, but the emphasis is more on independent living and the right to make choices equal to others. Community seems to be the same as society, understood as the entity in which disabled persons have to be included. How independence exactly relates to participation in the community is not really worked out, not even in the explanation published later. This explanation, the so-called General Comment 5 of the Committee on the Rights of Persons with Disabilities, focused on independent living, but mentions only very briefly a concept that has the potential to explore the link between individual and community. It recalls that "the Universal Declaration of Human Rights stresses in article 29 (1) the *interdependence* of an individual's personal development and the social aspect of being part of the community: 'Everyone has duties to the community in which alone the free and full development of his personality is possible.'"[78] Interdependence comes close to the notion of shared personhood that could be seen as a consequence of Article 12 of the convention.[79] During the diplomatic negotiations, however, the main focus was on independence.

Third, this also seems at first sight to be the case when we examine how support of family and professionals was discussed in relation to legal capacity during the drafting of the convention. In the draft of the working group legal capacity was, according to Theresia Degener, "at the core of many of the rights in the text, and historically the denial of legal capacity had led to many violations of individual rights."[80] Equal recognition as a person before the law was written into draft Article 9 (later Article 12) and reflected the wish of disabled people to be acknowledged as subjects of law "rather than being seen as objects of the law, without the capacity to exercise their own rights."[81] Moreover, the article promoted supported (instead of substituted) decision-making by stating that "where assistance is necessary to exercise that legal capacity: the assistance is proportional to the degree of assistance required by the person concerned and tailored to their circumstances, and does not interfere with the legal capacity, rights and freedoms of the person." Many state representatives asked for substitute decision-making in some cases, which supported a prominent role for families and professionals, but the working group simply added that "only in exceptional circumstances ... legal safeguards must be provided."[82] Although the article remained contested during the negotiations, the final text was close to what the working group intended and limited the influence of professionals.

It is striking that the concept of the family seems hardly to have played a role in the discussions about legal capacity, whereas support by the family was for so long taken for granted in global disability policies. Disabled self-advocates involved in the CRPD negotiations probably wanted to get rid of paternalistic understandings of legal capacity and to limit as much as possible representation through family members or others. As I have shown elsewhere, the role of the family was also limited in other articles. In the end only the reference to the family in the preamble was strengthened during the negotiations. It stated that "the family is the natural and fundamental group unit of society and is entitled to protection by society and the State, and that persons with disabilities and their family members should receive the necessary protection and assistance to enable families to contribute towards the full and equal enjoyment of the rights of persons with disabilities," whereas the draft preamble in 2004 did not even mention the family.[83] The convention therefore made a strong positive statement about the family, but contained few indications of the role families would need to play in disabled peoples' lives.

As Gerard Quinn has argued, the convention and Article 12 are not only about independence, but also challenge us to acknowledge "shared personhood" and "the myriad of supports—formal and informal—that we all rely on."[84] By looking toward the state for this support, the convention breaks away from a popular neoliberal approach that wants families and communities to support those who cannot meet the standard of being independent and live independently.[85] The structural support articulated in the convention is not a logical outcome of the struggle for equal rights by the global disability movement. People with mental disabilities, for whom the issue of legal capacity is the most pressing, became involved relatively late in the movement, and for a long time legal capacity, in contrast to other issues, had a low priority on the disability rights agenda. The way in which the United Nations framed legal capacity in the convention could therefore be considered an unforeseen development, after the unforeseen diplomatic intervention of Mexico discussed earlier.

This chapter took as its starting point a statement by Tina Minkowitz, during a meeting in Mexico City in 2002, about the right of disabled persons to be recognized as persons before the law. This meeting illustrates the surprising way in which people with disabilities became subjects of human rights. Subsequently the chapter contextualized this statement by following the concepts of the family, the community, and the professional in UN disability policies since the 1970s. It has shown that global disability policies for a long time assumed that people with (mental) disabilities were in need of care and supervision from another, who was often imagined to be a family member or a professional. The further development of a human rights perspective on disability and the increasing popularity of the Independent Living Movement undermined the assumed role of others, but it was not until the drafting of the UN convention on the rights of persons with disabilities that this was recognized at the international level.

We have also seen that the community became important in WHO policies in the 1970s as the provider of local knowledge and support in contrast to professional (medical) expertise. The so-called CBR approach of the WHO was in line with UN disability policies of the 1970s and 1980s. During the 1990s, however, UN policy documents prioritized disabled people over communities in terms of their involvement in disability policies. An initiative of the WHO, ILO, and UNESCO to give new impetus to CBR did not change that. Also the convention from 2006 emphasized the independence of disabled people and did not elaborate on the interdependence between individuals and communities.

This chapter supplements existing literature on the history of international disability law and human rights in two ways. First, it shows that recognition of the equality of people with (mental) disabilities in international law is not a logical outcome of a longer process, but an unexpected legal innovation. Although the emphasis in the convention is on independent individuals, it also opens the door to the notion of shared personhood, and a supportive role for others that does not threaten people with disabilities. Related to this is the second contribution of this chapter: It shows how the family and the community have been seen as an important resource and agency in social policies. In contrast to neoliberal approaches which tend to maintain the traditional role of the family in the lives of people with disabilities and to transfer social responsibility from the state to communities, the convention clearly limits the power of others over people with (mental) disabilities, and expects states to support persons with disabilities.

EPILOGUE

The history of the human rights of disabled persons which culminated in the Convention on the Rights of Persons with Disabilities (CRPD) is often written as a long road with many cobbles, a history of slow progress that started when cross-disability organizations began to claim their rights.[1] Too often, however, these histories have been built on the assumption that human rights have been a fixed concept. That is why this book has followed an historicizing approach, investigating as precisely as possible how disability has been framed in terms of international human rights, by whom, how this was related to the use of other concepts, and how and why this framing changed over time. This has resulted in a narrative of discontinuous progress from the margins, in the words of Ian Dury's "Spasticus Autisticus": a hobbling and wobbling narrative without a central "knobbled I" character. Although the United Nations comes closest to being this character, since it is in its various manifestations involved in almost all the histories in this book. This narrative of discontinuous progress from the margins will hopefully be further enriched, complicated, and contested by histories that remain to be told, for instance the role of actors from the African continent or from organizations such as the International Labour Organization (ILO). But it has already made the following two things clear.

First, the human rights of disabled persons as we know them today were invented only during the drafting of the convention in the early 2000s. Only then did human rights appear as a leading concept in the context of global disability policies and become a focus for the global disability movement. Before the negotiations, this book argues, the human rights of people with disabilities were framed differently: as part of normalization policies that intended to integrate people with mental disabilities into society (chapter 1); as appendix to a global vision on socioeconomic equality (chapter 2); subordinated to representation (chapter 3) and to development (chapter 4); as an extra layer to welfare policies (chapter 5); and as rights that could not apply to every person with a disability (chapter 6). Moreover, these framings came from unexpected actors: It turns out that self-advocates were not always in favor of the human rights approach to disability, and that diplomats without much disability background sometimes played a decisive role in the international recognition of disability rights. Nevertheless, the role played by self-advocates in shaping their own human rights during the drafting of the convention was unprecedented and hardly ever addressed in human rights historiography. By highlighting the novelty and uniqueness of the convention, the emphasis of this book is different from that prevailing in the current literature, which tends to interpret the convention as the outcome of an earlier shift to an approach based on human rights.

This does not mean, however, that the convention was not influenced by developments in the previous decades. Several parts of the process and content of the convention were, as I have shown, informed by the foregoing history. Moreover—and this is the second important point that I want to highlight here—almost all the framings of disability in terms of international human rights analyzed in this book have one thing in common: They have approached human rights within a national framework. Unlike human rights organizations such Amnesty International that have focused on a limited set of human rights beyond the nation-state, advocates for disability human rights have used international institutions mainly to provide nation-states and national self-advocates with instruments to improve the human rights situation in their own countries, not only incidentally but in a more structural way. This national use of human rights is often seen as something belonging to the first decades after the Second World War, in the words of Roland Burke: "Later obscured by the avowed anti-statism of the transnational nongovernmental organization (NGO) 'breakthrough' of the 1970s, this first variant of a global human rights enterprise, which commenced in 1945, reconfirmed and institutionalized the primacy of nation states as the emancipatory instrument of first and best resort."[2] But does this book and the convention in particular not show that the nation-state in the case of disability is still seen by many as an instrument of emancipation? And does this not challenge the view that human rights are insufficiently political?

POLITICS

Interestingly, the convention is criticized by scholars of disability because it contributed little to address material equality, to empower local self-advocacy and to provide for representation of everyone with a disability while it offers a lot on those points in comparison with other international law.[3] I do not deny that the convention may hinder emancipation in particular contexts, but seen from the critical perspective of human rights historiography the convention with its attention to state obligations, structural improvement, and the involvement of people with disabilities seems at least partly to address the criticism that human rights are insufficiently political.[4] According to the convention human rights are not only "norms to be enforced by judges" but may also "involve a transformation in steps."[5] The convention seems to see the nation-state as an emancipatory instrument and redirects attention to national political communities that, as Hannah Arendt has famously argued, are necessary to make human rights meaningful.[6] The large number of ratifications, the reports of the UN Committee on the Rights of Persons with Disabilities, and the ever-increasing literature on the convention indicate that many countries and actors around the world are indeed working on its implementation. This points to a use of human rights that is not only overlooked by human rights historiography with its focus on "high" international politics but seems also to be ignored by prophets of the end-times of human rights.[7]

There may be good reasons for skepticism about this national use of human rights. What does it mean for instance that "China has been able to develop so comprehensive a legislative and regulatory framework [for disabled persons] in a relatively compressed timeframe" at the same time as it violates the political rights of its citizens and minorities; and what does a change in its disability language "in line with the introduction of global human rights-based discourses" mean if China still tends to "stress the passivity and weakness of disabled people, rather than their self-determination and agency?"[8] The many ways in which human rights can be framed may of course always be used against human rights. But as I have shown throughout this book, the convention and its history contain elements which make it difficult to ignore the political and structural dimensions and to consider human rights only as a moral issue.

In human rights (law) scholarship the past has been used recently to provide inspiration for understandings of or alternatives to human rights that do justice to structural equality, not infrequently in a search for utopias that aim for material equality, and which could overturn the currently dominant neoliberal utopia that scarcely hinders increasing social inequality within and between countries.[9] I am not sure if this search for utopias is the way forward in the case of disability rights. Not only because I doubt if international law can go any further than the CRPD with its attention to structures and the innovative notion of shared personhood, but also because we can learn from the past that utopias often have a strongly exclusive side—particularly for people with disabilities. That is why I want to close this book with a critical reflection on utopias and a plea for heterotopias, as places in which to live, from which to learn and/or in which to do research; and as places that problematize the distance between what Ian Dury called Spasticus Autisticus and Normal Land and could encourage the hobbling and wobbling road of progress from the margins.

UTOPIA

Throughout this book we have encountered a variety of utopias, but we have not met a concrete imagination of a world that embraces disability—except Ratzka's Crip Utopia in chapter 1. Self-advocate Irving Kenneth Zola, however, did discover a crip utopia in real life and wrote a book about it: *Missing Pieces: A Chronicle of Living with a Disability*. This deals with his experience of "Het Dorp" (The Village), a fully accessible neighborhood in the Dutch city of Arnhem, designed to promote the optimum happiness of people with physical disabilities. Zola, a professor of sociology at Brandeis University, spent his sabbatical year in 1971–1972 as consultant-in-residence in the Netherlands at the Institute of Preventive Medicine in Leiden. He visited Het Dorp for a day in January 1972, and five months later he was resident visitor for a week. Zola approached Het Dorp, in his own words, as "I do many things, exploring and uncommitted," but "it became the setting for this chronicle and the stimulus for the search for my missing piece, my physical handicap." As a result of polio and a car accident Zola wore a long leg brace and a steel-reinforced back support.[10]

Zola actually uses the word utopia very sparingly. He describes his first, one-day visit to Het Dorp under the title "Several Hours in a Utopia." It becomes clear that Zola is not using the word here in an unequivocally positive way. He was clearly impressed: "Het Dorp was unlike any long-term care center" he had seen. But he also observed that "Het Dorp was so self-consciously a total institution, that it sought to provide everything, including happiness." "It was," as Zola continues, "rooted in the tradition of long-term medical care institutions and idealistically linked to the utopian communities."[11] Zola's unease with the utopia of Het Dorp was based on the fact that this utopia was not the utopia *of* people with disabilities but one *for* people with disabilities. It did not come from the people with disabilities themselves but was imagined and realized by able-bodied people. The idea of Het Dorp came from Arie Klapwijk, a physician working on the rehabilitation of people with physical disabilities, who wanted as he put it "to find and help severe invalids achieve optimal human development and optimal human happiness."[12] Klapwijk wanted to realize a place, and here I quote from Zola's translation of the founding documents, "where life could begin anew, where its physically handicapped inhabitants could live with dignity and independence, without the sense of futility and hopelessness of being restricted in medical institutions."[13]

I cannot give all the details of Zola's experience here, but his decision to use a wheelchair during his stay, combined with the fact that the residents knew that he was an American professor with a disability, led to many revealing conversations. Het Dorp seriously promoted the six rights that its founders had specified: the right to privacy, work, recreation, religion, culture, and self-governance; but the very existence of this special village and the way residents were approached showed the often-unequal relations between the "handicapped" and the "normal." Moreover, what residents, including Zola, found important was often ignored.[14] To paraphrase one of the most important slogans of the disability movement: The utopia was produced for them, not with them.[15] It was therefore not their utopia. His experience in Het Dorp made Zola realize that his disability was more important in his life than he thought. During his stay he realized that he felt "truly on someone's side, the side of the Village against the world."[16]

DYSTOPIA

Remarkably, Zola does not really develop an alternative utopia, but at most an implied minimalist utopia. This can be understood if we situate Zola in the context of the postwar Western welfare state, which gave social security to people with disability, but often not the emancipation and freedom for which they hoped. What we see in the Anglo-American disability movement, as inspired by Zola and others, is the fight against a paternalistic, welfarist utopia, in favor of an inclusive society that gives people with disabilities equal rights, independence, and a voice. However, I doubt if this inclusive society has often been imagined as a utopia. Forms of independent living since the 1970s and anti-discrimination laws in the 1990s are often seen as the most important achievements of the Anglo-American disability movement.[17] Both of these achievements focus on the individual: Independent living gives an individual with a disability the opportunity to live his or her own life with minimal dependence on others; anti-discrimination law gives an individual with a disability the possibility to go to court when he, she, or they are treated unequally. These achievements are huge, especially given how people with disabilities were treated in the past, but I doubt if they reflect an alternative society or city—a utopia. I would not say that the Anglo-American disability movement is without utopias and alternative imaginations of the social but fighting against the utopias formulated by others and finding ways to improve the lives of individuals with disabilities seems to have become more urgent.

It is not by chance that Zola presents at the beginning of his book a visit to a rehabilitation center in New Delhi, where his broken brace must be repaired. Under the title "With Hieronymus Bosch in India" he sketched a non-Western dystopia, before embarking on his critical investigation of a Western utopia. It is part of his narrative about disclosure; he ends the story as follows: "My three-hour experience was just another piece of information, just another incident in their busy day, recorded and quickly forgotten. But not for me, not for me."[18] Zola presented his visit to India, which took place shortly before he visited Het Dorp, as a first step in the search for his missing piece. So let us delve a bit deeper into this part of his book.

In India, Zola was shocked by two things. First, people asked him directly what had happened with his leg. That is, as Zola writes, "as any American would know . . . hardly a typical opening between strangers." It was an "intrusion into what Americans regard as so private a matter." Second, he was shocked by what he saw when he entered the Nehru Rehabilitation Centre: "Within comfortable touching distance was a panorama of physical suffering. An old man in a turban, toothless, blind in one eye, with his foot missing below the ankle, stood quite straight, almost proud; a young man, twentyish, wandered around, speaking to many but with no one returning the attention; countless children limped to and fro."[19] After this description Zola concludes that he "seemed to be the only one showing signs of discomfort."[20] These shocks helped Zola to discover his disability, but also made clear that the way people in India dealt with disability was not really attractive to him.

Thus, in this founding text of the Anglo-American disability movement a position is taken between a Western utopia and a non-Western dystopia, with some preference for the first. At its center we find an individual who is uncomfortable with the interference of others. This discomfort is understandable given the history of disabled people, but also questionable in the postcolonial context. The story of Zola indicates that there are good reasons to be skeptical about utopias, whether they be comprehensive welfare utopias or minimalist utopias focused on negative individual freedom. That is why I think another approach to the politics of time is more promising than utopianism, an approach moreover that challenges us to explore further the transformative potential of the convention.

HETEROTOPIA

Such an approach must take fraternity seriously: The concept from the triad of the French Revolution with which modern people have found it most difficult to identify.[21] Freedom and equality are contested and interpreted very differently, but people still tend to identify positively with these concepts. Fraternity has a slightly different story. It defines our relationship with others in a way that could be threatening for our imagined individuality, and it immediately raises the question of who those fraters, or brothers and sisters, really are. The ambivalent relationship between community and individual is particularly true for people with disabilities. Although "independent living" and "self-determination" have been core concepts of the global disability movement, many with disabilities have remained (partly) dependent on others who have been more or less organized as a community. Therefore, members of the disability movement and their allies have started to rethink their central concepts and to come up with alternatives such as interdependence and shared personhood, in which not only interhuman networks are addressed but also relations between humans, nonhumans, and the material environment.[22]

In chapter 6 I referred to this rethinking when mentioning Gerard Quinn's interpretation of Article 12. In addition to the reflections of Quinn and others on the convention, I think we also need stories that show or imagine how we could live alternative understandings of the human subject. Here I want to return to the (international) communities in which people with and without disabilities lived together, as described by Dagmar Herzog and others and as mentioned in chapter 1, and to discuss the case of Adam Arnett and Henri Nouwen. What I offer here is a brief analysis of the book *Adam, God's Beloved* (1996, translated and published in Dutch in 1997) and not an extensive investigation into their relationship based on different historical sources. The book is written mainly by the theologian Henri Nouwen, but because of his sudden death in 1996 it was finished and edited by his friend Sue Mosteller. The reason for the book was the death of Adam Arnett, a man with severe disabilities who died a couple of months before Nouwen. Arnett and Nouwen got to know each other in the L'Arche Daybreak community in Toronto, Canada. Arnett had lived in this community since 1985, and Nouwen came there on his sabbatical in 1995–1996. Nouwen had planned to write a book about the credo—the confession of Christian faith. When Arnett died in February 1996, Nouwen started to write a book about him that turned out to be a book about faith. For Nouwen, Arnett was a friend, teacher, and mentor. According to him Arnett was sent by God into the world to heal other people. Therefore, in writing about Arnett's life he related it to elements of Jesus's life. Nouwen saw in Adam the image of God, just as Jesus is perceived in the Christian tradition as "God with us."[23]

Although Nouwen's book is profoundly religious, the relationship between the two men can also be understood without focusing on religion. Arnett and Nouwen developed a friendship or became fraters because the latter was asked by the community to care in particular for the former. This shows that their relationship was not equal in every sense—there is a care and thus a power relationship in which Arnett's disabilities make him different from and dependent on Nouwen. In writing about Arnett, Nouwen balances difference and equality by saying that Arnett fulfilled his role as friend, teacher, and mentor in an uncommon way, because he could not communicate as people "usually" do. At the same time Nouwen stresses that Arnett was not extraordinary, not an angel, but a human being like everyone else. Interestingly, Nouwen challenges the view that he is the more powerful in their relationship by calling Arnett not only a friend but also a teacher and mentor. As becomes clear in his book, this process was no less than a reevaluation of values, as Nouwen wrote with an implicit reference to Nietzsche.[24]

What Nouwen and others experienced in their relationship with Arnett might therefore be seen as a variation on the social model—at the start they see people with disabilities as objects of care, but during the course of the relationship they learn to see their own view of disability as actually disabled and to perceive people with disabilities as individuals who inhabit the world partly in the same and partly in different ways.[25] This reevaluation is not without danger: People with disabilities could be seen as "instrumental" for able-bodied people to discover their own vulnerabilities, for instance.[26] While being aware of this, it is nevertheless worthwhile to examine stories of this kind because they further diversify disability studies. Arnett seems to have played a transformational role in the lives of several people, on account of his way of being in the world. Of course, we must reflect critically on the fact that Adam is "used" for religious narratives, but not more so than we do when reflecting on the more familiar resistance stories within the disability movement.

The case of Arnett and Nouwen not only reveals surprising forms of agency or personhood, but also points to the importance of space—which brings me back to utopias. In this case relationships were developed within a community in which people with and without disabilities lived closely together. It is striking that the agency of people with cognitive disabilities is respected and taken seriously, an attitude that cannot be taken for granted in society as a whole. Therefore, these communities could be seen as heterotopias, a Foucauldian concept of space applied by ethicist Herman Meininger to the inclusion of disabled persons. Foucault considers heterotopias to be "counter-sites" that "have the curious property of being in relation to all the other sites, but in such a way as to suspect, neutralize, or invert the set of relations that they happen to designate, mirror or reflect."[27] On the one hand heterotopias are a symptom of societies that exclude deviance, while on the other hand they can support the position of excluded people, because they occupy the space that society has abandoned as abnormal.[28] Meininger advocates heterotopias as spaces of encounter between people with and without intellectual disabilities because inclusion in public spaces "often turns out to be a space of discrimination."[29] According to Meininger heterotopias offer a "continuing dialogue between the 'normal' and 'abnormal' instead of adjusting 'the abnormal' to the 'normal,' an adjustment that cannot always be avoided in the politics of inclusion." In heterotopias the meetings between "we" and "the others" result in experiments with "new models of interaction, communication, connection, participation and power relations" and in "laboratories of new meaning and of alternative modes of social ordering."[30]

The history of people with cognitive disabilities seems in particular to contain such alternative narratives, although their history is rarely written from a more critical disability studies perspective. As already mentioned, the challenge of writing this history is that people with severe cognitive disabilities have hardly ever produced historical sources of their own—the sources they have left are often reproduced by other people. However, we do not always have to be dependent upon the able-bodied actor who dominates the sources; it is also possible to go beyond the focus on the individual and to look at the relationship between people as part of a broader network.[31] We need to realize, as Robbie Shilliam has pointed out, that "canons necessarily limit our understandings and imaginations" and "try to glean the margins of powers."[32] This enables us to articulate diverse ways of being in the world and to see how power relations could be shaped in order to make space for this diversity. Such investigations reveal how rights might be exercised within relations with the other and might therefore add usefully to the dominant narratives within the global disability movement that otherwise focus mostly on negative freedom rights. One may hope that disability history can uncover from the past more alternative narratives that will inspire people in the present to work toward a common future beyond the distinction between Spasticus Autisticus and Normal Land.

ACKNOWLEDGMENTS

I am not entirely sure when this book project started, but thanks to the encouragement of the Dutch historian Maarten van den Bos, I presented my first paper on the history of human rights and disability in 2013. A few years later, I became postdoc in the Rethinking Disability Project, led by Monika Baár and funded by the European Research Council, in which I received all the support needed to work further on the historical intersection of disability and international human rights. Because this project is long in the making, it is almost impossible to make a complete list of all the people who made a contribution to the book in one way or another. But let me give it a try: I want to thank Monika Baár, Gildas Brégain, Roland Burke, Christian O. Christiansen, Caelyn Cobb, Theresia Degener, Anna Derksen, Sam De Schutter, Yvonne Donders, Jan Eckel, Anaïs van Ertvelde, Patrick van Geest, Maartje Janse, Steven L. B. Jensen, Marisa Lastres, Natashe Lemos Dekker, Janet Lord, Julia Moses, Samuel Moyn, Simon Northwood, Nagase Osamu, Alanna O'Malley, Lis Pearson, Sander Rooijakkers, Brian Shaev, Emily Simon, Daniel Stahl, Marlies van der Kroft, Lotta Vikström, the anonymous reviewers, and all the other colleagues, archivists, and librarians without whom this book would not have been possible. Writing a book without people who do not directly contribute to it is also impossible, as is making a list of them. But let me make an exception for Marlies,

Lieke, Eefje, and Karlijn, who I thank for simply being with me when I was trying to make progress on this book within the margins of our household.

Parts of *Progress from the Margins* have been published elsewhere and are reused with permission. The Introduction and chapter 2 are partly published in "Inequality in Global Disability Policies Since the 1970s," in *Histories of Global Inequality: New Perspectives*, edited by Christian Olaf Christiansen and Steven L. B. Jensen (London: Palgrave Macmillan, 2019) 187–206; chapter 1 in "Equal Reproduction Rights? The Right to Found a Family in United Nation's Disability Policy Since the 1970s," *The History of the Family* 25, no. 2 (August 2019): 202–13; chapter 4 in "Belated Integration: Disability in International Human Rights Law," in *Embattled Visions: Human Rights Since 1990*, edited by Jan Eckel and Daniel Stahl (Göttingen: Wallstein Verlag, 2022) 101–20; chapter 5 in "Farewell to Social Europe? An Entangled Perspective on European Disability Policies in the 1980s and 1990s," in *Marginalized Groups, Inequalities and the Post-War Welfare State: Whose Welfare?*, edited by Monika Baár and Paul van Trigt (London: Routledge, 2020) 69–80; and the Epilogue in "Missing Utopia: Reconsidering the Politics of Time in the Global Disability Movement," in *Urban Utopias: Memory, Rights and Speculation*, edited by Barnita Bagchi (Kolkata: Jadavpur University Press, 2020) 120–39.

NOTES

INTRODUCTION

1. Ian Dury and the Blockheads, *Spasticus Autisticus, Lord Upminster* (Nassau: Compass Point Studios, 1981), live performance, https://www.youtube.com/watch?v=6isXNVdguI8.
2. Gerard Quinn and Anna Arstein-Kerslake, "Restoring the 'Human' in 'Human Rights': Personhood and Doctrinal Innovation in the UN Disability Convention," in *The Cambridge Companion to Human Rights Law*, ed. Conor Gearty and Costas Douzinas (New York: Cambridge University Press, 2012), 36–55; Frédéric Mégret, "The Disabilities Convention: Towards a Holistic Concept of Rights," *The International Journal of Human Rights* 12, no. 2 (2008): 261–77; Cf. Dagmar Herzog, *Unlearning Eugenics Sexuality, Reproduction, and Disability in Post-Nazi Europe* (Madison: University of Wisconsin Press, 2018).
3. Cf. Lys Kulamadayil, "Ableism in the College of International Lawyers: On Disabling Differences in the Professional Field," *Leiden Journal of International Law* 36, no. 3 (2023): 549–63.
4. Cf. Paul Ricoeur, *The Rule of Metaphor: The Creation of Meaning in Language* (London: Routledge, 2015).
5. Katharina Heyer, *Rights Enabled: The Disability Revolution, from the US, to Germany and Japan, to the United Nations* (Ann Arbor: University of Michigan Press, 2015), 2.
6. Robert F. Drake, "Welfare States and Disabled People," in *Handbook of Disability Studies*, ed. Gary L. Albrecht et al. (Thousand Oaks, CA: Sage Publications, 2001), 412–30, 416.
7. Jane Campbell and Mike Oliver, *Disability Politics: Understanding Our Past, Changing Our Future* (London: Routledge, 1996), 62. See for differences between the United States and the United Kingdom: Heyer, *Rights Enabled*, 47–50.

8. Heyer, *Rights Enabled*.
9. Gildas Brégain, "An Entangled Perspective on Disability History: The Disability Protests in Argentina, Brazil and Spain," in *The Imperfect Historian: Disability Histories in Europe*, ed. Sebastian Barsch et al. (Frankfurt am Main: Peter Lang, 2013), 133–53, 153.
10. Monika Baár, "Informal Networks, International Developments and the Founding of the First Interest-Representing Associations of Disabled People in Hungary in the Late Socialist Period (1970s–1980s)," *Moving the Social* 53 (2015): 39–62, 39.
11. Herbert Muyinda, "Negotiating Disability: Mobilization and Organization Among Landmine Survivors in Late Twentieth-Century Northern Uganda," in *Disability Histories*, ed. Susan Burch and Michael Rembis (Urbana: University of Illinois Press, 2014), 98–115, 112–13.
12. Gareth Millward, "Social Security Policy and the Early Disability Movement—Expertise, Disability, and the Government, 1965–77," *Twentieth Century British History* 26, no. 2 (2015): 274–97.
13. Dipesh Chakrabarty, *Provincializing Europe: Postcolonial Thought and Historical Difference* (Princeton, NJ: Princeton University Press, 2008).
14. Shaun Grech and Karen Soldatic, eds., *Disability in the Global South: The Critical Handbook* (Cham: Springer, 2016); Stephen J. Meyers, *Civilizing Disability Society: The Convention on the Rights of Persons with Disabilities Socializing Grassroots Disabled Persons' Organizations in Nicaragua* (Cambridge: Cambridge University Press, 2019).
15. Cf. Christopher Krentz, *Elusive Kinship: Disability and Human Rights in Postcolonial Literature* (Philadelphia: Temple University Press, 2022); Gildas Brégain, "Transnational History of Disability: Reflections," in *Handbook of Disability: Critical Thought and Social Change in a Globalizing World*, ed. Marcia H. Rioux et al. (Singapore: Springer, 2024), 137–57.
16. Samuel Moyn, "On the Nonglobalization of Ideas," in *Global Intellectual History*, ed. Samuel Moyn and Andrew Sartori (New York: Columbia University Press, 2013), 187–204, 188–89.
17. Moyn, "On the Nonglobalization of Ideas," 191–97.
18. Theresia Degener and Andrew Begg, "From Invisible Citizens to Agents of Change: A Short History of the Struggle for the Recognition of the Rights of Persons with Disabilities at the United Nations," in *The United Nations Convention on the Rights of Persons with Disabilities: A Commentary*, ed. Valentina Della Fina et al. (Cham: Springer, 2017), 1–39; Arlene S. Kanter, *The Development of Disability Rights Under International Law: From Charity to Human Rights* (New York: Routledge Taylor & Francis Group, 2017); Andrea Broderick, *The Long and Winding Road to Equality and Inclusion for Persons with Disabilities: The United Nations Convention on the Rights of Persons with Disabilities* (Cambridge: Intersentia, 2015); Rosemary Kayess and Phillip French, "Out of Darkness into Light? Introducing the Convention on the Rights of Persons with Disabilities," *Human Rights Law Review* 8, no. 1 (2008): 1–34.
19. Samuel Moyn, *The Last Utopia: Human Rights in History* (Cambridge, MA: Belknap Press of Harvard University Press, 2012); Cf. Jan Eckel, *The Ambivalence of Good:*

Human Rights in International Politics Since the 1940s (New York: Oxford University Press, 2019).

20. For a recent intervention in the debate about human rights and neoliberalism see Jessica Whyte, *The Morals of the Market: Human Rights and the Rise of Neoliberalism* (London: Verso, 2019).
21. Stephen Hopgood, *The Endtimes of Human Rights* (Ithaca, NY: Cornell University Press, 2015).
22. Benjamin Möckel, "Endtimes of Human Rights? Neue Forschungen zur Geschichte der Menschenrechte," *Neue Politische Literatur: Berichte aus Geschichts-und Politikwissenschaft* 65, no. 3 (2020): 473–501.
23. Stefan-Ludwig Hoffmann, "Human Rights and History," *Past & Present* 232, no. 1 (2016): 279–310, 282.
24. Antony Anghie, "Whose Utopia? Human Rights, Development, and the Third World," *Qui Parle* 22, no. 1 (2013): 63–80, 73–74.
25. Hoffmann, "Human Rights and History," 304.
26. Monika Baár, "Vegetables of the World Unite! Grassroots Internationalization of Disabled Citizens in the Post-War Period," in *Internationalists in European History: Rethinking the Twentieth Century*, ed. Jessica Reinisch and David Brydan (London: Bloomsbury Academic, 2021), 182–97; Cf. Glenda Sluga and Patricia M. Clavin, eds., *Internationalisms: A Twentieth-Century History* (Cambridge: Cambridge University Press, 2017); Matthew Connelly, "The Cold War in the Longue Durée: Global Migration, Public Health and Population Control," in *The Cambridge History of the Cold War*, ed. M. Leffler and O. Westad (Cambridge: Cambridge University Press, 2010), 466–88.
27. Cf. the approach of Vijay Prashad, *The Darker Nations: A People's History of The Third World* (New York: The New Press, 2007).

1. JERUSALEM 1968

1. Richard Sterner, "FN:S rättighetsförklaring för utvecklingsstörda från 1971," *Handikappsamverkan* 6 (1973): 14–17. Quoted from Inger Persson, *Ledare och artiklar av Richard Sterner: Ordförande i HCK—Handikapporganisationernas Centralkommitte 1963–1974* (Stockholm: Handikappförbundens samarbetsorgan/Handikapphistoriska Föreningen, 2009), 47f, http://u8628957.fsdata.se/wp-content/uploads/2015/03/ledare_sterner.pdf. I thank Anna Derksen for translating, and suggesting Swedish *frisläppta* as "promiscuous" instead of "liberated"—a more literal, but less fitting translation.
2. International League of Societies for the Mentally Handicapped (ILSMH), *Conclusions*, Legislative Aspects of Mental Retardation Symposium, Stockholm (June 11–17, 1967), https://mn.gov/mnddc/parallels2/pdf/60s/67/67-ILS-ILS.pdf.
3. Gildas Brégain, *Pour une histoire du handicap au XXe siècle: Approches transnationales (Europe et Amériques)* (Rennes: Presses Universitaires de Rennes, 2018), 164–66;

Dagmar Herzog, *Unlearning Eugenics: Sexuality, Reproduction, and Disability in Post-Nazi Europe* (Madison: University of Wisconsin Press, 2018), 73.
4. Sterner, "FN:S rättighetsförklaring."
5. Herzog, *Unlearning Eugenics*, 70–72.
6. Theresia Degener and Andrew Begg, "From Invisible Citizens to Agents of Change: A Short History of the Struggle for the Recognition of the Rights of Persons with Disabilities at the United Nations," in *The United Nations Convention on the Rights of Persons with Disabilities: A Commentary*, ed. Valentina Della Fina et al. (Cham: Springer, 2017), 4; Cf. the explanation of disability models in the Introduction.
7. Peter Mittler, *Thinking Globally, Acting Locally: A Personal Journey* (Central Milton Keynes: Authorhouse, 2010), 313.
8. Katharina Heyer, *Rights Enabled: The Disability Revolution, from the US, to Germany and Japan, to the United Nations* (Ann Arbor: University of Michigan Press, 2015), 2.
9. For an overview see Paul van Trigt, "De invoering van het Persoonsgebonden Budget in de gezondheidszorg in 1996 en het ontstaan van 'vrijemarktbureaucratie,'" *Tijdschrift Sociologie* 15 no. 3 (2019): 271–87.
10. Degener and Begg, "From Invisible Citizens to Agents of Change," 20.
11. Adolf Ratzska, "Crip Utopia," Independent Living Institute, 1998, https://www.independentliving.org/docs4/ratzkacu.html.
12. Gildas Brégain, "The Role of International Institutions in the Process of Categorization of 'Disabled People' (1930s–1975)," in *The Routledge History of Disability*, ed. Roy Hanes et al. (London: Routledge, 2018), 117–32, 118; Florian Kiuppis, "Why (Not) Associate the Principle of Inclusion with Disability? Tracing Connections from the Start of the 'Salamanca Process,'" *International Journal of Inclusive Education* 18, no. 7 (2014): 746–61, 749.
13. Cf. Glenda Sluga, *Internationalism in the Age of Nationalism* (Philadelphia: University of Pennsylvania Press, 2013).
14. Henri-Jacques Stiker, *A History of Disability* (Ann Arbor: University of Michigan Press, 2019); Sam de Schutter, "A Global Approach to Local Problems? How to Write a Longer, Deeper, and Wider History of the International Year of Disabled Persons in Kenya," *Diplomatica* 1, no. 2 (2019): 221–42.
15. Brégain, "The Role of International Institutions," 126–31.
16. Alison Bashford, *Global Population History, Geopolitics, and Life on Earth* (New York: Columbia University Press, 2016); Matthew James Connelly, *Fatal Misconception: The Struggle to Control World Population* (Cambridge, MA: Belknap Press of Harvard University Press, 2009).
17. Steven L. B. Jensen, "Da Danmark forsøgte at gøre tvangssterilisering til beskyttet praksis i international menneskeret," *Handicaphistorisk Tidsskrift* 51 (2024): 22–38. I thank Steven L. B. Jensen, who provided me with this article and a translation of the main findings.
18. Herzog, *Unlearning Eugenics*.
19. Herzog, *Unlearning Eugenics*, 72.

20. World Health Organization (WHO), *Co-ordinated International Programme on Rehabilitation of Physically Handicapped Persons*, Vol. 1952 (Geneva: WHO, 1952), 4. Thanks to Sam de Schutter for this quotation.
21. Herzog, *Unlearning Eugenics*, 86–90.
22. WHO Archives, R4/372/3 (WHO/ILO Collaboration in the field of rehabilitation), letter from Sterner to the WHO.
23. Karl Grunewald, "Scandinavian Influences on Intellectual Disability Policy in Other Parts of the World," *Scandinavian Journal of Disability Research* 5, no. 2 (2003): 203–7.
24. Grunewald, "Scandinavian Influences," 206.
25. Stanley S. Herr, "Rights into Action: Protecting Human Rights of the Mentally Handicapped," *Catholic University Law Review* 26, no. 2 (1977): 203–318, 206.
26. Mittler, *Thinking Globally, Acting Locally*, 340.
27. ILSMH, *Conclusions*.
28. Benjamin N. Schoenfeld, "Human Rights for the Mentally Retarded: Their Recognition by the Providers of Service," *Human Rights* 4, no. 1 (1974): 31–65, 45.
29. Schoenfeld, "Human Rights," 47.
30. Mittler, *Thinking Globally, Acting Locally*, 340.
31. Mittler, *Thinking Globally, Acting Locally*, 340.
32. Sterner, "FN:S rättighetsförklaring"; Cf. Mittler, *Thinking Globally, Acting Locally*, 340–41.
33. Sterner, "FN:S rättighetsförklaring"; United Nations Archives and Records Management Section (UNARMS), Archives Secretary General (ASG), s-0445-0344-0006, Declaration of General and Special Rights of the Mentally Retarded (1968).
34. UNARMS, ASG, s-0445-0344-0006, letter from Portray to Kosunen (June 10, 1971).
35. UNARMS, ASG, s-0445-0344-0006, draft text of the Declaration of the Rights of the Mentally Retarded (1970, E/CN.5/468). These sentences were probably proposed by Norman Acton, who worked at Rehabilitation International and will be introduced in chapter 2.
36. Mittler, *Thinking Globally, Acting Locally*, 341.
37. UN General Assembly, Convention on the Rights of Persons with Disabilities (CRPD), A/RES/61/106 (December 13, 2006), https://www.ohchr.org/en/instruments-mechanisms/instruments/convention-rights-persons-disabilities.
38. Degener and Begg, "From Invisible Citizens to Agents of Change," 26; David Mitchell and Sharon Snyder, "The Eugenic Atlantic: Race, Disability, and the Making of an International Eugenic Science, 1800–1945," *Disability & Society* 18, no. 7 (2003): 843–64.
39. Bret Shaffer, "The Right to Life, the Convention on the Rights of Persons with Disabilities, and Abortion," *Penn State International Law Review* 28, no. 2 (2009): 265–87.
40. Marta Schaaf, "Negotiating Sexuality in the Convention on the Rights of Persons with Disabilities," *Sur: International Journal on Human Rights* 8, no. 14 (2011): 113–31; Felipe Jaramillo Ruiz, "The Committee on the Rights of Persons with Disabilities and Its Take on Sexuality," *Reproductive Health Matters* 25, no. 50 (2017): 92–103.
41. Brégain, *Pour une histoire du handicap*, 164–66.

42. UN General Assembly, Resolution 3447, Declaration on the Rights of Disabled Persons (December 9, 1975), http://www.ohchr.org/EN/ProfessionalInterest/Pages/RightsOfDisabledPersons.aspx.
43. UN General Assembly, Resolution 31/123, International Year of Disabled Persons, A/RES/31/123 (December 16, 1976), http://www.un-documents.net/a31r123.htm.
44. UN General Assembly, World Programme of Action Concerning Disabled Persons, A/37/351/Add.1 (September 15, 1982), https://digitallibrary.un.org/record/36690/files/A_37_351_Add.1-EN.pdf?ln=en, 19.
45. UN General Assembly, Resolution 31/123, 1976.
46. UN General Assembly, Resolution 37/52, World Programme of Action Concerning Disabled Persons, A/RES/37/52 (December 3, 1982), http://www.un-documents.net/a37r52.htm.
47. UN General Assembly, A/37/351/Add.1, 1982, 8.
48. Leandro Despouy, *Human Rights and Disabled Persons* (New York: United Nations, 1993), https://www.un.org/esa/socdev/enable/dispaperdeso.htm.
49. UN General Assembly, Views Submitted by Governments, Intergovernmental Organizations and United Nations Bodies Concerning a Comprehensive and Integral International Convention on the Protection and Promotion of the Rights and Dignity of Persons with Disabilities, A/AC.265/2003/4 (May 6, 2003), http://uvallsc.s3.amazonaws.com/travaux/s3fs-public/A-AC_265-2003-4.pdf?null.
50. UN General Assembly, A/AC.265/2003/4, 2003.
51. UN General Assembly, Resolution 48/96, Standard Rules on the Equalization of Opportunities for Persons with Disabilities, A/RES/48/96 (March 4, 1994), 18, https://www.un.org/disabilities/documents/gadocs/standardrules.pdf.
52. Schaaf, "Negotiating Sexuality."
53. Isaiah Berlin, *Four Essays on Liberty* (Oxford: Oxford University Press, 1969), 118.
54. Tom Shakespeare, *Disability Rights and Wrongs Revisited* (London: Routledge, 2014), 214.
55. Schaaf, "Negotiating Sexuality," 114.
56. Schaaf, "Negotiating Sexuality," 116.
57. Irving Kenneth Zola, *Missing Pieces: A Chronicle of Living with a Disability* (Philadelphia: Temple University Press, 1982), 215.
58. UN General Assembly, Progress Report on the Preparations for the International Conference on Population and Development, A/48/430/Add.1 (October 14, 1993), http://uvallsc.s3.amazonaws.com/travaux/s3fs-public/A-48-430-Add_1.pdf?null, 17.
59. Schaaf, "Negotiating Sexuality," 118; Cf. Stefan-Ludwig Hoffmann, "Human Rights and History," *Past & Present* 232, no. 1 (2016): 302.
60. Quoted in Hoffmann, "Human Rights and History," 302.
61. Despouy, *Human Rights and Disabled Persons*.
62. Gerard Quinn and Theresia Degener, *Human Rights and Disability: The Current Use and Future Potential of United Nations Human Rights Instruments in the Context of Disability* (New York: United Nations, 2002), 35, https://www.ohchr.org/sites/default/files/Documents/Publications/HRDisabilityen.pdf.

63. UN General Assembly, Resolution 48/96, 1994, 5.
64. UN Economic and Social Council, Report of the Ad Hoc Open-Ended Working Group to Elaborate Standard Rules on the Equalization of Opportunities for Disabled Persons, E/CN.5/1993/5 (November 11, 1992), 6, http://uvallsc.s3.amazonaws.com/travaux/s3fs-public/E-CN_5-1993-5.pdf?null.
65. Quinn and Degener, *Human Rights and Disability*, 24.
66. Quinn and Degener, *Human Rights and Disability*, 75.
67. Heyer, *Rights Enabled*, 172–73.
68. Paul van Trigt, "A Blind Spot of a Guiding Country? Human Rights and Dutch Disability Groups Since 1981," *Moving the Social* 53 (2015): 87–102; Degener and Begg, "From Invisible Citizens to Agents of Change"; Herzog, *Unlearning Eugenics*.
69. Arlene S. Kanter, *The Development of Disability Rights Under International Law: From Charity to Human Rights* (New York: Routledge Taylor & Francis Group, 2017).
70. Degener and Begg, "From Invisible Citizens to Agents of Change."
71. Frédéric Mégret, "The Disabilities Convention: Human Rights of Persons with Disabilities or Disability Rights?," *Human Rights Quarterly* 30, no. 2 (2008): 494–516.
72. Schaaf, "Negotiating Sexuality," 121–23; Cf. Ruiz, "The Committee."
73. Ruiz, "The Committee," 92.
74. Cf. Ingo Venzke, "Situating Contingency in the Path of International Law," in *Contingency in International Law: On the Possibility of Different Legal Histories*, ed. Ingo Venzke and Kevin Jon Heller (Oxford: Oxford University Press, 2021), 3–19.

2. BELGRADE 1975

1. The World Council for the Welfare of the Blind, The International Federation of the Blind & the Union of the Blind of Yugoslavia, *Proceedings of the International Conference on the Situation of the Blind Women, November 18–20, 1975* (Belgrade, 1976), 12. I want to thank Gildas Brégain for making the proceedings accessible to me.
2. Samuel Moyn, "What Happened to the Dream of Global Justice?," *ABC Religion & Ethics* (October 31, 2019), https://www.abc.net.au/religion/samuel-moyn-what-happened-to-the-dream-of-global-justice/11658576; Nils Gilman, "The New International Economic Order: A Reintroduction," *Humanity: An International Journal of Human Rights, Humanitarianism, and Development* 6, no. 1 (2015): 1–16; Samuel Moyn, *Not Enough: Human Rights in an Unequal World* (Cambridge, MA: The Belknap Press of Harvard University Press, 2018).
3. Anaïs van Ertvelde, "Welfare: Defended, Questioned, Complemented? Belgian Welfare Arrangements in the 1970s–1980s from the Perspective of Disability Organizations," in *Marginalized Groups, Inequalities and the Post-War Welfare State: Whose Welfare?*, ed. Monika Baár and Paul van Trigt (London: Routledge, 2020), 137–54, 144–45; Gildas Brégain, "La fabrique de la Déclaration des droits des personnes handicapées de l'ONU (1975): un succès diplomatique rapide en temps de guerre froide," *Droit et société* 113, no. 1 (2023): 31–53.

4. Nora Groce, *From Charity to Disability Rights: Global Initiatives of Rehabilitation International, 1922-2002* (New York: Rehabilitation International, 2002); Gildas Brégain, "The Role of International Institutions in the Process of Categorization of 'Disabled People' (1930s-1975)," in *The Routledge History of Disability*, ed. Roy Hanes et al. (London: Routledge, 2018), 117-32.
5. Henri-Jacques Stiker, *A History of Disability* (Ann Arbor: University of Michigan Press, 2019); Gildas Brégain, *Pour une histoire du handicap au XXe siècle: Approches transnationales (Europe et Amériques)* (Rennes: Presses Universitaires de Rennes, 2018); Sam de Schutter, "A Global Approach to Local Problems? How to Write a Longer, Deeper, and Wider History of the International Year of Disabled Persons in Kenya," *Diplomatica* 1, no. 2 (2019): 221-42.
6. Cf. Kristen Rogheh Ghodsee, *Second World, Second Sex: Socialist Women's Activism and Global Solidarity During the Cold War* (Durham, NC: Duke University Press, 2019).
7. Gildas Brégain, "The ILO and the Shift Towards Economic Liberalization in the International Professional Rehabilitation Policies of People with Disabilities After World War II," in *Marginalized Groups,* 49-68, 56.
8. Groce, *From Charity to Disability Rights*, 38-39.
9. Groce, *From Charity to Disability Rights*, 43-44.
10. Groce, *From Charity to Disability Rights*, 55.
11. "Appendix" in Rehabilitation International, *Proceedings Second International Conference on Legislation Concerning the Disabled, Manila 1978* (New York: Rehabilitation International, 1978), 284.
12. Rehabilitation International, *Proceedings*, 285.
13. Rehabilitation International, *Proceedings*, 285-86.
14. Van Ertvelde, "Welfare: Defended, Questioned, Complemented?," 144-45; Brégain, *Pour une histoire du handicap.*
15. Brégain, *Pour une histoire du handicap*, 179-80.
16. Groce, *From Charity to Disability Rights*, 55.
17. "Manila Statement," in Rehabilitation International, *Proceedings*, 193.
18. A distinction not made in Groce, *From Charity to Disability Rights*, 55.
19. "The Impact of the International Year of Disabled Persons: An Interview with Norman Acton," *International Rehabilitation Review* 50, no. 1 (2000): 10-12; Cf. Groce, *From Charity to Disability Rights*, 66. I want to thank Osamu Nagase for the information about Kikhia.
20. Cf. Steven L. B. Jensen, *The Making of International Human Rights: The 1960s, Decolonization, and the Reconstruction of Global Values* (New York: Cambridge University Press, 2016); Simon Jackson and Alanna O'Malley, eds., *The Institution of International Order: From the League of Nations to the United Nations* (London: Routledge, 2020); Vijay Prashad, *The Darker Nations: A People's History of The Third World* (New York: The New Press, 2007).
21. Fatima Shah, *Sunshine & Shadows: The Autobiography of Dr. Fatima Shah* (Karachi: Ferozsons, 1999), 133-35.

22. Shah, *Sunshine & Shadows*, 136–37.
23. Shah, *Sunshine & Shadows*, 152–53. Shah became president of International Federation of the Blind (IFB) in 1974.
24. Shah, *Sunshine & Shadows*, 165. Later the IFB and World Council for the Welfare of the Blind (WCWB) amalgamated as the World Blind Union.
25. Brégain, *Pour une histoire du handicap*, 162–65.
26. The World Council, *Proceedings of the International Conference*, 1–2.
27. The World Council, *Proceedings of the International Conference*, 15.
28. The World Council, *Proceedings of the International Conference*, 16.
29. The World Council, *Proceedings of the International Conference*, 17.
30. The World Council, *Proceedings of the International Conference*, 22–23.
31. The World Council, *Proceedings of the International Conference*, 41–48.
32. The World Council, *Proceedings of the International Conference*, 132.
33. Shah, *Sunshine & Shadows*, 181.
34. Shah, *Sunshine & Shadows*, 201.
35. Shah, *Sunshine & Shadows*, 211–12.
36. Shah, *Sunshine & Shadows*, 237.
37. Brégain, "The Role of International Institutions."
38. UN Division for Social Policy and Development, *The United Nations and Disability: 70 Years of the Work Towards a More Inclusive World* (New York: United Nations, 2018), https://www.un.org/development/desa/disabilities/wp-content/uploads/sites/15/2018/01/History_Disability-in-the-UN_jan23.18-Clean.pdf.
39. Brégain, *Pour une histoire du handicap*.
40. UN Division, *The United Nations and Disability*. For the development of the declaration see Brégain, *Pour une histoire du handicap*; Van Ertvelde, "Welfare: Defended, Questioned, Complemented?"
41. UN General Assembly, Resolution 3447, 1975, Article 3.
42. UN General Assembly, A/37/351/Add.1, 1982.
43. For first version see UN General Assembly, Resolution 31/123, 1976.
44. Monika Baár, "The European 'Disability Revolts' of 1981: How Were They Related to the Youth Movement?," in *A European Youth Revolt: European Perspectives on Youth Protest and Social Movements in the 1980s*, ed. Knud Andersen and Bart van der Steen (Houndmills: Palgrave MacMillan, 2016), 159–71.
45. Diane Driedger, *The Last Civil Rights Movement: Disabled Peoples' International* (London: Hurst, 1989), 1.
46. Driedger, *The Last Civil Rights Movement*, 97.
47. Nationaal Archief, Den Haag (NL-HaNA), Ministerie van Volksgezondheid en Milieuhygiëne: Stichting Nationale Commissie Internationaal Jaar van de Gehandicapten 1981, nummer toegang 2.27.07, inventarisnummer 6, attachment to the meeting of September 17, 1981. Translations of Dutch quotations are my own.
48. For the Dutch case see Paul van Trigt, "Gelijkheid zonder beperking: Over de Algemene Wet Gelijke Behandeling (1994) en de constructive van handicap in politieke instituties," *BMGN—Low Countries Historical Review* 134, no. 1 (2019): 3–27; For

the International Year for Disabled Persons in a Scandinavian context see Anna Derksen, "'To Action for Full Participation and Equality.' Re-framing International Solidarity in 1980s Nordic Disability Rights Activism," in *Towards Solidarity. The Use and Abuse of Concepts of Compassion*, ed. Irène Hermann and Renata Latała (Chêne-Bourg: Georg Editeur, 2024), 179–205.

49. UN Economic and Social Council, Resolution 1921 (LVIII), Prevention of Disability and Rehabilitation of Disabled Persons, E/CN.5/565 (December 19, 1978), 5, https://digitallibrary.un.org/record/2105?ln=en.
50. NL-HaNA, Cie. Internationaal Jaar Gehandicapten, 2.27.07, inv.nr. 10, speech by Queen Juliana of the Netherlands (r. 1948–1980).
51. UN General Assembly, A/37/351/Add.1, 1982.
52. UN General Assembly, A/37/351/Add.1, 1982.
53. Shaun Grech, "Disability and Development: Critical Connections, Gaps and Contradictions," in *Disability in the Global South: The Critical Handbook*, ed. Shaun Grech and Karen Soldatic (Cham: Springer, 2016), 3–19; Shaun Grech, "Disability and Poverty: Complex Interactions and Critical Reframings," in *Disability in the Global South*, 217–35.
54. Cf. Moyn, *Not Enough*.
55. UN General Assembly, A/37/351/Add.1, 1982.
56. For this distinction see Samuel Moyn, *The Last Utopia: Human Rights in History*, (Cambridge, MA: Belknap Press of Harvard University Press, 2012).
57. Einar Helander, "The Origins of Community Based Rehabilitation," *Behindering und internationale Entwicklung/Disability and International Development* 24, no. 1 (2013): 4–14, 11. Helander writes about the UN High Commissioner of Human Rights, but this institution did not exist at the time. My thanks to Sam de Schutter for drawing this paper to my attention.
58. Leandro Despouy, *Human Rights and Disabled Persons* (New York: United Nations, 1993), https://www.un.org/esa/socdev/enable/dispaperdeso.htm.
59. UN Centre for Social Development and Humanitarian Affairs (CSDHA), Global Meeting of Experts to Review the Implementation of the World Programme of Action Concerning Disabled Persons at Midpoint of the United Nations Decade of Disabled Persons, CSDHA/DDP/GME/7 (September 1, 1987), 5.
60. UN CSDHA, CSDHA/DDP/GME/7, 1987, 8.
61. UN CSDHA, CSDHA/DDP/GME/7, 1987, 6.
62. Despouy, *Human Rights and Disabled Persons*.
63. Despouy, *Human Rights and Disabled Persons*.
64. UN Economic and Social Council, Draft resolution VII, United Nations Decade of Disabled Persons, E/1989/25, E/CN.5/1989/12 (March 22, 1989), 15, http://uvallsc.s3.amazonaws.com/travaux/s3fs-public/E-1989-25__E-CN_5-1989-12_0.pdf?null.
65. UN General Assembly, A/AC.265/2003/4, 2003.
66. Gerard Quinn and Theresia Degener, *Human Rights and Disability: The Current Use and Future Potential of United Nations Human Rights Instruments in the Context of Disability* (New York: United Nations, 2002), 35.

67. UN General Assembly, Resolution 48/96, A/RES/48/96, 1994, 5–6.
68. UN General Assembly, Resolution 48/96, A/RES/48/96, 1994, 8; Cf. Moyn, who shows in *Not Enough* how the human needs paradigm was used by the World Bank, among others, to deal with (global) poverty without contesting structural material inequality.
69. UN General Assembly, Resolution 48/96, A/RES/48/96, 1994, 4.
70. UN General Assembly, Resolution 48/96, A/RES/48/96, 1994, 6.
71. Moyn, *Not Enough*, 3.
72. UN General Assembly, Resolution 48/96, A/RES/48/96, 1994, 7.
73. UN General Assembly, Resolution 48/96, A/RES/48/96, 1994, 17.
74. Stefan-Ludwig Hoffmann, "Introduction: Genealogies of Human Rights and History," in *Human Rights in the Twentieth Century*, ed. Stefan-Ludwig Hoffmann (New York: Cambridge University Press, 2010), 24; Cf. Julia Dehm, "Rights as Potential Sites of Distributive Struggle," *Tocqueville21* (July 10, 2018), https://tocqueville21.com/focus/rights-as-potential-sites-of-distributive-struggle/. In her blog Dehm writes in response to Moyn, *Not Enough*: "There was [in the late 1980s] a call for rights advocates to retreat from an ideal that 'might call for equality for all' and instead focus on the pragmatic realization of rights through 'consistent vigilance to improve the conditions for the most vulnerable, without expecting dramatic and abrupt transformations of comprehensive and interlocking economic and social systems.'"
75. UN General Assembly, Summary Record of the 5th Meeting: 3rd Committee, 60th session, A/C.3/60/SR.5 (October 26, 2005), http://uvallsc.s3.amazonaws.com/travaux/s3fs-public/A-C_3-60-SR_5.pdf?null. In 2001 the "argument for a disability convention was framed in light of the recently released Millenium Development Goals" by Mexico. See Katharina Heyer, *Rights Enabled: The Disability Revolution, from the US, to Germany and Japan, to the United Nations* (Ann Arbor: University of Michigan Press, 2015), 172–73.
76. Helen Meekosha and Karen Soldatic, "Human Rights and the Global South: The Case of Disability," *Third World Quarterly* 32, no. 8 (2011): 1383–97, 1389.
77. Frédéric Mégret, "The Disabilities Convention: Human Rights of Persons with Disabilities or Disability Rights?" *Human Rights Quarterly* 30, no. 2 (2008): 494–516.

3. SINGAPORE 1981

1. Singapore Organising Committee, *Souvenir Magazine of the Disabled Peoples' International First World Congress, Singapore, November 29–December 4, 1981* (Singapore 1981), 11.
2. Jiyoung Song, ed., *A History of Human Rights Society in Singapore, 1965–2015* (Abingdon: Routledge, 2017).
3. Singapore Organising Committee, *Souvenir Magazine*, 11.
4. UN Committee on the Rights of Persons with Disabilities, General Comment No. 7 (2018) on the Participation of Persons with Disabilities, Including Children with

Disabilities, Through Their Representative Organizations, in the Implementation and Monitoring of the Convention, CRPD/C/GC/7 (November 9, 2018), https://digitallibrary.un.org/record/3899396?ln=en; Meredith Raley, "The Drafting of Article 33 of the Convention on the Rights of Persons with Disabilities: The Creation of a Novel Mechanism," *The International Journal of Human Rights* 20, no. 1 (2016): 138–52, https://doi.org/10.1080/13642987.2015.1073714.

5. Archives of Manitoba, Disabled Peoples' International Fonds (AM–DPIf, 11823), Box 1, Press Release from DPI, February 27, 1981. I want to thank Anaïs van Ertvelde for sharing her archival material from the Archives of Manitoba with me.

6. AM–DPIf, 11823, Box 1, paper titled, "How Disabled People Are Organizing Themselves in the World," presented by Henry Enns at the Latin American Symposium on Rehabilitation (May 24–29, 1981); Cf. Henry Enns and Alfred H. Neufeldt, eds., *In Pursuit of Equal Participation: Canada and Disability at Home and Abroad* (Concord, ON: Captus Press, 2003).

7. AM–DPIf, 11823, DPI Manifesto, which was adopted at the Disabled Peoples' International First World Congress in Singapore, November 29–December 4, 1981.

8. UN General Assembly, General Assembly official records, 34th session: 3rd Committee, 56th meeting, A/C.3/34/SR.56 (November 26, 1979), https://digitallibrary.un.org/record/129877?ln=en. From the UN documents, including the UN Advisory Committee for the International Year of Disabled Persons' report of the first session, it is not clear who exactly made this proposal. See UN General Assembly, International Year for Disabled Persons, Meeting of the Advisory Committee for the International Year for Disabled Persons: Report of the Secretary-General, A/34/158 (March 19–23, 1979), https://digitallibrary.un.org/record/3844?ln=en. Susan Burch has claimed it was Frank Bowe, a Deaf self-advocate from the United States, while the Disabled Peoples' International fonds claims the request came from the Canadian representative. See respectively Susan Burch, ed., *Encyclopedia of American Disability History* (New York: Facts on File, 2009); AM–DPIf, 11823, Box 3.

9. Diane Driedger, *The Last Civil Rights Movement: Disabled Peoples' International* (London: Hurst, 1989), 58–59.

10. James I. Charlton, *Nothing About Us Without Us: Disability Oppression and Empowerment* (Berkeley: University of California Press, 1998).

11. Sharon Barnett, "The Globalization of Disability Protests, 1970–2005: Pushing the Limits of Cross-Cultural Research?," *Comparative Sociology* 9 (2010): 222–40; Michael Rembis, "Yes We Can Change: Disability Studies—Enabling Equality," *Journal of Postsecondary Education and Disability* 23, no. 1 (2010): 19–27; Katharina Heyer, *Rights Enabled: The Disability Revolution, from the US, to Germany and Japan, to the United Nations* (Ann Arbor: University of Michigan Press, 2015).

12. Devaki Jain, "Gender: From Eliminating Discrimination to Promoting Women's Rights and Empowerment," in *UN Ideas That Changed the World*, ed. Richard Jolly et al. (Bloomington: Indiana University Press, 2009), 68–82; Jocelyn Olcott, *International Women's Year: The Greatest Consciousness-Raising Event in History* (New York: Oxford University Press, 2017); Paul van Trigt, "Introduction: Scripts for a New Stage:

United Nations' Observances and New Perspectives on Diplomatic History," *Diplomatica* 1, no. 2 (2019): 145–56.

13. Adaly M. Rodriquez, *The Rise of Women's Rights in Curaçao: The Potential of the Women's Convention to the Empowerment and Equal Rights of Women in Curaçao* (Amsterdam: Caribpublishing/SWP, 2015), 100.

14. Rodriquez, *The Rise of Women's Rights*, 100–101.

15. Paul van Trigt, "Gelijkheid zonder beperking: Over de Algemene Wet Gelijke Behandeling (1994) en de constructie van handicap in politieke instituties," *BMGN—Low Countries Historical Review* 134, no. 1 (2019): 3–27.

16. NL–HaNA, Cie. Internationaal Jaar Gehandicapten, 2.27.07, inv.nr. 9, attachment to the meeting of December 18, 1980. Translation of Dutch quotations is my own.

17. A. D. C. Gomez, "Stichting voor Rehabilitatie van gehandicapten," *Amigoe* (November 6, 1978).

18. "Voorbereidingen voor Jaar van Gehandicapte," *Amigoe* (January 23, 1980).

19. NL–HaNA, Cie. Internationaal Jaar Gehandicapten, 2.27.07, inv.nr. 10, attachment to the meeting of January 29, 1981. Translation of Dutch quotations is my own.

20. "Aruba ervaart opnieuw handicap-imperialisme," *Amigoe* (March 30, 1981); Cf. the articles in *Amigoe* (April 2, April 7, and May 12, 1981).

21. NL–HaNA, Cie. Internationaal Jaar Gehandicapten, 2.27.07, inv.nr. 30, eindverslag (*final report*). Translation of Dutch quotations is my own.

22. "Gehandicaptenzorg is méér dan verzorging alleen," *Amigoe* (January 22, 1982).

23. Leetz-Cijntje became chairperson in April 1982. See "Nieuwe voorzitter Raad gehandicapten," *Amigoe* (July 20, 1982).

24. "Min Croes: proces gaat te langzaam. Adviesraad Gehandicapten bijeen," *Amigoe* (November 29, 1982).

25. Rodriquez, *The Rise of Women's Rights*.

26. Joan Tucker, "Local Strategies in a Global Network: Disability Rights in Jamaica," PhD Diss. (University of South Florida, 2007), https://digitalcommons.usf.edu/etd/2388/.

27. Van Trigt, "Gelijkheid zonder beperking"; Dora Vargha, *Polio Across the Iron Curtain: Hungary's Cold War with an Epidemic* (Cambridge: Cambridge University Press, 2018); Charlton, *Nothing About Us Without Us*.

28. Monika Baár, "The European 'Disability Revolts' of 1981: How Were They Related to the Youth Movement?," in *A European Youth Revolt: European Perspectives on Youth Protest and Social Movements in the 1980s*, ed. Knud Andersen and Bart van der Steen (Houndmills: Palgrave MacMillan, 2016) 159–71; Monika Baár, "Vegetables of the World Unite! Grassroots Internationalization of Disabled Citizens in the Post-War Period," in *Internationalists in European History: Rethinking the Twentieth Century*, ed. Jessica Reinisch and David Brydan (London: Bloomsbury Academic, 2021) 182–97.

29. Matthew Kohrman, *Bodies of Difference: Experiences of Disability and Institutional Advocacy in the Making of Modern China* (Berkeley: University of California Press, 2005).

30. Van Trigt, "Gelijkheid zonder beperking"; Sam de Schutter, "A Global Approach to Local Problems? How to Write a Longer, Deeper, and Wider History of the International Year of Disabled Persons in Kenya," *Diplomatica* 1, no. 2 (2019): 221–42.
31. Cf. Michele Friedner et al., "'Cross-Disability' in India? On the Limits of Disability as a Category and the Work of Negotiating Impairments," *South Asia Multidisciplinary Academic Journal* (April 5, 2018), https://doi.org/10.4000/samaj.4516.
32. Steven L. B. Jensen, *The Making of International Human Rights: The 1960s, Decolonization, and the Reconstruction of Global Values* (New York: Cambridge University Press, 2016), 100.
33. Maria Cristina Galmarini, *Ambassadors of Social Progress: A History of International Blind Activism in the Cold War* (Ithaca, NY: Northern Illinois University Press, 2024), 92.
34. Anne Derksen, "Bengt Olof Lennart Lindqvist (1936–2016)," *nordics.info* (December 4, 2019), https://nordics.info/show/artikel/bengt-olof-lennart-lindqvist-1936-2016.
35. Kalle Könkkölä and Heini Saraste, *The World Became My Room* (Juva: WSOY, 1996), 189.
36. Shaffiq Alkhatib, "Blind Activist and Handicap Welfare Champion Ron Chandran-Dudley Dies," *TNP Singapore* (December 31, 2015); Cf. Ron Chandran-Dudley, *The Man with a Mission: A Life Well-lived* (Singapore: Pagesetters Services, 2017).
37. Singapore Association of the Visually Handicapped (SAVH), *Walk Unafraid* (Singapore: The Association, 2001), 78.
38. SAVH, *Walk Unafraid*, 61; National Library Board Singapore, *Magazine Independent Society of the Blind* (1991), 9.
39. National Co-ordinating Committee for the International Year of Disabled Persons (Singapore), *Rights Issue: International Year of Disabled Persons—Full Participation and Integration* (Singapore: National Co-ordinating Committee (IYDP), 1981); Cf. Kuansong Victor Zhuang, "At the Margins of Society: Disability Rights and Inclusion in 1980s Singapore," *Disability and the Global South* 7, no. 1 (2020): 1813–29.
40. Baár, "Vegetables."
41. Disabled Peoples' International, *The Disabled Peoples' International Anniversary Journal* (Singapore: Disabled Peoples' International, 1984), 7.
42. Theresia Degener and Andrew Begg, "From Invisible Citizens to Agents of Change: A Short History of the Struggle for the Recognition of the Rights of Persons with Disabilities at the United Nations," in *The United Nations Convention on the Rights of Persons with Disabilities: A Commentary*, ed. Valentina Della Fina et al. (Cham: Springer, 2017), 11–12.
43. Diane Driedger, "The Origins and History of Disabled Peoples' International (DPI) 1945–1985," MA Thesis (University of Manitoba, 1987), https://mspace.lib.umanitoba.ca/xmlui/handle/1993/9408.
44. UN General Assembly, A/37/351/Add.1, 1982.
45. UN CSDHA, CSDHA/DDP/GME/7, 1987.

46. UN General Assembly, Resolution 48/96, 1994, 5–6.
47. UN General Assembly, A/37/351/Add.1, 1982.
48. Fatima Shah, *Sunshine & Shadows: The Autobiography of Dr. Fatima Shah* (Karachi: Ferozsons, 1999), 239–40.
49. Joseph J. Murray, "Linguistic Human Rights Discourse in Deaf Community Activism," *Sign Language Studies* 15, no. 4 (2015): 379–410, 391.
50. Maartje De Meulder, "Sign Language Recognition: Tensions Between Specificity and Universalism in International Deaf Discourses," in *It's a Small World: International Deaf Spaces and Encounters*, ed. Michele Ilana Friedner and Annelies Kusters (Washington, D.C.: Gallaudet University Press, 2015), 160–72. However, the Deaf were very early in using human rights for their self-advocacy. How human rights were used before the 1980s is not well explored in the literature. Corrie Tijsseling has mentioned that the World Federation of the Deaf, founded in 1951, had already celebrated ten years of Universal Declaration and initiated a World Deaf Day in 1958, which sought, first, to translate and explain human rights in sign language, and second, to draw the public's attention to the disadvantaged societal position of the Deaf. The first World Deaf Day was successful and became a tradition. See Corrie Tijsseling, "'School, waar?' Een onderzoek naar de betekenis van het Nederlandse dovenonderwijs voor de Nederlandse dovengemeenschap, 1790–1990," PhD diss. (University of Utrecht, 2014), 208.
51. Joseph J. Murray et al., "An Education in Sign Language as a Human Right? The Sensory Exception in the Legislative History and Ongoing Interpretation of Article 24 of the UN Convention on the Rights of Persons with Disabilities," *Human Rights Quarterly* 40, no. 1 (2018): 37–60.
52. Liisa Kauppinen and Markku Jokinen, "Including Deaf Culture and Linguistic Rights," in *Human Rights and Disability Advocacy*, ed. Maya Sabatello and Marianne Schulze (Philadelphia: University of Pennsylvania Press, 2014), 131–45.
53. Pamela Molina Toledo, "At the United Nations . . .'The South Also Exists,'" in *Human Rights and Disability Advocacy*, 170–87, 175.
54. For a recent overview of the literature see *Histories of Global Inequality: New Perspectives*, edited by Christian Olaf Christiansen and Steven L. B. Jensen (London: Palgrave Macmillan, 2019).
55. AM–DPIf, 11823, Box 2, document "Role, Mandate and Structures of Committees in DPI (1984–85)."
56. AM–DPIf, 11823, Box 4, "Resolution RE DPI Human Rights Committee" from the DPI World Council Meeting in Stockholm, August 1983.
57. AM–DPIf, 11823, Box 4, letter from James Donald to the members of the DPI Human Rights Committee about the "Report on Human Rights Committee Progress in UN (1984)"; Driedger, "The Origins and History," 136.
58. AM–DPIf, 11823, Box 3, document "Human Rights Background (abridged)."
59. AM–DPIf, 11823, Box 4, document "Suggested Outline for Reports of Violations of Human Rights of Disabled Individuals."
60. AM–DPIf, 11823, Box 3, document "Human Rights Background (abridged)."

4. NEW YORK 1987

1. UNARMS, ASG, s-1048-0089-02, note from Florence to Mr. Dayal, October 6, 1987.
2. UN Education, Scientific and Cultural Organization (UNESCO), International Year of Disabled Persons (IYDP), 114 EX/INF.3 (April 5, 1982), 10, https://digital.archives.unesco.org/en/collection/governing-documents/detail/8ace5686-7902-9275-1ec0-04559c76cf00/media/58a1d072-dbda-3078-5315-10fb0c9614a3.
3. "International Year of Disabled Persons: New Ways to Learning," *The UNESCO Courier* (June 1981, 14), https://en.unesco.org/courier/june-1981.
4. Bengt Lindqvist, *Blindstyre* (Åsele: Tundell Salmson Audio, 2012), 181. I would like to thank my colleague Anna Derksen for translating parts of this book for me; Osamu Nagase, "Difference, Equality and Disabled People: Disability Rights and Disability Culture," MA Thesis (International Institute of Social Studies, The Hague, 1995).
5. UN General Assembly, Summary record of the 16th meeting: 3rd Committee, 42nd session, A/C.3/42/SR.16 (October 19, 1987), https://digitallibrary.un.org/record/154951?ln=en; Cf. Nagase, "Difference, Equality and Disabled People."
6. Stefan-Ludwig Hoffmann, "Human Rights and History," *Past & Present* 232, no. 1 (2016): 282.
7. Hoffmann, "Human Rights and History," 302.
8. Antony Anghie, "Whose Utopia? Human Rights, Development, and the Third World," *Qui Parle* 22, no. 1 (2013): 63–80; Samuel Moyn, *The Last Utopia: Human Rights in History* (Cambridge, MA: Belknap Press of Harvard University Press, 2012).
9. UN Standard Rules on the Equalization of Opportunities for Persons with Disabilities, see chapter 2.
10. United Nations Research Institute for Social Development (UNRISD), "Our History," accessed October 13, 2022, https://www.unrisd.org/en/about/our-history.
11. Jessica Whyte, *The Morals of the Market: Human Rights and the Rise of Neoliberalism* (London: Verso, 2019).
12. Samuel Moyn, *Not Enough: Human Rights in an Unequal World* (Cambridge, MA: The Belknap Press of Harvard University Press, 2018), 204.
13. UNARMS, ASG, s-1048-0003-10, Alan Reich's résumé.
14. Katharina Heyer, *Rights Enabled: The Disability Revolution, from the US, to Germany and Japan, to the United Nations* (Ann Arbor: University of Michigan Press, 2015).
15. National Archives and Records Administration (NARA), General Records of the Department of Education (Record Group 441), Committee for the International Year of Disabled Persons, 1979–82 (CIYDP), Box 2, Folder 3/7, document "IYDP—Its Promise and Potential."
16. Cf. Moyn, *Not Enough*; Whyte, *The Morals of the Market*.
17. NARA, Record Group 441, CIYDP, Box 2, File 3/7, speech by O'Flaherty.
18. UNARMS, ASG, s-0913-0020-09, press release wherein the District of Columbia presents the UN Day Award to the US Council for IYDP, October 23, 1981.
19. NARA, Record Group 441, CIYDP, Box 2, File 3/7, speech by O'Flaherty.
20. NARA, Record Group 441, CIYDP, Box 2, File 4/7, US council for the IYDP's resolution "Continuing the Momentum of IYDP," October 22, 1981.

21. Heyer, *Rights Enabled*; Judith Heumann and Kristen Joiner, *Being Heumann: An Unrepentant Memoir of a Disability Rights Activist* (Boston: Beacon Press, 2021), 155.
22. Heumann and Joiner, *Being Heumann*, 199.
23. Mark Mazower, *Governing the World: The History of an Idea* (London: Penguin Press, 2012), xv, 310.
24. Richard Jolly et al., *UN Contributions to Development Thinking and Practice* (Bloomington: Indiana University Press, 2004).
25. Jolly et al., *UN Contributions to Development Thinking and Practice*; Christian Olaf Christiansen, "Partnerships Against Global Poverty: When 'Inclusive Capitalism' Entered the United Nations," in *Histories of Global Inequality: New Perspectives*, edited by Christian Olaf Christiansen and Steven L. B. Jensen (London: Palgrave Macmillan, 2019), 277–300; Thomas G. Weiss et al., "The 'Third' United Nations," *Global Governance* 15, no. 1 (2009): 123–42.
26. UNARMS, ASG, s-0908-0012-01, letter to Reich, December 17, 1981.
27. UNARMS, ASG, s-1028-0011-0013, note for the secretary-general by Angela Knippenberg-Uther, April 28, 1982.
28. UNARMS, ASG, s-0971-0013-03, letter from Reich to Waldheim, October 15, 1981.
29. UNARMS, ASG, s-0971-0013-03, letter from Reich and the US council for the IYDP to Secretary-General Kurt Waldheim, November 30, 1981.
30. UNARMS, ASG, s-1028-0011-0013, letter from Reich to the secretary-general, December 8, 1982.
31. UNARMS, ASG, s-1048-0003-10, meeting with the secretary-general concerning the "Bimillenneum Project," November 29, 1982.
32. UNARMS, ASG, s-1048-0009-11, note of May 10 concerning the letter of April 26, 1983; UNARMS, ASG, s-1028-0011-0013, Letter of the secretary-general to Reich, January 7, 1983.
33. UNARMS, ASG, s-1048-0013-06, remarks by the secretary-general for the luncheon organized by Ambassador Kirkpatrick in honor of the International Decade of Disabled Persons (1983–1992), October 29, 1984.
34. Jolly et al., *UN Contributions to Development Thinking and Practice*.
35. UNARMS, ASG, s-1048-0041-05, note added to Yolah's letter to Reich, September 9, 1986. The letter mentions that Reich and Acton were collaborators. The file also contains the correspondence between Yolah and Acton, who operated on behalf of the International Council on Disability, the former Council of World Organizations Interested in the Handicapped initiated by the United Nations in 1952.
36. AM-DPIf, 11823, Box 3, letter from Henry Enns to John Wilson, October 3, 1986.
37. AM-DPIf, 11823, Box 4, letter from Enns to Mr. Javier Perez de Cuellar, September 26, 1986.
38. UNARMS, ASG, s-1048-0090-02, letter from Reich to the secretary-general, January 7, 1989.
39. UNARMS, ASG, s-1028-0011-0013, letter from A. Cielens to the secretary-general, March 5, 1985.

40. UNARMS, ASG, s-1028-0011-0013, letter from the secretary-general to Cielens, August 19, 1985.
41. Lindqvist, *Blindstyre*, 181.
42. Lindqvist, *Blindstyre*, 181, 184.
43. UNARMS, ASG, s-1048-0089-02, note from Florence to Mr. Dayal, October 6, 1987.
44. UNARMS, ASG, s-1028-0011-0013, notes from Paul Kavanagh and Shuaib U. Yolah to the secretary-general, November 6, 1986.
45. UNARMS, ASG, s-1028-0011-0013, document with remarks from Reich on the Decade of Disabled Persons during the International Rehabilitation Week Conference in April 1986.
46. UNARMS, ASG, s-1048-0041-05, letter from Yolah to Reich, December 30, 1986.
47. UNARMS, ASG, s-1048-0090-02, letter from Basnayake to Jopling, February 14, 1989; Daniel Markovits, "How McKinsey Destroyed the Middle Class: Technocratic Management, No Matter How Brilliant, Cannot Unwind Structural Inequalities," *The Atlantic* (February 3, 2020), https://www.theatlantic.com/ideas/archive/2020/02/how-mckinsey-destroyed-middle-class/605878/.
48. Christiansen, "Partnerships Against Global Poverty."
49. UNARMS, ASG, s-1028-0011-0014, letter from the committee to the members, January 1, 1988. This letter was probably sent as an attachment to the correspondence between Reich and the secretary-general.
50. Lindqvist, *Blindstyre*, 186f; UNARMS, ASG, s-1086-0053-04-00001, letter from the Minister for Foreign Affairs of Sweden, May 4, 1994.
51. Alexander Buettger and Ezra Zubrow, "Bengt Lindqvist: A Prominent Figure and Advocate," in *Handbook of Disability: Critical Thought and Social Change in a Globalizing World*, ed. Marcia H. Rioux et al. (Singapore: Springer, 2024), 47–56.
52. Buettger and Zubrow, "Bengt Lindqvist."
53. Theresia Degener and Yolan Koster-Dreese, "Preface," in *Human Rights and Disabled Persons*, ed. Theresia Degener and Yolan Koster-Dreese (Leiden: Brill, 1995) xi–xiv; cf. Paul van Trigt, "A Blind Spot of a Guiding Country? Human Rights and Dutch Disability Groups Since 1981," *Moving the Social* 53 (2015): 87–102.
54. UN Special Rapporteur on Disability, *Let the World Know. Report of a Seminar on Human Rights and Disability Held at Almåsa Conference Centre Stockholm Sweden, November 5–9, 2000* (United Nations, 2001).
55. Theresia Degener and Andrew Begg, "From Invisible Citizens to Agents of Change: A Short History of the Struggle for the Recognition of the Rights of Persons with Disabilities at the United Nations," in *The United Nations Convention on the Rights of Persons with Disabilities: A Commentary*, ed. Valentina Della Fina et al. (Cham: Springer, 2017), 10.
56. Degener and Begg, "From Invisible Citizens to Agents of Change," 13.
57. UN Special Rapporteur on Disability, *Let the World Know*, 10.
58. Lindqvist, *Blindstyre*, 189.
59. UNARMS, ASG, s-1086-105-10, notes from the secretary-general's meeting with Disability Awareness in Action and DPI, October 13, 1992; UNARMS, ASG, s-1086-0081-04-00001, correspondence with DPI in 1995.

60. UNARMS, ASG, s-1086-0060-02-00001, announcement of the UN award.
61. UNARMS, ASG, s-1096-0177-07-00004, correspondence with Reich, December 4, 2002.
62. Heumann and Joiner, *Being Heumann*, 188.
63. UNARMS, ASG, s-1096-0217-07-00011, letter to Reich, December 7, 2001.
64. Heyer, *Rights Enabled*, 172f; Degener and Begg, "From Invisible Citizens to Agents of Change," 13.
65. Degener and Begg, "From Invisible Citizens to Agents of Change," 16.
66. Degener and Begg, "From Invisible Citizens to Agents of Change," 18.
67. Janet E. Lord, "Disability Rights and the Human Rights Mainstream: Reluctant Gate-Crashers?," in *The International Struggle for New Human Rights*, ed. Clifford Bob (Philadelphia: University of Pennsylvania Press, 2009), 83–92, 89.
68. Stefan Tromel, "A Personal Perspective on the Drafting History of the United Nations Convention on the Rights of Persons with Disabilities," *European Yearbook of Disability Law* 1 (2009): 115–38, 117.
69. Julia Dehm, "'A Pragmatic Compromise Between the Ideal and the Realistic:' Debates Over Human Rights, Global Distributive Justice and Minimum Core Obligations in the 1980s," in *Histories of Global Inequality*, 157–85; Anghie, "Whose Utopia?"
70. Degener and Begg, "From Invisible Citizens to Agents of Change"; Lord, "Disability Rights and the Human Rights Mainstream."
71. Hoffmann, "Human Rights and History."
72. Frédéric Mégret, "The Disabilities Convention: Human Rights of Persons with Disabilities or Disability Rights?," *Human Rights Quarterly* 30, no. 2 (2008): 494–516.
73. Lynn Hunt, "The Long and the Short of the History of Human Rights," *Past & Present* 233, no. 1 (2016): 323–31.
74. Michael Ashley Stein, "China and Disability Rights," *Loyola of Los Angeles International and Comparative Law Review* 33, no. 1 (Fall 2010): 7–26.

5. VIENNA 1993

1. Roland Burke, "The 1993 World Conference on Human Rights and the Retreat of a Redistributive Rights Vision," *London Review of International Law* 8, no. 2 (2020): 233–60, https://doi.org/10.1093/lril/lraa023.
2. Theresia Degener and Andrew Begg, "From Invisible Citizens to Agents of Change: A Short History of the Struggle for the Recognition of the Rights of Persons with Disabilities at the United Nations," in *The United Nations Convention on the Rights of Persons with Disabilities: A Commentary*, ed. Valentina Della Fina et al. (Cham: Springer, 2017), 13–14; UN World Conference on Human Rights in Vienna, *Vienna Declaration and Programme of Action* (June 25, 1993), https://www.ohchr.org/en/professionalinterest/pages/vienna.aspx.
3. "Disabled Pushed Aside at Conference," *Terra Viva—NGO News* (June 15, 1993). I would like to thank Roland Burke for sharing this article with me.

4. AM–DPIf, 11823, Box 2, report titled "Disabled People Storm UN Headquarters," by Henry Enns (n.d., stamp from 1988).
5. AM–DPIf, 11823, Box 4, DPI Communique to the National Assemblies, (n.d.), 2. By contacting Degener in January 2022, I learned that Frank Newman, who was Degener's professor at Berkeley Law School, helped her get this internship.
6. Monika Baár, "The European 'Disability Revolts' of 1981: How Were They Related to the Youth Movement?," in *A European Youth Revolt: European Perspectives on Youth Protest and Social Movements in the 1980s*, ed. Knud Andersen and Bart van der Steen (Houndmills: Palgrave MacMillan, 2016), 159–71.
7. Katharina Heyer, *Rights Enabled: The Disability Revolution, from the US, to Germany and Japan, to the United Nations* (Ann Arbor: University of Michigan Press, 2015), 150; AM–DPIf, Box 4, the Disabled Peoples' International Human Rights Committee's preliminary report titled "The Institutionalized Mentally Ill in Japan (1985)," and the DPI Human Rights Committee Report for 1987/1988.
8. AM–DPIf, Box 4, report on the Symposium on the Evaluation of the Decade Concerning Disabled Persons 1983–1992 on August 13–4, 1987 in Stockholm.
9. AM–DPIf, Box 3, a preliminary information note on "The Global Meeting of Experts to Review Implementation of the World Programme of Action Concerning Disabled Persons at the Mid-Point of the United Nations Decade of Disabled Persons (UN, V.87-85873)."
10. AM–DPIf, Box 3, drafted suggestion for the General Assembly Resolution (1987).
11. UN General Assembly, Summary record of the 19th meeting: 3rd Committee ... 42nd session, A/C.3/42/SR.19 (October 21, 1987), https://digitallibrary.un.org/record/151734?ln=en.
12. AM–DPIf, Box 4, the DPI Human Rights Committee Report for 1987/8.
13. UN General Assembly, A/C.3/44/SR.16, 1989.
14. AM–DPIf, Box 4, project plan "International Monitoring Mechanism for Human Rights Violations Against Disabled Persons."
15. AM–DPIf, Box 4, the DPI Human Rights Committee Report of 1990.
16. AM–DPIf, Box 4, the DPI Human Rights Committee Report of 1990.
17. Archive United Nations Office Geneva, Registry Second Period, G/SO 214 (48), Promotion and Protection of Human Rights of Disabled Persons, file 5 (1990–1996), Letter of DPI to Assistant Secretary-General for Human Rights Ibrahima Fall, August 8, 1994.
18. Bengt Lindqvist, *Blindstyre* (Åsele: Tundell Salmson Audio, 2012), 184–86; AM–DPIf, Box 4, funding proposal to "Develop Guidelines in the Areas of Equalization of Opportunities as Defined in the World Programme of Action at III World Congress of DPI in Bogotá, Colombia," November 27–December 1, 1989.
19. AM–DPIf, Box 4, statement by World Chairperson DPI Joshua T. Malinga to the UN General Assembly in New York, October 12, 1992.
20. Sandrine Kott, "Social Europe, Democracy and Brexit," *Contemporary European History* 28, no. 1 (2019): 46–49.
21. Sebastian Conrad, *What is Global History?* (Princeton, NJ: Princeton University Press, 2016), esp. Chapter 4; Mark Priestley, "In Search of European Disability

Policy: Between National and Global," *ALTER: European Journal of Disability Research/Revue européenne de recherche sur le handicap* 1, no. 1 (2007): 61–74, https://doi.org/10.1016/j.alter.2007.08.006.

22. Anne Waldschmidt, "Behindertenpolitik (in) der Europäischen Union," in *Aufbrüche und Barrieren: Behindertenpolitik und Behindertenrecht in Deutschland und Europa seit den 1970er-Jahren*, ed. Theresia Degener and Marc von Miquel (Bielefeld: Transcript, 2019), 79–106, 86.

23. Commission of the European Communities (CEC), COM(73) 1958 final, Proposal for a Decision of the Council on Action by the European Social Fund to Assist the Social and Occupational Integration of Handicapped Persons, V/661/2/73-E (November 16, 1973), https://eur-lex.europa.eu/legal-content/EN/TXT/PDF/?uri=CELEX:51973PC1958&from=GA. Since the archives of the European Disability Forum are not yet (publicly) available, my analysis is partly derived from Baár's paper "From Social Welfare to Human Rights: Disability Policy." Baár based her argument on an analysis of the reports on the social situation in Europe. She presented her findings at the conference *Experts and Expertise in European International Organizations*, held in Maastricht, 2014.

24. Cf. Mark Priestley, "We're All Europeans Now! The Social Model of Disability and European Social Policy," in *The Social Model of Disability: Europe and the Majority World*, ed. Colin Barnes and Geof Mercer (Leeds: The Disability Press), 17–31.

25. Monika Baár and Anna Derksen, "Das Internationale Jahr der Behinderten 1981 in historischer Perspektive," in *Aufbrüche und Barrieren*, 161–84; Baár, "The European 'Disability Revolts' of 1981."

26. Priestley, "We're All Europeans Now!," 19.

27. Baár, "The European 'Disability Revolts' of 1981"; Diane Driedger, *The Last Civil Rights Movement: Disabled Peoples' International* (London: Hurst, 1989).

28. Anne Waldschmidt, "Disability Policy of the European Union: The Supranational Level," *ALTER, European Journal of Disability* 3 (2009): 8–23; Priestley, "We're All Europeans Now!"

29. CEC, Council Recommendation of July 24, 1986 on the Employment of Disabled People in the Community, 86/379/EEC (July 24, 1986), https://eur-lex.europa.eu/legal-content/EN/TXT/PDF/?uri=CELEX:31986H0379&from=EN; Priestley, "In Search of European Disability Policy."

30. Waldschmidt, "Behindertenpolitik (in) der Europäischen Union," 99.

31. Baár, "The European 'Disability Revolts' of 1981"; Baár and Derksen, "Das Internationale Jahr der Behinderten 1981 in historischer Perspektive."

32. Waldschmidt, "Disability Policy of the European Union."

33. Osamu Nagase, "Difference, Equality and Disabled People: Disability Rights and Disability Culture," MA Thesis (International Institute of Social Studies, The Hague, 1995); Penny Price and Yutaka Takamine, "The Asian and Pacific Decade of Disabled Persons 1993–2002: What Have We Learned?," *Asia Pacific Disability Rehabilitation Journal* 14, no. 2 (2003): 115–27; Cf. Antony Anghie, "Whose Utopia? Human Rights, Development, and the Third World," *Qui Parle* 22, no. 1 (2013).

34. Rachel Hurst, "Disabled Peoples' International: Europe and the Social Model of Disability," in *The Social Model of Disability*, 65–79, 67–68.
35. Hurst, "Disabled Peoples' International," 68.
36. CEC, COM(91) 350 final, Proposal for a Council Decision Establishing a Third Community Action Programme to Assist Disabled People (HELIOS II (1992–96)) (October 23, 1991), https://eur-lex.europa.eu/legal-content/EN/TXT/PDF/?uri =CELEX:51991PC0350&rid=2.
37. CEC, COM(92) 482 final, Amended Proposal for a Council Decision Establishing a Third Community Action Programme to Assist Disabled People—Helios II (1993 to 1997), 93/C 24/01 (January 28, 1993), https://eur-lex.europa.eu/legal-content/EN/TXT /PDF/?uri=CELEX:51992PC0482&rid=39.
38. Hurst, "Disabled Peoples' International," 71.
39. Hurst, "Disabled Peoples' International," 73.
40. Hurst, "Disabled Peoples' International," 73–74; Cf. Monika Baár and Paul van Trigt, "British and European Citizenship: Entanglements Through the Lens of Disability," *Contemporary European History* 28, no. 1 (2019): 50–52.
41. CEC, COM(96)8 final, Interim Evaluation Report on the HELIOS II Programme (January 23, 1996), https://eur-lex.europa.eu/legal-content/EN/TXT/PDF/?uri=CELEX:51996 DC0008&rid=97.
42. CEC, COM(1998) 15 final, On the Evaluation of the Third Community Action Programme to Assist Disabled People (Helios II) 1993–1996 (January 20, 1998), https:// eur-lex.europa.eu/legal-content/EN/TXT/PDF/?uri=CELEX:51998DC0015&rid=3.
43. Priestley, "We're All Europeans Now!"
44. AM–DPIf, Box 2, DPI International Seminar on Human Rights in Lisbon, Portugal (May 30, 1988).
45. Paul van Trigt, "A Blind Spot of a Guiding Country? Human Rights and Dutch Disability Groups Since 1981," *Moving the Social* 53 (2015): 95.
46. Theresia Degener, "A New Human Rights Model of Disability," in *The United Nations Convention on the Rights of Persons with Disabilities*, 41–59.
47. Quoted by Katharina Heyer in *Rights Enabled*, 33–34.
48. Aart Hendriks, "Promoting Disability Equality After the Treaty of Amsterdam: New Legal Directions and Practical Expansion Strategies," in *Disability Rights in Europe: From Theory to Practice*, ed. Anna Lawson and Caroline Gooding (London: Bloomsbury Publishing 2005), 187–98, 190; European Disability Forum, *Guide to the Amsterdam Treaty* (Brussels: European Disability Forum, 1998), https:// www.independentliving.org/docs3/edf98.html.
49. Theresia Degener and Gerard Quinn, "A Survey of International, Comparative and Regional Disability Law Reform," in *Disability Rights Law and Policy: International and National Perspectives*, ed. Mary Lou Breslin and Silvia Lee (Leiden: Brill, 2002), 3–125, 106.
50. Degener and Quinn, "A Survey of International, Comparative and Regional Disability Law Reform," 106–7.
51. Priestley, "In Search of European Disability Policy."

52. Lisa Waddington, *From Rome to Nice in a Wheelchair: The Development of a European Disability Policy* (Groningen: Europa Law Publishing, 2006).
53. Baár and Van Trigt, "British and European Citizenship"; Deborah Mabbett, "The Development of Rights-Based Social Policy in the European Union: The Example of Disability Rights," *Journal of Common Market Studies* 43, no. 1 (2005): 97–120, esp. 110.
54. Priestley, "We're All Europeans Now!"
55. Heyer, *Rights Enabled*, 47–48; Priestley, "In Search of European Disability Policy."
56. Waldschmidt, "Disability Policy of the European Union," 21.
57. Hendriks, "Promoting Disability Equality after the Treaty of Amsterdam," 188; Lisa Waddington and Matthew Diller, "Tensions and Coherence in Disability Policy: The Uneasy Relationship Between Social Welfare and Civil Rights Models of Disability in American, European and International Employment Law," in *Disability Rights Law and Policy*, 241–80.
58. Mabbett, "The Development of Rights-Based Social Policy in the European Union," 103–4, 106.
59. Gerard Quinn and Theresia Degener, *Human Rights and Disability: The Current Use and Future Potential of United Nations Human Rights Instruments in the Context of Disability* (New York: United Nations, 2002), 118–19; Waddington and Diller, "Tensions and Coherence in Disability Policy," 278–79.
60. Waldschmidt, "Disability Policy of the European Union," 8, emphasis added.
61. Degener and Begg, "From Invisible Citizens to Agents of Change."
62. Degener and Begg, "From Invisible Citizens to Agents of Change," 14–15; Janet E. Lord, "Disability Rights and the Human Rights Mainstream: Reluctant Gate-Crashers?," in *The International Struggle for New Human Rights*, ed. Clifford Bob (Philadelphia: University of Pennsylvania Press, 2009) 83–92; Theresia Degener, "International Disability Law—A New Legal Subject on the Rise: The Interregional Experts' Meeting in Hong Kong, December 13–17, 1999," *Berkeley Journal of International Law* 18, no. 1 (2000): 180–95.
63. Annie Herro, "The Pre-Negotiation of UN Human Rights Treaties: The Case of the Convention on the Rights of Persons with Disabilities," *International Negotiation* 24, no. 2 (2019): 240–65, 257.
64. Lord, "Disability Rights and the Human Rights Mainstream."
65. Herro, "The Pre-Negotiation of UN Human Rights Treaties," 257.

6. MEXICO CITY 2002

1. Tina Minkowitz, "WNUSP Statement to Mexico City Meeting Before Beginning of CRPD Negotiations" (June 2002), https://www.academia.edu/8753018/WNUSP_statement_to_Mexico_City_meeting_before_beginning_of_CRPD_negotiations.
2. Tina Minkowitz, "CRPD Advocacy by the World Network of Users and Survivors of Psychiatry: The Emergence of an User/Survivor Perspective in Human Rights" (August 14, 2012), https://dx.doi.org/10.2139/ssrn.2326668.

3. Gerard Quinn and Anna Arstein-Kerslake, "Restoring the 'Human' in 'Human Rights:' Personhood and Doctrinal Innovation in the UN Disability Convention," in *The Cambridge Companion to Human Rights Law*, ed. Conor Gearty and Costas Douzinas (New York: Cambridge University Press, 2012), 40.
4. Maya Sabatello, "The New Diplomacy," in *Human Rights and Disability Advocacy*, ed. Maya Sabatello and Marianne Schulze (Philadelphia: University of Pennsylvania Press, 2014), 239–58.
5. Janet E. Lord, "Disability Rights and the Human Rights Mainstream: Reluctant Gate-Crashers?," in *The International Struggle for New Human Rights*, ed. Clifford Bob (Philadelphia: University of Pennsylvania Press, 2009), 83–89.
6. Theresia Degener and Andrew Begg, "From Invisible Citizens to Agents of Change: A Short History of the Struggle for the Recognition of the Rights of Persons with Disabilities at the United Nations," in *The United Nations Convention on the Rights of Persons with Disabilities: A Commentary*, ed. Valentina Della Fina et al. (Cham: Springer, 2017), 12.
7. Lord, "Disability Rights and the Human Rights Mainstream," 88–90.
8. Lord, "Disability Rights and the Human Rights Mainstream," 89.
9. Degener and Begg, "From Invisible Citizens to Agents of Change," 12–13; Bengt Lindqvist, *Blindstyre* (Åsele: Tundell Salmson Audio, 2012), 193.
10. Lord, "Disability Rights and the Human Rights Mainstream," 89.
11. Annie Herro, "The Pre-Negotiation of UN Human Rights Treaties: The Case of the Convention on the Rights of Persons with Disabilities," *International Negotiation* 24, no. 2 (2019): 256.
12. Herro, "The Pre-Negotiation of UN Human Rights Treaties," 249–51; Christy Thornton, *Revolution in Development: Mexico and the Governance of the Global Economy* (Oakland: University of California Press, 2021).
13. Herro, "The Pre-Negotiation of UN Human Rights Treaties," 254; Degener and Begg, "From Invisible Citizens to Agents of Change," 18.
14. Lord, "Disability Rights and the Human Rights Mainstream," 88–90.
15. Degener and Begg, "From Invisible Citizens to Agents of Change," 19; Sabatello, "The New Diplomacy."
16. Allison C. Carey et al., eds., *Allies and Obstacles: Disability Activism and Parents of Children with Disabilities* (Philadelphia: Temple University Press, 2020).
17. See chapter 1.
18. Danielle Celermajer and Alexandre Lefebvre, eds., *The Subject of Human Rights* (Stanford, CA: Stanford University Press, 2020).
19. UN Committee on the Rights of Persons with Disabilities, General comment No. 1 (2014): Article 12: Equal Recognition Before the Law, CRPD/C/GC/1 (May 19, 2014), 1, https://www.ohchr.org/en/documents/general-comments-and-recommendations/general-comment-no-1-article-12-equal-recognition-1.
20. Quinn and Arstein-Kerslake, "Restoring the 'Human' in 'Human Rights,'" 40.
21. Quinn and Arstein-Kerslake, "Restoring the 'Human' in 'Human Rights,'" 38; Cf. Gerard Quinn, "Personhood and Legal Capacity: Perspectives on the Paradigm Shift

of Article 12 CRPD," paper presented at the *Conference on Disability and Legal Capacity Under the CRPD*, Boston, Harvard Law School (2010), https://www.nuigalway.ie/media/centrefordisabilitylawandpolicy/files/archive/Submission-on-Legal-Capacity-to-the-Oireachtas-Committee-on-Justice,-Defence-&-Equality-(August,-2011).pdf.

22. However, policies inspired by Article 12 could promote "a form of private family ordering that is antithetical to individual rights," as is shown for the United States by Nina A. Kohn, "Legislating Supported Decision-Making," *Harvard Journal on Legislation* 58, no 2 (2021): 313–56.

23. Natasha Wheatley, "New Subjects in International Law and Order," in *Internationalisms: A Twentieth-Century History*, ed. Glenda Sluga and Patricia M. Clavin (Cambridge: Cambridge University Press, 2017), 265–86.

24. Samuel Moyn, *Not Enough: Human Rights in an Unequal World* (Cambridge, MA: The Belknap Press of Harvard University Press, 2018); Jessica Whyte, *The Morals of the Market: Human Rights and the Rise of Neoliberalism* (London: Verso, 2019).

25. Mark Goodale, "Dark Matter: Toward a Political Economy of Indigenous Rights and Aspirational Politics," *Critique of Anthropology* 36, no. 4 (2016): 439–57.

26. Moyn, *Not Enough*.

27. Dagmar Herzog, *Unlearning Eugenics Sexuality, Reproduction, and Disability in Post-Nazi Europe* (Madison: University of Wisconsin Press, 2018).

28. Sigrid Graumann, "Assistierte Freiheit: Von einer Behindertenpolitik der Wohltätigkeit zu einder Politik der Menschenrechte," PhD diss. (University of Utrecht, 2009); Adolf Ratzska, *Independent Living and Attendant Care in Sweden: A Consumer Perspective* (New York: International Exchange of Experts and Information in Rehabilitation, World Rehabilitation Fund, 1986).

29. Paul van Trigt, "A History of 'Legal Capacity' and the 'Family' in the United Nations' Disability Policies since the 1970s," in *Family, Human Rights and Internationalism*, ed. Julia Moses (forthcoming).

30. UNARMS, ASG, s-0445-0344-0006, letter of Brian M. Mcann representing the National Association for Retarded Children to Esko Kosunen at the United Nations, September 15, 1971.

31. UNARMS, ASG, s-0445-0344-0006, letter of Kosunen representing the UN Rehabilitation Unit for the Disabled to K. Jansson at the UN Social Development Division, October 6, 1970.

32. UN General Assembly, Resolution 2856 (XXVI), 1971.

33. UNARMS, ASG, S-0445-0344-0006, letter of Rosemary F. Dybwad representing the International League of Societies for the Mentally Handicapped (ISLMH) to Kosunen at the United Nations, May 20, 1971.

34. International League of Societies for the Mentally Handicapped (ILSMH), *Conclusions*, Legislative Aspects of Mental Retardation Symposium, Stockholm (June 1967), https://mn.gov/mnddc/parallels2/pdf/60s/67/67-ILS-ILS.pdf.

35. UN General Assembly, Resolution 3447, 1975; , Gildas Brégain, *Pour une histoire du handicap au XXe siècle: Approches transnationales (Europe et Amériques)* (Rennes:

Presses Universitaires de Rennes, 2018); Anaïs Van Ertvelde, "Welfare: Defended, Questioned, Complemented? Belgian Welfare Arrangements in the 1970s–1980s from the Perspective of Disability Organizations," in *Marginalized Groups, Inequalities and the Post-War Welfare State: Whose Welfare?*, ed. Monika Baár and Paul van Trigt (London: Routledge, 2020): 137–54.

36. UN General Assembly, Resolution 3447, 1975.
37. UN General Assembly, Resolution 3447, 1975.
38. Brégain, *Pour une histoire du handicap*, 126.
39. Randall M. Packard, *A History of Global Health: Interventions into the Lives of Other Peoples* (Baltimore, MD: John Hopkins University Press, 2016), 234.
40. See the introduction.
41. Corinna R. Unger, *International Development: A Postwar History* (London: Bloomsbury Academic, 2019), 108.
42. WHO and UNICEF, *Alma-Ata Declaration* (September 6–12, 1978), https://www.who.int/publications/i/item/WHO-EURO-1978-3938-43697-61471.
43. Einar Helander et al., *Training Disabled People in the Community: A Manual on Community-Based Rehabilitation for Developing Countries* (World Health Organization, 1983), https://iris.who.int/handle/10665/69298.
44. Einar Helander, "The Origins of Community Based Rehabilitation," *Behindering und Internationale Entwicklung/Disability and International Development* 24, no. 1 (2013): 4–14.
45. David Werner, *Where There Is No Doctor: A Village Health Care Handbook* (London: Macmillan, 1977), introduction to the English edition; Packard, *History of Global Health*, 240–41.
46. UN General Assembly, A/37/351/Add.1, 1982, 10.
47. UN General Assembly, A/37/351/Add.1, 1982, 20.
48. UN General Assembly, A/37/351/Add.1, 1982, 22.
49. UN General Assembly, A/37/351/Add.1, 1982, 32–33, 40.
50. Erica-Irene A. Daes, *Principles, Guidelines and Guarantees for the Protection of Persons Detained on Grounds of Mental Ill-Health or Suffering from Mental Disorder* (New York: United Nations, 1986), iv–v.
51. Harold Hongju Koh and Lawrence O. Gostin, "Introduction: The Human Rights Imperative," in *The Human Rights of Persons with Intellectual Disabilities: Different but Equal*, ed. Stanley S. Herr et al. (Oxford: Oxford University Press, 2003), 1–22, 2–3.
52. UN General Assembly, Resolution 46/119, Principles for the Protection of Persons with Mental Illness and the Improvement of Mental Health Care (December 17, 1991), https://www.ohchr.org/en/instruments-mechanisms/instruments/principles-protection-persons-mental-illness-and-improvement.
53. Peter Bartlett et al., *Mental Disability and the European Convention on Human Rights* (Leiden: Brill, 2006).
54. Degener and Begg, "From Invisible Citizens to Agents of Change," 25.
55. UN CSDHA, CSDHA/DDP/GME/7, 1987, 8–9, recommendation 37.

56. UN CSDHA, CSDHA/DDP/GME/7, 1987, 13.
57. UN General Assembly, Resolution 48/96, A/RES/48/96, 1994, 8.
58. UN General Assembly, Resolution 48/96, A/RES/48/96, 1994, 7–8, 12.
59. UN General Assembly, Resolution 48/96, A/RES/48/96, 1994, 24.
60. See chapter 1.
61. In UN Resolution 48/96, the formulation "and their families" appears in Rules 1.1, 1.5, 2.1, 3.2, 3.4, 5.5 (including their advocates), 13.3, 18.1, as well as in Rule 6 as the "parents of disabled children." Viz. UN General Assembly, Resolution 48/96, A/RES/48/96, 1994.
62. Peter Mittler, *Thinking Globally, Acting Locally: A Personal Journey* (Central Milton Keynes: Authorhouse, 2010), 313–20.
63. Stanley S. Herr, "Self-Determination, Autonomy, and Alternatives for Guardianship," in *The Human Rights of Persons with Intellectual Disabilities*, 429–50.
64. World Health Organization (WHO), UNESCO, and International Labour Organization (ILO), *Community-Based Rehabilitation for and with People with Disabilities: 1994 Joint Position Paper* (World Health Organization, 1994), https://iris.who.int/handle/10665/75842.
65. WHO, UNESCO, ILO, *Community-Based Rehabilitation*.
66. Mike Miles, "The 'Community Base' in Rehabilitation Planning: Key or Gimmick?," in *Practical Approaches to Childhood Disability in Developing Countries: Insights from Experience and Research*, ed. Marigold J. Thorburn and Kofi Marfo (Tampa, FL: Global Age Publishing, 1994), 287–302, 291.
67. Raymond Lang, "The Role of NGOs in the Process of Empowerment and Social Transformation of People with Disabilities," *Asia Pacific Disability Rehabilitation Journal: Selected Readings in Community Based Rehabilitation* 1 (2000): 1–20, 5.
68. Geert Vanneste, "Current Status of CBR in Africa: A Review," *Asia Pacific Disability Rehabilitation Journal: Selected Readings in Community Based Rehabilitation* 1 (2000): 127–135, 127.
69. Frank Huisman and Nancy Tomes, "A World South-Side Up?: Global Health and the Provincializing of Europe," *European Journal for the History of Medicine and Health* 78, no. 1 (2021): 195–212, 205, https://doi.org/10.1163/26667711-78010019.
70. Packard, "History of Global Health," 264.
71. William Boyce and John Paterson, "Community Based Rehabilitation for Children in Nepal," *Asia Pacific Disability Rehabilitation Journal: Selected Readings in Community Based Rehabilitation* 2 (2002): 67–81, 67.
72. DPI, "Position Paper on Community-Based Rehabilitation." Part of the Marlies van der Kroft Papers, temporarily stored in my Leiden office.
73. DPA Singapore Vox Nostra, *Integrator, Medium for the Promotion of Equalization of Opportunities* 7, no. 1 (January–March 1997): 15–16.
74. Corinne L. Mason, "'Cripping' the World Bank: Disability, Empowerment and the Cost of Violence Against Women," *International Feminist Journal of Politics* 17, no. 3 (2014): 435–53, 438.
75. Degener and Begg, "From Invisible Citizens to Agents of Change"; Rachel Hurst, "Disabled Peoples' International: Europe and the Social Model of Disability," in *The*

Social Model of Disability: Europe and the Majority World, ed. Colin Barnes and Geof Mercer (Leeds: The Disability Press, 2005), 65–79.
76. UN General Assembly, A/RES/61/106 (December 13, 2006).
77. WHO and World Bank, *World Report on Disability 2011* (Geneva: World Health Organization, 2011).
78. UN Committee on the Rights of Persons with Disabilities, CRPD/C/GC/5, 2017, emphasis added.
79. See for a more detailed discussion: Van Trigt, "History of 'Legal Capacity.'"
80. Degener and Begg, "From Invisible Citizens to Agents of Change," 23.
81. Degener and Begg, "From Invisible Citizens to Agents of Change," 23.
82. Degener and Begg, "From Invisible Citizens to Agents of Change," 23; Cf. the draft article: UN General Assembly Ad Hoc Committee on a Comprehensive and Integral International Convention on the Protection and Promotion of the Rights and Dignity of Persons with Disabilities Working Group (UNGA-AHC-WG), Report of the Working Group to the Ad Hoc Committee, A/AC.265/2004/WG/1 (January 27, 2004), 14–5, https://www.un.org/esa/socdev/enable/documents/ahcwgreport.pdf.
83. Degener and Begg, "From Invisible Citizens to Agents of Change," 33; UNGA-AHC-WG, A/AC.265/2004/WG/1, 2004, 7–9; Cf. Van Trigt, "A History of 'Legal Capacity.'"
84. Quinn and Arstein-Kerslake, "Restoring the 'Human' in 'Human Rights,'" 38; Cf. Quinn, "Personhood and Legal Capacity."
85. Melinda Cooper, *Family Values: Between Neoliberalism and the New Social Conservatism* (New York: Zone Books, 2017).

EPILOGUE

1. "I'm knobbled on the cobbles" is a line from Ian Dury and the Blockheads, *Spasticus Autisticus, Lord Upminster* (Nassau: Compass Point Studios, 1981), https://www.youtube.com/watch?v=6isXNVdguI8.
2. Roland Burke, "The Internationalism of Human Rights," in *Internationalisms: A Twentieth-Century History*, ed. Glenda Sluga and Patricia M. Clavin (Cambridge: Cambridge University Press, 2017), 287–314.
3. For examples of criticism see Helen Meekosha and Karen Soldatic, "Human Rights and the Global South: The Case of Disability," *Third World Quarterly* 32, no. 8 (2011): 1383–97; Gabor Petri et al., "'More Honoured in the Breach than in the Observance'—Self-Advocacy and Human Rights," *Laws* 6, no. 4 (2017): 26, https://doi.org/10.3390/laws6040026; Stephen J. Meyers, *Civilizing Disability Society: The Convention on the Rights of Persons with Disabilities Socializing Grassroots Disabled Persons' Organizations in Nicaragua* (Cambridge: Cambridge University Press, 2019).
4. Samuel Moyn, *Not Enough: Human Rights in an Unequal World* (Cambridge, MA: The Belknap Press of Harvard University Press, 2018); Jessica Whyte, *The Morals of the Market: Human Rights and the Rise of Neoliberalism* (London: Verso, 2019).

5. Samuel Moyn, *Human Rights and the Uses of History* (London: Verso, 2014), 143.
6. Hannah Arendt, *The Origins of Totalitarianism* (Cleveland, OH: The World Publishing Company 1958), 296–97; Cf. Samuel Moyn, *The Last Utopia: Human Rights in History* (Cambridge, MA: Belknap Press of Harvard University Press, 2012), 12–13.
7. Lynn Hunt, "The Long and the Short of the History of Human Rights," *Past & Present* 233, no. 1 (2016): 323–31; Stephen Hopgood, *The Endtimes of Human Rights* (Ithaca, NY: Cornell University Press, 2015).
8. William P. Alford, "Editor's Note, FOCUS: Disability Rights in China and in the World," *Frontiers of Law in China* 11, no. 1 (2016): 1–3; Sarah Dauncey, *Disability in Contemporary China: Citizenship, Identity and Culture* (Cambridge: Cambridge University Press, 2020), 187.
9. See Ingo Venzke and Kevin Jon Heller, eds., *Contingency in International Law: On the Possibility of Different Legal Histories* (Oxford: Oxford University Press, 2021).
10. Irving Kenneth Zola, *Missing Pieces: A Chronicle of Living with a Disability* (Philadelphia: Temple University Press, 1982), 3.
11. Zola, *Missing Pieces*, 34.
12. Zola, *Missing Pieces*, 9.
13. Zola, *Missing Pieces*, 10.
14. Zola, *Missing Pieces*, 213–14, 84.
15. James I. Charlton, *Nothing About Us Without Us: Disability Oppression and Empowerment* (Berkeley: University of California Press, 1998).
16. Zola, *Missing Pieces*, 194.
17. Katharina Heyer, *Rights Enabled: The Disability Revolution, from the US, to Germany and Japan, to the United Nations* (Ann Arbor: University of Michigan Press, 2015).
18. Zola, *Missing Pieces*, 22.
19. Zola, *Missing Pieces*, 17–18.
20. Zola, *Missing Pieces*, 19.
21. Cf. Julia Kristeva, "Liberty, Equality, Fraternity, and . . . Vulnerability," *Women's Studies Quarterly* 38, no. 1–2 (2010): 251–68; Pierre Rosanvallon, *The Society of Equals*, trans. Arthur Goldhammer (Cambridge, MA: Harvard University Press, 2013).
22. See Aimi Hamraie and Kelly Fritsch, "Crip Technoscience Manifesto," *Catalyst: Feminism, Theory, Technoscience* 5, no. 1 (2019): 1–34, https://catalystjournal.org/index.php/catalyst/article/view/29607/24772.
23. Henri Nouwen, *Adam: Een vriendschap*, trans. Maria ter Steeg (Tielt: Lannoo, 1997), 11–14.
24. Nouwen, *Adam*, 12–14, 49, 54.
25. Cf. Patrick McKearney, "Receiving the Gift of Cognitive Disability: Recognizing Agency in the Limits of the Rational Subject," *The Cambridge Journal of Anthropology* 36, no. 1 (2018): 40–60.
26. Moreover, Nouwen's description of caregiving deserves a critical evaluation from a gender perspective, see Laura MacGregor, "A Holy Mess of a Story: Maternal Reflections on Caregiving, Chaos, and Intellectual Disability," *Journal of Disability & Religion* 27, 1 (2021): 124–37, doi:10.1080/23312521.2021.1932688; see for a critical evaluation

of a theologian related to Nouwen: Brian Brock, "The Troubled Inheritance of Jean Vanier: Locating the Fatal Theological Mistakes," *Studies in Christian Ethics* 36, no. 3 (2023): 433–56.

27. Michel Foucault and Jay Miskowiec, "Of Other Spaces," *Diacritics* 16, no. 1 (1986): 22–7, 24.
28. Herman Meininger, "Inclusion as Heterotopia: Spaces of Encounter Between People with and Without Intellectual Disability," *Journal of Social Inclusion* 4, no. 1 (2013): 24–44, 28.
29. Meininger, "Inclusion as Heterotopia," 24.
30. Meininger, "Inclusion as Heterotopia," 33.
31. Cf. Paul van Trigt and Susan Legêne, "Writing Disability into Colonial Histories of Humanitarianism," *Social Inclusion* 4, no. 4 (2016): 188–96.
32. Robbie Shilliam, *Decolonizing Politics: An Introduction* (Cambridge: Polity Press, 2021), 17.

BIBLIOGRAPHY

PRIMARY SOURCES

ARCHIVES OF MANITOBA, WINNIPEG, CANADA (AM)

Disabled Peoples' International fonds (DPIf, 11823)

COMMISSION OF THE EUROPEAN COMMUNITIES, ONLINE ARCHIVE (CEC)

86/379/EEC (July 24, 1986)
COM(73) 1958 final, V/661/2/73-E (November 16, 1973)
COM(91) 350 final (October 23, 1991)
COM(92) 482 final, 93/C 24/01 (January 28, 1993)
COM(96) 8 final (January 23, 1996)
COM(1998) 15 final (January 20, 1998)

NATIONAAL ARCHIEF, DEN HAAG, THE NETHERLANDS (NL-HANA)

Ministerie van Volksgezondheid en Milieuhygiëne
Stichting Nationale Commissie Internationaal Jaar van de Gehandicapten 1981 (2.27.07)

NATIONAL ARCHIVES AND RECORDS ADMINISTRATION, WASHINGTON, D.C. (NARA)

General Records of the Department of Education (Record Group 441)
Committee for the International Year of Disabled Persons, 1979–82 (CIYDP)

UNITED NATIONS EDUCATION, SCIENTIFIC AND CULTURAL ORGANIZATION, ONLINE ARCHIVE (UNESCO)

International Year of Disabled Persons (IYDP)
114 EX/INF.3 (April 5, 1982)

UNITED NATIONS ARCHIVES AND RECORDS MANAGEMENT SECTION, NEW YORK, NY (UNARMS)

Archives Secretary-General (ASG)

UNITED NATIONS OFFICE, GENEVA, SWITZERLAND (UNOG)

Registry Second Period, G/SO 214 (48), Promotion and Protection of Human Rights of Disabled Persons 1983–1996

WORLD HEALTH ORGANIZATION ARCHIVES, GENEVA, SWITZERLAND (WHO)

WHO/ILO Collaboration in the Field of Rehabilitation, file R4/372/3

PUBLISHED DOCUMENTS, UNITED NATIONS AND SPECIALIZED AGENCIES

Daes, Erica-Irene A. *Principles, Guidelines and Guarantees for the Protection of Persons Detained on Grounds of Mental Ill-Health or Suffering from Mental Disorder*. New York: United Nations, 1986.

Despouy, Leandro. *Human Rights and Disabled Persons*. New York: United Nations, 1993. https://www.un.org/esa/socdev/enable/dispaperdeso.htm.

Helander, Einar, Padmani Mendis, and Gunnel Nelson. *Training Disabled People in the Community: A Manual on Community-Based Rehabilitation for Developing Countries*. World Health Organization, 1983. https://iris.who.int/handle/10665/69298.

Quinn, Gerard, and Theresia Degener. *Human Rights and Disability: The Current Use and Future Potential of United Nations Human Rights Instruments in the Context of Disability*. New York: United Nations, 2002. https://www.ohchr.org/sites/default/files/Documents/Publications/HRDisabilityen.pdf.

UNESCO Courier. "International Year of Disabled Persons: New Ways to Learning" (June 1981). https://courier.unesco.org/en/articles/international-year-disabled-persons-new-ways-learning.

United Nations Centre for Social Development and Humanitarian Affairs (CSDHA)
    CSDHA/DDP/GME/7 (September 1, 1987)

United Nations Committee on the Rights of Persons with Disabilities
    CRPD/C/GC/1 (May 19, 2014)

CRPD/C/GC/5 (October 27, 2017)

CRPD/C/GC/7 (November 9, 2018)

United Nations Division for Social Policy and Development. *The United Nations and Disability. 70 Years of the Work Towards a More Inclusive World*. New York: United Nations, 2018. https://www.un.org/development/desa/disabilities/wp-content/uploads/sites/15/2018/01/History_Disability-in-the-UN_jan23.18-Clean.pdf.

United Nations Economic and Social Council

E/1989/25, E/CN.5/1989/12 (March 22, 1989)

E/CN.5/1993/5 (November 11, 1992)

Resolution 1921 (LVIII), E/CN.5/565 (December 19, 1978)

United Nations General Assembly

A/34/158 (March 19–23, 1979)

A/37/351/Add.1 (September 15, 1982)

A/48/430/Add.1 (October 14, 1993)

A/59/360 (September 14, 2004)

A/60/266 (August 17, 2005)

A/AC.265/2003/4 (May 6, 2003)

A/AC.265/2004/5 (June 9, 2004)

A/AC.265/2004/WG/1 (January 27, 2004)

A/AC.265/2005/2 (February 23, 2005)

A/AC.265/2006/1 (October 24, 2005)

A/C.3/34/SR.56 (November 26, 1979)

A/C.3/42/SR.16 (October 19, 1987)

A/C.3/48/SR.16 (October 25, 1993)

A/C.3/60/SR.5 (October 26, 2005)

A/RES/61/106 (December 13, 2006)

Resolution 31/123, A/RES/31/123 (December 16, 1976)

Resolution 37/52, A/RES/37/52 (December 3, 1982)

Resolution 46/119 (December 17, 1991)

Resolution 48/96, A/RES/48/96 (March 4, 1994)

Resolution 2856 (XXVI) (December 20, 1971)

Resolution 3447 (December 9, 1975)

United Nations Research Institute for Social Development (UNRISD). "Our History." https://www.unrisd.org/en/about/our-history.

United Nations Special Rapporteur on Disability. *Let the World Know. Report of a Seminar on Human Rights and Disability Held at Almåsa Conference Centre Stockholm Sweden, November 5–9, 2000*. New York: United Nations, 2001.

UN World Conference on Human Rights in Vienna. *Vienna Declaration and Programme of Action*, June 25, 1993. https://www.ohchr.org/en/professionalinterest/pages/vienna.aspx.

World Health Organization and UNICEF. *Alma-Ata Declaration*. September 6–12, 1978. https://www.who.int/publications/i/item/WHO-EURO-1978-3938-43697-61471.

World Health Organization, UNESCO, and International Labour Organization. *Community-Based Rehabilitation for and with People with Disabilities: 1994 Joint Position Paper*. World Health Organization, 1994. https://iris.who.int/handle/10665/75842.

WHO and World Bank. *World Report on Disability 2011.* Geneva: World Health Organization, 2011.
World Health Organization. *Co-ordinated International Programme on Rehabilitation of Physically Handicapped Persons.* Geneva: World Health Organization, 1952.

OTHER PRIMARY SOURCES

Amigoe. "Aruba ervaart opnieuw handicap-imperialisme." *Amigoe,* March 30, 1981.
Amigoe. "Gehandicaptenzorg is méér dan verzorging alleen." *Amigoe,* January 22, 1982.
Amigoe. "Min Croes: proces gaat te langzaam. Adviesraad Gehandicapten bijeen." *Amigoe,* November 29, 1982.
Amigoe. "Nieuwe voorzitter Raad gehandicapten." *Amigoe,* July 20, 1982.
Amigoe. "Voorbereidingen voor Jaar van Gehandicapte." *Amigoe,* January 23, 1980.
Disabled Peoples' International. *The Disabled Peoples' International Anniversary Journal.* Singapore: Disabled Peoples' International, 1984.
Disabled Peoples' International, "Position Paper on Community-Based Rehabilitation." Marlies van der Kroft Papers, Leiden.
DPA Singapore Vox Nostra. *Integrator, Medium for the Promotion of Equalization of Opportunities* 7, no. 1 (January–March 1997).
Dury, Ian, and the Blockheads. *Spasticus Autisticus, Lord Upminster.* Nassau: Compass Point Studios, 1981. https://www.youtube.com/watch?v=6isXNVdguI8.
European Disability Forum. *Guide to the Amsterdam Treaty.* Brussels: European Disability Forum, 1998. https://www.independentliving.org/docs3/edf98.html.
Gomez, A. D. C. "Stichting voor Rehabilitatie van gehandicapten." *Amigoe,* November 6, 1978.
International League of Societies for the Mentally Handicapped (ILSMH). *Conclusions.* Legislative Aspects of Mental Retardation Symposium, Stockholm, June 11–17, 1967. https://mn.gov/mnddc/parallels2/pdf/60s/67/67-ILS-ILS.pdf.
National Co-ordinating Committee for the International Year of Disabled Persons (Singapore). *Rights Issue: International Year of Disabled Persons—Full Participation and Integration.* Singapore: National Co-ordinating Committee (IYDP), 1981.
National Library Board Singapore. *Magazine Independent Society of the Blind* (1991).
Ratzska, Adolf. "Crip Utopia." Independent Living Institute, 1998. https://www.independentliving.org/docs4/ratzkacu.html.
Rehabilitation International. *Proceedings Second International Conference on Legislation Concerning the Disabled, Manila 1978.* New York: Rehabilitation International, 1978.
Singapore Association of the Visually Handicapped (SAVH). *Walk Unafraid.* Singapore: The Association, 2001.
Singapore Organising Committee. *Souvenir Magazine of the Disabled Peoples' International First World Congress, Singapore, November 29–December 4, 1981.* Singapore, 1981.
Sterner, Richard. "FN:S rättighetsförklaring för utvecklingsstörda från 1971." In *Handikappsamverkan* 6 (1973): 14–17. Quoted from Persson, Inger. *Ledare och artiklar av Richard Sterner. Ordförande i HCK—Handikapporganisationernas Centralkommitte 1963–1974.* Stockholm: Handikappförbundens samarbetsorgan/Handikapphistoriska

Föreningen 2009, 47f. http://u8628957.fsdata.se/wp-content/uploads/2015/03/ledare_sterner.pdf.

Terra Viva—NGO News. "Disabled Pushed Aside at Conference" (June 15, 1993).

World Council for the Welfare of the Blind, the International Federation of the Blind & the Union of the Blind of Yugoslavia. *Proceedings of the International Conference on the Situation of the Blind Women, November 18–20, 1975*. Belgrade, 1976.

SECONDARY SOURCES

Alford, William P. "Editor's Note, FOCUS: Disability Rights in China and in the World." *Frontiers of Law in China* 11, no. 1 (2016): 1–3.

Alkhatib, Shaffiq. "Blind Activist and Handicap Welfare Champion Ron Chandran-Dudley Dies." *TNP Singapore*, December 31, 2015. https://tnp.straitstimes.com/news/singapore/blind-activist-and-handicap-welfare-champion-ron-chandran-dudley-dies.

Anghie, Antony. "Whose Utopia? Human Rights, Development, and the Third World." *Qui Parle* 22, no. 1 (2013): 63–80.

Arendt, Hannah. *The Origins of Totalitarianism*. Cleveland, OH: The World Publishing Company, 1958.

Baár, Monika. "The European 'Disability Revolts' of 1981: How Were They Related to the Youth Movement?" In *A European Youth Revolt: European Perspectives on Youth Protest and Social Movements in the 1980s*, edited by Knud Andersen and Bart van der Steen, 159–71. Houndmills: Palgrave MacMillan, 2016.

Baár, Monika. "Informal Networks, International Developments and the Founding of the First Interest-Representing Associations of Disabled People in Hungary in the Late Socialist Period (1970s–1980s)." *Moving the Social* 53 (2015): 39–62.

Baár, Monika. "Vegetables of the World Unite! Grassroots Internationalization of Disabled Citizens in the Post-War Period." In *Internationalists in European History: Rethinking the Twentieth Century*, edited by Jessica Reinisch and David Brydan, 182–97. London: Bloomsbury Academic, 2021.

Baár, Monika, and Anna Derksen. "Das Internationale Jahr der Behinderten 1981 in historischer Perspektive." In *Aufbrüche und Barrieren: Behindertenpolitik und Behindertenrecht in Deutschland und Europa seit den 1970er-Jahren*, edited by Theresia Degener and Marc von Miquel, 161–84. Bielefeld: Transcript, 2019.

Baár, Monika, and Paul van Trigt. "British and European Citizenship: Entanglements Through the Lens of Disability." *Contemporary European History* 28, no. 1 (2019): 50–52.

Barnett, Sharon. "The Globalization of Disability Protests, 1970–2005: Pushing the Limits of Cross-Cultural Research?" *Comparative Sociology* 9 (2010): 222–40.

Bartlett, Peter, Oliver Lewis, and Oliver Thorold, eds. *Mental Disability and the European Convention on Human Rights*. Boston: Brill, 2006.

Bashford, Alison. *Global Population History, Geopolitics, and Life on Earth*. New York: Columbia University Press, 2016.

Berlin, Isaiah. *Four Essays on Liberty*. Oxford: Oxford University Press, 1969.

Boyce, William, and John Paterson. "Community Based Rehabilitation for Children in Nepal." *Asia Pacific Disability Rehabilitation Journal: Selected Readings in Community Based Rehabilitation* 2 (2002): 67–81.

Brégain, Gildas. "An Entangled Perspective on Disability History: The Disability Protests in Argentina, Brazil and Spain." In *The Imperfect Historian: Disability Histories in Europe*, edited by Sebastian Barsch, Anne Klein, and Pieter Verstraete, 133–53. Frankfurt am Main: Peter Lang, 2013.

Brégain, Gildas. "La fabrique de la Déclaration des droits des personnes handicapées de l'ONU (1975): un succès diplomatique rapide en temps de guerre froide." *Droit et société* 113, no. 1 (2023): 31–53.

Brégain, Gildas. "The ILO and the Shift Towards Economic Liberalization in the International Professional Rehabilitation Policies of People with Disabilities After World War II." In *Marginalized Groups, Inequalities and the Post-War Welfare State: Whose Welfare?*, edited by Monika Baár and Paul van Trigt, 49–68. London: Routledge, 2020.

Brégain, Gildas. *Pour une histoire du handicap au XXe siècle: Approches transnationales (Europe et Amériques)*. Rennes: Presses Universitaires de Rennes, 2018.

Brégain, Gildas. "The Role of International Institutions in the Process of Categorization of 'Disabled People' (1930s–1975)." In *The Routledge History of Disability*, edited by Roy Hanes, Ivan Brown, and Nancy E. Hansen, 117–32. London: Routledge, 2018.

Brégain, Gildas. "Transnational History of Disability: Reflections." In *Handbook of Disability: Critical Thought and Social Change in a Globalizing World*, edited by Marcia H. Rioux, Alexis Buettgen, Ezra Zubrow, and José Viera, 137–57. Singapore: Springer, 2024.

Brock, Brian. "The Troubled Inheritance of Jean Vanier: Locating the Fatal Theological Mistakes." *Studies in Christian Ethics* 36, no. 3 (2023): 433–56.

Broderick, Andrea. *The Long and Winding Road to Equality and Inclusion for Persons with Disabilities: The United Nations Convention on the Rights of Persons with Disabilities*. Cambridge: Intersentia, 2015.

Buettger, Alexander, and Ezra Zubrow. "Bengt Lindqvist: A Prominent Figure and Advocate." In *Handbook of Disability: Critical Thought and Social Change in a Globalizing World*, edited by Marcia H. Rioux, Alexis Buettgen, Ezra Zubrow, and José Viera, 47–56. Singapore: Springer, 2024.

Burch, Susan, ed. *Encyclopedia of American Disability History*. New York: Facts on File, 2009.

Burke, Roland. "The Internationalism of Human Rights." In *Internationalisms: A Twentieth-Century History*, edited by Glenda Sluga and Patricia M. Clavin, 287–314. Cambridge: Cambridge University Press, 2017.

Burke, Roland. "The 1993 World Conference on Human Rights and the Retreat of a Redistributive Rights Vision." *London Review of International Law* 8, no. 2 (2020): 233–60. https://doi.org/10.1093/lril/lraa023.

Campbell, Jane, and Mike Oliver, *Disability Politics: Understanding Our Past, Changing Our Future*. London: Routledge, 1996.

Carey, Allison C., Pamela Block, and Richard K. Scotch, eds. *Allies and Obstacles. Disability Activism and Parents of Children with Disabilities*. Philadelphia: Temple University Press, 2020.

Celermajer, Danielle, and Alexandre Lefebvre, eds. *The Subject of Human Rights*. Stanford, CA: Stanford University Press, 2020.

Chakrabarty, Dipesh. *Provincializing Europe: Postcolonial Thought and Historical Difference*. Princeton, NJ: Princeton University Press, 2008.

Chandran-Dudley, Ron. *The Man with a Mission: A Life Well-lived*. Singapore: Pagesetters Services, 2017.

Charlton, James I. *Nothing About Us Without Us: Disability Oppression and Empowerment*. Berkeley: University of California Press, 1998.

Christiansen, Christian Olaf. "Partnerships Against Global Poverty: When 'Inclusive Capitalism' Entered the United Nations." In *Histories of Global Inequality: New Perspectives*, edited by Christian Olaf Christiansen and Steven L. B. Jensen, 277–300. London: Palgrave Macmillan, 2019.

Connelly, Matthew. "The Cold War in the Longue Durée: Global Migration, Public Health and Population Control." In *The Cambridge History of the Cold War*, edited by Melvyn Leffler and Odd Westad, 466–88. Cambridge: Cambridge University Press, 2010.

Connelly, Matthew. *Fatal Misconception: The Struggle to Control World Population*. Cambridge, MA: Belknap Press of Harvard University Press, 2009.

Conrad, Sebastian. *What is Global History?* Princeton, NJ: Princeton University Press, 2016.

Dauncey, Sarah. *Disability in Contemporary China: Citizenship, Identity and Culture*. Cambridge: Cambridge University Press, 2020.

De Meulder, Maartje. "Sign Language Recognition: Tensions Between Specificity and Universalism in International Deaf Discourses." In *It's a Small World: International Deaf Spaces and Encounters*, edited by Michele Ilana Friedner and Annelies Kusters, 160–72. Washington, D.C.: Gallaudet University Press, 2015.

De Schutter, Sam. "A Global Approach to Local Problems? How to Write a Longer, Deeper, and Wider History of the International Year of Disabled Persons in Kenya." *Diplomatica: A Journal of Diplomacy and Society* 1, no. 2 (2019): 221–42.

Degener, Theresia. "International Disability Law—A New Legal Subject on the Rise: The Interregional Experts' Meeting in Hong Kong, December 13–17, 1999." *Berkeley Journal of International Law* 18, no. 1 (2000): 180–95.

Degener, Theresia. "A New Human Rights Model of Disability." In *The United Nations Convention on the Rights of Persons with Disabilities: A Commentary*, edited by Valentina Della Fina, Rachele Cera, and Giuseppe Palmisano, 41–59. Cham: Springer, 2017.

Degener, Theresia, and Andrew Begg. "From Invisible Citizens to Agents of Change: A Short History of the Struggle for the Recognition of the Rights of Persons with Disabilities at the United Nations." In *The United Nations Convention on the Rights of Persons with Disabilities: A Commentary*, edited by Valentina Della Fina, Rachele Cera, and Giuseppe Palmisano, 1–39. Cham: Springer, 2017.

Degener, Theresia, and Yolan Koster-Dreese. "Preface." In *Human Rights and Disabled Persons*, edited by Theresia Degener and Yolan Koster-Dreese, xi–xiv. Leiden: Brill, 1995.

Degener, Theresia, and Gerard Quinn. "A Survey of International, Comparative and Regional Disability Law Reform." In *Disability Rights Law and Policy: International and National Perspectives*, edited by Mary Lou Breslin and Silvia Lee, 3–125. Leiden: Brill, 2002.

Dehm, Julia. "'A Pragmatic Compromise Between the Ideal and the Realistic': Debates Over Human Rights, Global Distributive Justice and Minimum Core Obligations in the 1980s." In *Histories of Global Inequality: New Perspectives*, edited by Christian Olaf Christiansen and Steven L. B. Jensen, 157–85. London: Palgrave Macmillan, 2019.

Dehm, Julia. "Rights as Potential Sites of Distributive Struggle." *Tocqueville21*, July 10, 2018. https://tocqueville21.com/focus/rights-as-potential-sites-of-distributive-struggle.

Derksen, Anna. "'To Action for Full Participation and Equality.' Re-framing International Solidarity in 1980s Nordic Disability Rights Activism." In *Towards Solidarity. The Use and Abuse of Concepts of Compassion*, edited by Irène Hermann and Renata Latała, 179–205. Chêne-Bourg: Georg Editeur, 2024.

Derksen, Anna. "Bengt Olof Lennart Lindqvist (1936–2016)." *Nordics.info*, December 4, 2019. https://nordics.info/show/artikel/bengt-olof-lennart-lindqvist-1936-2016.

Drake, Robert F. "Welfare States and Disabled People." In *Handbook of Disability Studies*, edited by Gary L. Albrecht, Katherine D. Seelman, and Michael Bury, 412–30. Thousand Oaks, CA: Sage Publications, 2001.

Driedger, Diane. *The Last Civil Rights Movement: Disabled Peoples' International*. London: Hurst, 1989.

Driedger, Diane. "The Origins and History of Disabled Peoples' International (DPI) 1945–1985." MA Thesis, University of Manitoba, 1987. https://mspace.lib.umanitoba.ca/xmlui/handle/1993/9408.

Eckel, Jan. *The Ambivalence of Good: Human Rights in International Politics Since the 1940s*. New York: Oxford University Press, 2019.

Emmerij, Louis, Dharam Ghai, Richard Jolly, and Frédéric Lapeyre. *UN Contributions to Development Thinking and Practice*. Bloomington: Indiana University Press, 2006.

Enns, Henry, and Alfred H. Neufeldt, eds. *In Pursuit of Equal Participation: Canada and Disability at Home and Abroad*. Concord, ON: Captus Press, 2003.

Foucault, Michel, and Jay Miskowiec. "Of Other Spaces." *Diacritics* 16, no. 1 (1986): 22–27.

Friedner, Michele, Nandini Ghosh, and Deepa Palaniappan. "'Cross-Disability' in India? On the Limits of Disability as a Category and the Work of Negotiating Impairments." *South Asia Multidisciplinary Academic Journal* (April 5, 2018). https://doi.org/10.4000/samaj.4516.

Galmarini, Maria Cristina. *Ambassadors of Social Progress: A History of International Blind Activism in the Cold War*. Ithaca, NY: Northern Illinois University Press, 2024.

Ghodsee, Kristen Rogheh. *Second World, Second Sex: Socialist Women's Activism and Global Solidarity During the Cold War*. Durham, NC: Duke University Press, 2019.

Gilman, Nils. "The New International Economic Order: A Reintroduction." *Humanity: An International Journal of Human Rights, Humanitarianism, and Development* 6, no. 1 (2015): 1–16.

Goodale, Mark. "Dark Matter: Toward a Political Economy of Indigenous Rights and Aspirational Politics." *Critique of Anthropology* 36, no. 4 (2016): 439–57.

Graumann, Sigrid. "Assistierte Freiheit: Von einer Behindertenpolitik der Wohltätigkeit zu einer Politik der Menschenrechte." PhD Thesis, University of Utrecht, 2009.

Grech, Shaun. "Disability and Development: Critical Connections, Gaps and Contradictions." In *Disability in the Global South: The Critical Handbook*, edited by Shaun Grech and Karen Soldatic, 3–19. Cham: Springer, 2016.

Grech, Shaun. "Disability and Poverty: Complex Interactions and Critical Reframings." In *Disability in the Global South: The Critical Handbook*, edited by Shaun Grech and Karen Soldatic, 217–35. Cham: Springer, 2016.

Grech, Shaun, and Karen Soldatic, eds. *Disability in the Global South: The Critical Handbook*. Cham: Springer, 2016.

Groce, Nora. *From Charity to Disability Rights: Global Initiatives of Rehabilitation International, 1922–2002*. New York: Rehabilitation International, 2002.

Grunewald, Karl. "Scandinavian Influences on Intellectual Disability Policy in other Parts of the World." *Scandinavian Journal of Disability Research* 5, no. 2 (2003): 203–7.

Hamraie, Aimi, and Kelly Fritsch. "Crip Technoscience Manifesto." *Catalyst: Feminism, Theory, Technoscience* 5, no. 1 (2019): 1–34. https://catalystjournal.org/index.php/catalyst/article/view/29607/24772.

Helander, Einar. "The Origins of Community Based Rehabilitation." *Behindering und Internationale Entwicklung/Disability and International Development* 24, no. 1 (2013): 4–14.

Hendriks, Aart. "Promoting Disability Equality After the Treaty of Amsterdam: New Legal Directions and Practical Expansion Strategies." In *Disability Rights in Europe: From Theory to Practice*, edited by Anna Lawson and Caroline Gooding, 187–98. London: Bloomsbury Publishing 2005.

Heumann, Judith, and Kristen Joiner. *Being Heumann: An Unrepentant Memoir of a Disability Rights Activist*. Boston: Beacon Press, 2021.

Herr, Stanley S. "Rights Into Action: Protecting Human Rights of the Mentally Handicapped." *Catholic University Law Review* 26, no. 2 (1977): 203–318.

Herr, Stanley S. "Self-Determination, Autonomy, and Alternatives for Guardianship." In *The Human Rights of Persons with Intellectual Disabilities: Different but Equal*, edited by Stanley S. Herr, Lawrence O. Gostin, and Harold Hongju Koh, 429–50. Oxford: Oxford University Press, 2003.

Herro, Annie. "The Pre-Negotiation of UN Human Rights Treaties: The Case of the Convention on the Rights of Persons with Disabilities." *International Negotiation* 24, no. 2 (2019): 240–65.

Herzog, Dagmar. *Unlearning Eugenics: Sexuality, Reproduction, and Disability in Post-Nazi Europe*. Madison: University of Wisconsin Press, 2018.

Heyer, Katharina. *Rights Enabled: The Disability Revolution, from the US, to Germany and Japan, to the United Nations*. Ann Arbor: University of Michigan Press, 2015.

Hoffmann, Stefan-Ludwig. "Human Rights and History." *Past & Present* 232, no. 1 (2016): 279–310.

Hoffmann, Stefan-Ludwig. "Introduction: Genealogies of Human Rights and History." In *Human Rights in the Twentieth Century*, edited by Stefan-Ludwig Hoffmann, 1–26. New York: Cambridge University Press, 2010.

Hopgood, Stephen. *The Endtimes of Human Rights*. Ithaca, NY: Cornell University Press, 2015.

Huisman, Frank, and Nancy Tomes. "A World South-Side Up?: Global Health and the Provincializing of Europe." *European Journal for the History of Medicine and Health* 78, no. 1 (2021): 195–212.

Hunt, Lynn. "The Long and the Short of the History of Human Rights." *Past & Present* 233, no. 1 (2016): 323–31.

Hurst, Rachel. "Disabled Peoples' International: Europe and the Social Model of Disability." In *The Social Model of Disability: Europe and the Majority World*, edited by Colin Barnes and Geof Mercer, 65–79. Leeds: The Disability Press, 2005.

International Rehabilitation Review, Editors of the. "The Impact of the International Year of Disabled Persons: An Interview with Norman Acton." *International Rehabilitation Review* 50, no. 1 (2000): 10–12.

Jackson, Simon, and Alanna O'Malley, eds. *The Institution of International Order: From the League of Nations to the United Nations*. London: Routledge, 2020.

Jain, Devaki. "Gender: From Eliminating Discrimination to Promoting Women's Rights and Empowerment." In *UN Ideas That Changed the World*, edited by Richard Jolly, Louis Emmerij, and Thomas G. Weiss, 68–82. Bloomington: Indiana University Press, 2009.

Jensen, Steven L. B. "Da Danmark forsøgte at gøre tvangssterilisering til beskyttet praksis i international menneskeret." *Handicaphistorisk Tidsskrift* 51 (2024): 22–38.

Jensen, Steven L. B. *The Making of International Human Rights: The 1960s, Decolonization, and the Reconstruction of Global Values*. New York: Cambridge University Press, 2016.

Jolly, Richard, Louis Emmerij, Dharam Ghai, and Frédéric Lapeyre. *UN Contributions to Development Thinking and Practice*. Bloomington: Indiana University Press, 2004.

Kanter, Arlene S. *The Development of Disability Rights Under International Law: From Charity to Human Rights*. New York: Routledge Taylor & Francis Group, 2017.

Kauppinen, Liisa, and Markku Jokinen. "Including Deaf Culture and Linguistic Rights." In *Human Rights and Disability Advocacy*, edited by Maya Sabatello and Marianne Schulze, 131–45. Philadelphia: University of Pennsylvania Press, 2014.

Kayess, Rosemary, and Phillip French. "Out of Darkness into Light? Introducing the Convention on the Rights of Persons with Disabilities." *Human Rights Law Review* 8, no. 1 (2008): 1–34.

Kiuppis, Florian. "Why (Not) Associate the Principle of Inclusion with Disability? Tracing Connections from the Start of the 'Salamanca Process.'" *International Journal of Inclusive Education* 18, no. 7 (2014): 746–61.

Koh, Harold Hongju, and Lawrence O. Gostin. "Introduction: The Human Rights Imperative." In *The Human Rights of Persons with Intellectual Disabilities. Different but Equal*, edited by Stanley S. Herr, Lawrence O. Gostin, and Harold Hongju Koh, 1–22. Oxford: Oxford University Press, 2003.

Kohn, Nina A. "Legislating Supported Decision-Making." *Harvard Journal on Legislation* 58, no. 2 (2021): 313–56.

Kohrman, Matthew. *Bodies of Difference: Experiences of Disability and Institutional Advocacy in the Making of Modern China*. Berkeley: University of California Press, 2005.

Könkkölä, Kalle, and Heini Saraste. *The World Became My Room*. Juva: WSOY, 1996.

Kott, Sandrine. "Social Europe, Democracy and Brexit." *Contemporary European History* 28, no. 1 (2019): 46–49.
Krentz, Christopher. *Elusive Kinship: Disability and Human Rights in Postcolonial Literature.* Philadelphia: Temple University Press, 2022.
Kristeva, Julia. "Liberty, Equality, Fraternity, and . . . Vulnerability." *Women's Studies Quarterly* 38, no. 1–2 (2010): 251–68.
Kulamadayil, Lys. "Ableism in the College of International Lawyers: On Disabling Differences in the Professional Field." *Leiden Journal of International Law* 36, no. 3 (2023): 549–63.
Lang, Raymond. "The Role of NGOs in the Process of Empowerment and Social Transformation of People with Disabilities." *Asia Pacific Disability Rehabilitation Journal: Selected Readings in Community Based Rehabilitation* 1 (2000): 1–20.
Lindqvist, Bengt. *Blindstyre.* Åsele: Tundell Salmson Audio, 2012.
Lord, Janet E. "Disability Rights and the Human Rights Mainstream: Reluctant Gate-Crashers?" In *The International Struggle for New Human Rights*, edited by Clifford Bob, 83–92. Philadelphia: University of Pennsylvania Press, 2009.
Mabbett, Deborah. "The Development of Rights-Based Social Policy in the European Union: The Example of Disability Rights." *Journal of Common Market Studies* 43, no. 1 (2005): 97–120.
MacGregor, Laura. "A Holy Mess of a Story: Maternal Reflections on Caregiving, Chaos, and Intellectual Disability." *Journal of Disability & Religion* 27, no. 1 (2021): 124–37.
Markovits, Daniel. "How McKinsey Destroyed the Middle Class: Technocratic Management, No Matter How Brilliant, Cannot Unwind Structural Inequalities." *The Atlantic*, February 3, 2020. https://www.theatlantic.com/ideas/archive/2020/02/how-mckinsey-destroyed-middle-class/605878/.
Mason, Corinne L. "'Cripping' the World Bank: Disability, Empowerment and the Cost of Violence Against Women." *International Feminist Journal of Politics* 17, no. 3 (2014): 435–53.
Mazower, Mark. *Governing the World: The History of an Idea.* London: Penguin Press, 2012.
McKearney, Patrick. "Receiving the Gift of Cognitive Disability: Recognizing Agency in the Limits of the Rational Subject." *The Cambridge Journal of Anthropology* 36, no. 1 (2018): 40–60.
Meekosha, Helen, and Karen Soldatic. "Human Rights and the Global South: The Case of Disability." *Third World Quarterly* 32, no. 8 (2011): 1383–97.
Mégret, Frédéric. "The Disabilities Convention: Human Rights of Persons with Disabilities or Disability Rights?" *Human Rights Quarterly* 30, no. 2 (2008): 494–516.
Mégret, Frédéric. "The Disabilities Convention: Towards a Holistic Concept of Rights." *The International Journal of Human Rights* 12, no. 2 (2008): 261–77.
Meininger, Herman. "Inclusion as Heterotopia: Spaces of Encounter Between People with and Without Intellectual Disability." *Journal of Social Inclusion* 4, no. 1 (2013): 24–44.
Meyers, Stephen J. *Civilizing Disability Society: The Convention on the Rights of Persons with Disabilities Socializing Grassroots Disabled Persons' Organizations in Nicaragua.* Cambridge: Cambridge University Press, 2019.

Miles, Mike. "The 'Community Base' in Rehabilitation Planning: Key or Gimmick?" In *Practical Approaches to Childhood Disability in Developing Countries: Insights from Experience and Research*, edited by Marigold J. Thorburn and Kofi Marfo, 287–302. Tampa, FL: Global Age Publishing, 1994.

Millward, Gareth. "Social Security Policy and the Early Disability Movement—Expertise, Disability, and the Government, 1965–77." *Twentieth Century British History* 26, no. 2 (2015): 274–97.

Minkowitz, Tina. "CRPD Advocacy by the World Network of Users and Survivors of Psychiatry: The Emergence of an User/Survivor Perspective in Human Rights." August 14, 2012. https://ssrn.com/abstract=2326668 or http://dx.doi.org/10.2139/ssrn.2326668.

Minkowitz, Tina. "WNUSP Statement to Mexico City Meeting Before Beginning of CRPD Negotiations." March 14, 2022. https://www.academia.edu/8753018/WNUSP_statement_to_Mexico_City_meeting_before_beginning_of_CRPD_negotiations.

Mitchell, David, and Sharon Snyder. "The Eugenic Atlantic: Race, Disability, and the Making of an International Eugenic Science, 1800–1945." *Disability & Society* 18, no. 7 (2003): 843–64.

Mittler, Peter. "Meeting the Needs of People with an Intellectual Disability: International Perspectives." In *The Human Rights of Persons with Intellectual Disabilities. Different but Equal*, edited by Stanley S. Herr, Lawrence O. Gostin, and Harold Hongju Koh, 25–48. Oxford: Oxford University Press, 2003.

Mittler, Peter. *Thinking Globally, Acting Locally: A Personal Journey*. Central Milton Keynes: Authorhouse, 2010.

Möckel, Benjamin. "Endtimes of Human Rights? Neue Forschungen zur Geschichte der Menschenrechte." *Neue Politische Literatur: Berichte aus Geschichts- und Politikwissenschaft* 65, no. 3 (2020): 473–501.

Moyn, Samuel. *Human Rights and the Uses of History*. London: Verso, 2014.

Moyn, Samuel. *Not Enough: Human Rights in an Unequal World*. Cambridge, MA: The Belknap Press of Harvard University Press, 2018.

Moyn, Samuel. "On the Nonglobalization of Ideas." In *Global Intellectual History*, edited by Samuel Moyn and Andrew Sartori, 187–204. New York: Columbia University Press, 2013.

Moyn, Samuel. *The Last Utopia: Human Rights in History*. Cambridge, MA: Belknap Press of Harvard University Press, 2012.

Moyn, Samuel. "What Happened to the Dream of Global Justice?" *ABC Religion & Ethics*, October 31, 2019. https://www.abc.net.au/religion/samuel-moyn-what-happened-to-the-dream-of-global-justice/11658576.

Murray, Joseph J., Maartje de Mulder, and Delphine le Maire. "An Education in Sign Language as a Human Right? The Sensory Exception in the Legislative History and Ongoing Interpretation of Article 24 of the UN Convention on the Rights of Persons with Disabilities." *Human Rights Quarterly* 40, no. 1 (2018): 37–60.

Murray, Joseph J. "Linguistic Human Rights Discourse in Deaf Community Activism." *Sign Language Studies* 15, no. 4 (2015): 379–410.

Muyinda, Herbert. "Negotiating Disability: Mobilization and Organization Among Landmine Survivors in Late Twentieth-Century Northern Uganda." In *Disability Histories*, edited by Susan Burch and Michael Rembis, 98–115. Urbana: University of Illinois Press, 2014.

Nagase, Osamu. "Difference, Equality and Disabled People: Disability Rights and Disability Culture." MA Thesis, International Institute of Social Studies, The Hague, 1995.

Nouwen, Henri. *Adam: Een vriendschap*. Translated by Maria ter Steeg. Tielt: Lannoo, 1997.

Olcott, Jocelyn. *International Women's Year: The Greatest Consciousness-Raising Event in History*. New York: Oxford University Press, 2017.

Packard, Randall M. *A History of Global Health: Interventions into the Lives of Other Peoples*. Baltimore, MD: John Hopkins University Press, 2016.

Petri, Gabor, Julie Beadle-Brown, and Jill Bradshaw. " 'More Honoured in the Breach than in the Observance'—Self-Advocacy and Human Rights." *Laws* 6, no. 4 (2017): 26. https://doi.org/10.3390/laws6040026.

Prashad, Vijay. *The Darker Nations: A People's History of The Third World*. New York: The New Press, 2007.

Price, Penny, and Yutaka Takamine. "The Asian and Pacific Decade of Disabled Persons 1993–2002: What Have We Learned?" *Asia Pacific Disability Rehabilitation Journal* 14, no. 2 (2003): 115–27.

Priestley, Mark. "In Search of European Disability Policy: Between National and Global." *ALTER: European Journal of Disability Research/Revue européenne de recherche sur le handicap* 1, no. 1 (2007): 61–74. https://doi.org/10.1016/j.alter.2007.08.006.

Priestley, Mark. "We're All Europeans Now! The Social Model of Disability and European Social Policy." In *The Social Model of Disability: Europe and the Majority World*, edited by Colin Barnes and Geof Mercer, 17–31. Leeds: The Disability Press, 2005.

Quinn, Gerard. "Personhood and Legal Capacity: Perspectives on the Paradigm Shift of Article 12 CRPD." Paper presented at the *Conference on Disability and Legal Capacity Under the CRPD*. Boston: Harvard Law School, 2010. https://www.nuigalway.ie/media/centrefordisabilitylawandpolicy/files/archive/Submission-on-Legal-Capacity-to-the-Oireachtas-Committee-on-Justice,-Defence-&-Equality-(August,-2011).pdf.

Quinn, Gerard, and Anna Arstein-Kerslake. "Restoring the 'Human' in 'Human Rights': Personhood and Doctrinal Innovation in the UN Disability Convention." In *The Cambridge Companion to Human Rights Law*, edited by Conor Gearty and Costas Douzinas, 36–55. New York: Cambridge University Press, 2012.

Raley, Meredith. "The Drafting of Article 33 of the Convention on the Rights of Persons with Disabilities: The Creation of a Novel Mechanism." *The International Journal of Human Rights* 20, no. 1 (2016): 138–52. https://doi.org/10.1080/13642987.2015.1073714.

Ratzska, Adolf. *Independent Living and Attendant Care in Sweden: A Consumer Perspective*. New York: International Exchange of Experts and Information in Rehabilitation, World Rehabilitation Fund, 1986.

Rembis, Michael. "Yes We Can Change: Disability Studies—Enabling Equality." *Journal of Postsecondary Education and Disability* 23, no. 1 (2010): 19–27.

Ricoeur, Paul. *The Rule of Metaphor: The Creation of Meaning in Language*. London: Routledge, 2015.

Rodriquez, Adaly M. *The Rise of Women's Rights in Curaçao: The Potential of the Women's Convention to the Empowerment and Equal Rights of Women in Curaçao*. Amsterdam: Caribpublishing/SWP, 2015.

Rosanvallon, Pierre. *The Society of Equals*. Translated by Arthur Goldhammer. Cambridge, MA: Harvard University Press, 2013.

Ruiz, Felipe Jaramillo. "The Committee on the Rights of Persons with Disabilities and Its Take on Sexuality." *Reproductive Health Matters* 25, no. 50 (2017): 92–103.

Sabatello, Maya. "The New Diplomacy." In *Human Rights and Disability Advocacy*, edited by Maya Sabatello and Marianne Schulze, 239–58. Philadelphia: University of Pennsylvania Press, 2014.

Sabatello, Maya, and Marianne Schulze, eds. *Human Rights and Disability Advocacy*. Philadelphia: University of Pennsylvania Press, 2014.

Schaaf, Marta. "Negotiating Sexuality in the Convention on the Rights of Persons with Disabilities." *Sur: International Journal on Human Rights* 8, no. 14 (2011): 113–31.

Schoenfeld, Benjamin N. "Human Rights for the Mentally Retarded: Their Recognition by the Providers of Service." *Human Rights* 4, no. 1 (1974): 31–65.

Shaffer, Bret. "The Right to Life, the Convention on the Rights of Persons with Disabilities, and Abortion." *Penn State International Law Review* 28, no. 2 (2009): 265–87.

Shah, Fatima. *Sunshine & Shadows: The Autobiography of Dr. Fatima Shah*. Karachi: Ferozsons, 1999.

Shakespeare, Tom. *Disability Rights and Wrongs Revisited*. London: Routledge, 2014.

Shilliam, Robbie. *Decolonizing Politics: An Introduction*. Cambridge: Polity Press, 2021.

Sluga, Glenda, and Patricia M. Clavin, eds. *Internationalisms: A Twentieth-Century History*. Cambridge: Cambridge University Press, 2017.

Sluga, Glenda. *Internationalism in the Age of Nationalism*. Philadelphia: University of Pennsylvania Press, 2013.

Song, Jiyoung, ed. *A History of Human Rights Society in Singapore, 1965–2015*. Abingdon: Routledge, 2017.

Stein, Michael Ashley. "China and Disability Rights." *Loyola of Los Angeles International and Comparative Law Review* 33, no. 1 (Fall 2010): 7–26.

Stiker, Henri-Jacques. *A History of Disability*. Ann Arbor: University of Michigan Press, 2019.

Thornton, Christy. *Revolution in Development. Mexico and the Governance of the Global Economy*. Oakland: University of California Press, 2021.

Tijsseling, Corrie. "'School, waar?' Een onderzoek naar de betekenis van het Nederlandse dovenonderwijs voor de Nederlandse dovengemeenschap, 1790–1990." PhD Dissertation, University of Utrecht, 2014.

Toledo, Pamela Molina. "At the United Nations...'The South Also Exists.'" In *Human Rights and Disability Advocacy*, edited by Maya Sabatello and Marianne Schulze, 170–87. Philadelphia: University of Pennsylvania Press, 2014.

Tromel, Stefan. "A Personal Perspective on the Drafting History of the United Nations Convention on the Rights of Persons with Disabilities." *European Yearbook of Disability Law* 1 (2009): 115–38.

Tucker, Joan. "Local Strategies in a Global Network: Disability Rights in Jamaica." PhD Dissertation, University of South Florida, 2007. https://digitalcommons.usf.edu/etd/2388/.
Unger, Corinna R. *International Development: A Postwar History*. London: Bloomsbury Academic, 2019.
Van Ertvelde, Anaïs. "Welfare: Defended, Questioned, Complemented? Belgian Welfare Arrangements in the 1970s–1980s from the Perspective of Disability Organizations." In *Marginalized Groups, Inequalities and the Post-War Welfare State: Whose Welfare?*, edited by Monika Baár and Paul van Trigt, 137–54. London: Routledge, 2020.
Vanneste, Geert. "Current Status of CBR in Africa: A Review." *Asia Pacific Disability Rehabilitation Journal: Selected Readings in Community Based Rehabilitation* 1 (2000): 127–35.
Van Trigt, Paul. "A Blind Spot of a Guiding Country? Human Rights and Dutch Disability Groups Since 1981." *Moving the Social* 53 (2015): 87–102.
Van Trigt, Paul. "Gelijkheid zonder beperking: Over de Algemene Wet Gelijke Behandeling (1994) en de constructie van handicap in politieke instituties." *BMGN—Low Countries Historical Review* 134, no. 1 (2019): 3–27.
Van Trigt, Paul. "A History of 'Legal Capacity' and the 'Family' in the United Nations' Disability Policies Since the 1970s." In *Family, Human Rights and Internationalism*, edited by Julia Moses (forthcoming).
Van Trigt, Paul. "Introduction: Scripts for a New Stage: United Nations' Observances and New Perspectives on Diplomatic History." *Diplomatica* 1, no. 2 (2019): 145–56.
Van Trigt, Paul. "De invoering van het Persoonsgebonden Budget in de gezondheidszorg in 1996 en het ontstaan van 'vrijemarktbureaucratie.'" *Tijdschrift Sociologie* 15 no. 3 (2019): 271–87.
Van Trigt, Paul, and Susan Legêne. "Writing Disability into Colonial Histories of Humanitarianism." *Social Inclusion* 4, no. 4 (2016): 188–96.
Vargha, Dora. *Polio Across the Iron Curtain: Hungary's Cold War with an Epidemic*. Cambridge: Cambridge University Press, 2018.
Venzke, Ingo, and Kevin Jon Heller, eds. *Contingency in International Law: On the Possibility of Different Legal Histories Get Access Arrow*. Oxford: Oxford University Press, 2021.
Venzke, Ingo. "Situating Contingency in the Path of International Law." In *Contingency in International Law: On the Possibility of Different Legal Histories*, edited by Ingo Venzke and Kevin Jon Heller, 3–19. Oxford: Oxford University Press, 2021.
Waddington, Lisa, and Matthew Diller. "Tensions and Coherence in Disability Policy: The Uneasy Relationship Between Social Welfare and Civil Rights Models of Disability in American, European and International Employment Law." In *Disability Rights Law and Policy: International and National Perspectives*, edited by Mary Lou Breslin and Silvia Lee, 241–80. Leiden: Brill, 2002.
Waddington, Lisa. *From Rome to Nice in a Wheelchair: The Development of a European Disability Policy*. Groningen: Europa Law Publishing, 2006.
Waldschmidt, Anne. "Behindertenpolitik (in) der Europäischen Union." In *Aufbrüche und Barrieren: Behindertenpolitik und Behindertenrecht in Deutschland und Europa seit den 1970er-Jahren*, edited by Theresia Degener and Marc von Miquel, 79–106. Bielefeld: Transcript, 2019.

Waldschmidt, Anne. "Disability Policy of the European Union: The Supranational Level." *ALTER, European Journal of Disability* 3 (2009): 8–23.

Weiss, Thomas G., Tatiana Carayannis, and Richard Jolly. "The 'Third' United Nations." *Global Governance* 15, no. 1 (2009): 123–42.

Werner, David. *Where There Is No Doctor: A Village Health Care Handbook*. London: Macmillan, 1977.

Wheatley, Natasha. "New Subjects in International Law and Order." In *Internationalisms. A Twentieth-Century History*, edited by Glenda Sluga and Patricia Clavin, 265–86. Cambridge: Cambridge University Press, 2017.

Whyte, Jessica. *The Morals of the Market: Human Rights and the Rise of Neoliberalism*. London: Verso, 2019.

Zhuang, Kuansong Victor. "At the Margins of Society: Disability Rights and Inclusion in 1980s Singapore." *Disability and the Global South* 7, no. 1 (2020): 1813–29.

Zola, Irving Kenneth. *Missing Pieces: A Chronicle of Living with a Disability*. Philadelphia: Temple University Press, 1982.

INDEX

Acton, Norman, 40, 42, 89, 90, 175n35
ADA. *See* Americans with Disabilities Act
Adam, God's Beloved (Nouwen), 152–53
Ad Hoc Committee on a Comprehensive and Integral International Convention on the Protection and Promotion of the Rights and Dignity of Persons with Disabilities, 32, 97–98, 121, 124
Americans with Disabilities Act (ADA) (1990), 3, 4, 84, 115–17
Amnesty International, 7, 27, 78, 99, 119, 122, 145
Amsterdam Treaty (1997), 116–17
Anghie, Antony, 8, 9, 82, 98–99
Annan, Kofi, 87, 96, 97
anti-discrimination, 4, 32, 51–52, 118, 120
anti-psychiatric movement, Nirje and Wolfensberger normalization principle, 20–21
Arnett, Adam, 152–53
Article 12, of CRPD, 13, 122, 141; on equal recognition of people with mental disabilities, 126–27; Herzog on, 128; Quinn on independence and, 142, 152
Article 19 of CRPD, on IL, 124, 127–28, 140

Article 23 of CRPD, on right to have family, 24, 25, 33–34
Article 25 of CRPD, on sexual and reproductive health, 25

Bank Mikkelsen, Erik, 21
Belgrade 1975: on disability and women rights in Global South, 43–47; on equality of blind persons, 37; rehabilitation and Cold War, 38–43; Shah on blind women in, 11, 43, 46; Standard Rules and, 51–56; WPA concerning disabled persons, 47–51, 134
blind persons, 123; Belgrade 1975 on equality of, 37; Global South PAB first organization of, 44; international activism for, 68, 105. *See also* international conference of blind women
Brégain, Gildas, 5, 41; comparison of 1971 and 1975 declarations, 130; on global disability policies, 39–40; on women issues, 44
British Disability Discrimination Act (1995), 117
Burke, Roland, 101, 146

Casseres, R. A., 62–63
CBR. *See* Community Based Rehabilitation
Centre for Social Development and Humanitarian Affairs, of ECOSOC, 47–48, 82
CESCR. *See* Committee on Economic, Social and Cultural Rights
Chandran-Dudley, Ron: as DPI founding member, 11, 69; on rehabilitation and socioeconomic inequality, 70; Singapore 1981, 69–71
Charlton, James, 61
Charter of Fundamental Rights, EU, 117
Chronically Sick and Disabled Act (1971), UK, 40
citizen rights, Enns lecture on, 59–60
cognitive disabilities, 38, 74; heterotopia and, 153–54
Cold War, 10, 38–43, 81, 99, 122
Commission on Human Rights, UN, 27–28, 52–53
Committee on Economic, Social and Cultural Rights (CESCR), 94, 103
Committee on the Rights of Persons with Disabilities, Ruiz on right to have family, 34–35
community: Declaration on the Rights of Disabled Persons addition of, 130; IL in, 139–42; Standard Rules mention of, 135; WPA on, 132
Community Action Programmes for Disabled People: HELIOS I (1988–1991), 112–13; HELIOS II (1993–1996), 112–13, 114
Community Based Rehabilitation (CBR), 128; Lang on medical model of disability in, 138; Nakanishi on IL same concept as, 138–39; primary health care and, 138, 140; Standard Rules criticism of, 135–36; UN unpopularity of, 134–39; WHO, ILO and UNESCO paper on, 136–37, 143; WHO development of, 131
Connelly, Matthew, 30

Convention on the Rights of Persons with Disabilities (CRPD), of UN, 1, 3–6; anti-discrimination law and, 32; Article 12 of, 13, 122, 126–28, 141, 142, 152; Article 19 on IL, 124, 127–28, 140; Article 23 concerning right to have family, 24, 25, 33–34; Article 25 on health, 25; disability movement human rights appropriation, 32; Gallardo at signing of, 33; global disability policies and, 83; human rights law and, 127; on international law granting equal rights to persons with disabilities, 126; legal capacity in, 2, 127; mentally disabled persons reproductive rights inclusion in, 16; Minkowitz at signing of, 125; nation-state framework, 7; negotiation of, 32–35; persons with disabilities implementation and monitoring of, 58–59; politics and, 146–47; selective domestic implementation of human rights, 13–14; self-advocacy role in, 145; sexuality word deleted, 34; on sign language, 75; socioeconomic rights in, 57; Standard Rules compared to, 33–35, 54; Toledo on Global South self-advocacy inclusion in, 74–75
Council of the Handicapped, Curaçao, 63, 65
Covenant on Civil and Political Rights, UN, forced sterilization rejection, 19
Crip Camp documentary, 17
Crip Utopia (Ratzka), 16–18, 148
cross-disability organizations: Charlton on, 61; Disabled Peoples' Federation of Pakistan as, 46–47; DPI as first run by disabled persons, 58; for self-advocacy, 19
CRPD. *See* Convention on the Rights of Persons with Disabilities
cultural diversity, DPI acceptance of, 71

Daes, Erica-Irene A., 133
DALY. *See* disability-adjusted life years

Deaf community: as minority language recognition, 12; seen as ethnic group or linguistic minority, 74–75; Standard Rule on sign language and education of, 75

Declaration of General and Special Rights of Mentally Retarded Persons, ILSMH Jerusalem 1968, 26

Declaration on the Rights of Disabled Persons (1975), UN, 10, 11, 27, 41, 129; addition of community to, 130; medical model approach to disability, 47; persons with disabilities limited involvement in creation of, 38; on reproductive rights in, 15; right to have family exclusion, 25–26, 35

Declaration on the Rights of Mentally Retarded Persons (1971), UN, 10, 23, 41; debate on reproductive rights in, 15; ILSMH *Step by Step* policy instrument for national level implementation, 24

Degener, Theresia, 12, 31–32, 94, 98, 103, 119; on legal capacity of persons with disabilities, 141; social development framework dissatisfaction, 95

Despouy, Leandro, 31, 53, 77

developing countries: DPI resources for, 112; Manila Statement for disability law in, 42; Singapore 1981 self-advocacy from, 58–59; Standard Rules on disability problems in, 76

disabilities: cognitive, 38, 74, 153–54; IYDP priority of prevention of, 26; Miles on, 136–38; Millennium Development Goals insufficiency for, 56, 82, 89, 123; rehabilitation for physical, 38–43; seen as development issue, 82; sensory and physical, 38. *See also* blind persons; Deaf community; medical model of disability; mental disabilities; persons with disabilities

disability-adjusted life years (DALY), of WHO, 139

disability historicization, Singapore and, 66–69

disability human rights: discontinuity element of, 2; long-term development of, 9–10

disability internationalism and normalization: anti-psychiatric movement influence on, 20–21; eugenics policies, 19, 20, 24–25; human rights adoption for ILSMH, 18; ILO vocational rehabilitation policies, 19; 1960s and 1970s movements impact on, 20; UNESCO special education program, 19; WHO medical rehabilitation policies, 19

disability policies: claiming rights in, 28–32; Deafness education recognition in UN, 75; European, 110–11, 118; internationalization of, 3; on negative freedom, 29, 35; on positive freedom, 29; UN trend for, 35. *See also* global disability policies

disability rights movements (DRM): Charlton on, 61; Independent Living Movement, 17, 18, 128; mental disabilities lack of inclusion in, 16

disability rights progress, 3–6; ADA and, 84, 115–17

Disabled Peoples' Federation of Pakistan, Shah cross-disability organization of, 46–47

Disabled Peoples' International (DPI), 80; on basic rights for persons with disabilities, 60; Chandran-Dudley as founding member of, 11, 69; collaboration with Despouy, 77, 104; on creation of structure to address disabled persons human rights violations, 106; cultural diversity acceptance by, 71; Driedger book on, 60–61; Enns of, 48–49, 59–60; first global cross-disability organization run by disabled persons, 58, 111; Human Rights Committee of, 31, 77–78, 101, 103, 105; as IDA member, 123; importance of self-advocacy, 72, 111; Lindqvist as founder of, 68; position to

Disabled Peoples' International (DPI) (*continued*)
discourage convention, 106; resources for developing countries, 112; self-advocacy and social development support by, 11; "Self-Help Leadership Training Seminars" of, 61; Shah at Singapore, 46, 74; in Singapore during IYDP, 11, 48; on social development policies importance, 71; support of Saulle convention initiative, 104; on UN lack of financial resources for Decade, 90; women protest against men dominance in, 74; WPA negotiations and, 72
disabled people's organizations (DPOs), 74
Disabled Persons and the International Organizations, The (Saulle), 80–81
diversity, Singapore 1981 and, 73–76
DPI. *See* Disabled Peoples' International
DPOs. *See* disabled people's organizations
Driedger, Diane, 60–61
DRM. *See* disability rights movement
Dury, Ian, 1, 144, 147
Dutch national committee, for IYDP, 62–65
Dybwad, Gunnar, 20–22
Dybwad, Rosemary, 21–22
dystopia, 149–51

Economic and Social Council (ECOSOC), UN, 23, 51; Centre for Social Development and Humanitarian Affairs organization of IYDP, 47–48, 82; disability policies main responsibility of, 27, 53; IDA organizations consultative status, 123; Kikhia on Acton speech at, 42
EDF. *See* European Disability Forum
Enns, Henry, 48–49, 59–60, 90, 102
EU. *See* European Union
eugenic policies, 19, 20, 24–25
European Disability Forum (EDF), 113, 118, 120
European disability policies: employment as focal point of, 110–11; Waldschmidt on equal rights and non-discrimination, 118

European Regional Meeting on Implementation of WPA, 81
European social model, 107–8, 120; with civil rights and anti-discrimination, 118; nation-states responsibility for welfare, 110–11
Europeans with Disabilities Act, 116–19
European Union (EU), 108–9; Charter of Fundamental Rights, 117

family, persons with disabilities and their, 141–42; CRPD Article 23 concerning right to found a, 24, 25, 33–34; Declaration on the Rights of Disabled Persons (1975) on, 25–26, 35, 130; Standard Rules on Equalization of Opportunities for Persons with Disabilities (1993) on, 28–29, 31, 33–34, 136
Fatal Misconception (Connelly), 30
forced sterilization attempts, in 1949 and 1950, 19
Framework Directive on Non-discrimination in Occupation and Employment (2000), EU, 117–18
Franklin D. Roosevelt International Disability Award, Reich and, 96, 97
From Charity to Rights rights declaration draft, of ILSMH, 22

Gallardo, Gilberto Rincón, 33
global disability policies, 18; Acton on, 42; as apolitical issue of rehabilitation, 56–57; Brégain on, 39–40; CRPD and, 83; human rights and socioeconomic equality addressed in, 47–51, 79–80, 142, 145; on human rights as human needs, 83; IYDP importance in development of, 85; potential turning point in, 88–91; rehabilitation and, 38–39; Reich development of, 84; shift to human needs in 1980s, 57, 83; for transfer of welfare state model, 42, 56; UN and other agency involvement in, 139

INDEX 209

Global Meeting of Experts, in Stockholm in 1987, 119; on CBR, 134–35; DPI and, 72–73; drafting of international disability convention, 81; Lindqvist instrumental in, 68; Saulle on international disability convention, 81; self-advocacy CBR criticism, 138–39; UN policy challenge by Lindqvist, 91; WPA Concerning Disabled Persons implementation review by, 79; on WPA implementation, 52

Global North: Enns from, 60; Global South development attempts by, 50, 68–69; IDC overrepresentation of, 76

Global South, 60; disability and women's rights in, 43–47; Global North development attempts for, 50, 68–69; IDC inclusion and, 76; PAB as first organization of blind in, 44; rehabilitation efforts in, 42; self-advocacy in, 43, 44, 75–76; support of utopia of development, 82

Grant, Isabella, 43–44

Groce, Nora, 39–40

Grunewald, Karl, 21

"Health Aspects of Mental Retardation," WHO memorandum, 129

HELIOS I (1988–1991), 112–13

HELIOS II (1993–1996), 112–13; rights-based perspective on disability, 114

Herzog, Dagmar, 152; on Article 12 of CRPD, 128; on selective domestic implementation of human rights, 13

Het Dorp utopia, 30, 148–49, 150

heterotopia, 151, 155; Arnett and Nouwen case, 152–53; persons with cognitive disabilities and, 153–54

Heumann, Judy, 17, 84, 96–97

Hoffmann, Stefan-Ludwig, 8–9, 27, 34–35, 55, 81, 98

human rights, of disabled persons, 1, 3; agenda of self-advocacy, 101–2; Degener and Koster-Dreese on instruments for, 94; discontinuity of history, 2; framed as needs by Standard Rules, 54, 107; international conference of blind women absence of language of, 44–45; International Decade of Disabled Persons approach of, 52; Jerusalem 1968 and, 25–28; national framework of, 145; new diplomacy for in 2000s, 122–24; self-advocacy on, 145; social development framework and, 89; Vienna Declaration and Programme of Action on, 101

Human Rights and Disability (Quinn and Degener), 31–32

Human Rights and Disabled Persons: Despouy report on specific disability rights, 53, 94; human rights 1993 report, 30–31

Human Rights Committee, of DPI, 31, 77–78, 101, 103, 105

human rights historiography, 2, 6, 99, 144; Amnesty International, 7; contribution of Jensen to, 67; Hoffmann on, 8–9; internationalisms and international relations, 9; legal capacity and, 127; Moyn model of truncation and fulfillment approach, 6–7; neoliberalism and, 7, 10, 37, 83, 86; shift from collective to individual rights, 7

human rights law, 147; CRPD support of exercise of, 2, 127; disability inclusion blocked in 1980s, 96; nation-states implementation role of, 83; persons with disabilities as subject and agents of, 13

human rights organizations: Amnesty International, 7, 27, 78, 99, 119, 122, 145; Human Rights Watch, 122

IDA. *See* International Disability Alliance

IDC. *See* International Disability Caucus

IFB. *See* International Federation of the Blind

IL. *See* Independent Living

ILO. *See* International Labour Organization

ILSMH. *See* International League of Societies for the Mentally Handicapped
Inclusion International, as IDA member, 123
Independent Living (IL), 17, 122; in community, 139–42; CRPD Article 19 on, 124, 127–28, 140; Nakanishi on CBR same concept of, 138–39
Independent Living Movement, 17, 18, 128
individual freedom rights: UN and WHO policies on human rights and, 134; World Conference on Human Rights focus on, 101
institutionalization, normalization principle as alternative for, 20–21
interdependence, Universal Declaration of Human Rights on, 140
International Bill of Human Rights, DPI on disability absence from, 77–78
international conference of blind women (1975), 37; human rights language absence in, 44–45; IFB and WCWB for, 44; Shah and, 11, 43, 46
International Convention to Promote and Protect the Rights and Dignity of Persons with Disabilities, in Mexico City, 121
International Decade of Disabled Persons (1983–1992), 48; human rights approach during, 52; UN observance of, 26, 27
International Disability Alliance (IDA), 95, 123
International Disability Caucus (IDC), 76
international disability law, US reluctance to, 87
International Federation of the Blind (IFB), 44
International Labour Organization (ILO), 19, 106, 144; publication on CBR, 136–37, 143
international law: self-advocacy research encouragement, 119; utopias and, 79–84
International League of Societies for the Mentally Handicapped (ILSMH), in Jerusalem, 129; adoption of human rights of, 18; blocking promiscuous Scandinavia, 15; lack of confirmation of reproductive rights by, 10; persons with disabilities rights to have family blocked, 35; Sterner and symposium in Stockholm in 1967, 15
International Society for the Rehabilitation of the Disabled. *See* Rehabilitation International
International Year of Disabled Persons (IYDP) (1981): change from "for" to "of" in title of, 48, 60, 170n8; Declaration on the Rights of Disabled People similarity, 47; as disability internationalism development catalyst, 11; DPI disability advocates and, 111; Dury song at, 1; full participation and equality theme, 48; goal of persons with disabilities integration, 109–10; prevention of disabilities as priority, 26; Reich on Third World disability policies support, 86–87; Shah involvement in seminars during, 46; social integration of disabled, 110; spread of disability perspectives from Global North to Global South, 60; UN observance of, 26; US joining of, 85, 86; various country response to, 66–67; WPA drafted during, 27
International Year of Women (1975), IFB and WCWB international conference on the situation of blind women, 44
IYDP. *See* International Year of Disabled Persons
IYDP in Dutch Caribbean, 54, 61, 63–64; Dutch national committee for, 62; intensification of programmes already in place, 66–67; WPA and International Decade of Disabled Persons not implemented after, 65

Jensen, Steven L. B., 67
Jerusalem 1968, 10, 15, 36; convention negotiation, 32–35; *Crip Utopia*, 16–18;

disability internationalism and
normalization, 18–24; human rights
before human rights, 25–28; ILSMH
Declaration of General and Special
Rights of Mentally Retarded Persons in,
26; ILSMH *From Charity to Rights* rights
declaration in, 22–23; mentally disabled
persons reproductive rights opposition
at ILSMH conference in, 15; from
planning policy to claiming rights,
28–32; reference to Universal
Declaration of Human Rights, 22;
reproductive rights, 24–25

Kikhia, Mansur R., 42
Klapwijk, Arie, 148–49
Könkkölä, Kalle Kustaa Topias, 68–69
Koster-Dreese, Yolan, 94

labor market, persons with disabilities
integration into, 108–9, 112
Lakhani, Zain, 30
Landmine Survivors Network, 124
Lang, Raymond, 138
Last Utopia (Moyn), 82
legal capacity of persons with disabilities,
122; CRPD support of, 2, 127; Degener
on, 141; family concept lacking in,
141–42; Minkowitz on, 13, 121
"Let the World Know" seminar on
disability and human rights, of Rioux
and Lindqvist, 95, 96
Lindqvist, Bengt Olof Lennart, 68, 91, 104–5

Maastricht Treaty (1992), 114–15
MacKay, Don, 125
maltreatment, DPI focus on, 11
Manila Statement, of RI, 41; for developing
countries disability law, 42; Global South
and, 42
material inequality, 57, 169n68
medical model of disability, 3–4; CRPD
and, 16; Declaration on the Rights of
Disabled Persons approach, 47;
Lang on CBR programs, 138; WHO
on, 51, 130
mental disabilities, 16, 129, 143; Article 12
on equal recognition for, 126–27; Daes
report on, 133; deprivation of legal status
and civil rights, 121; Standard Rules
limitations for protection and support
of, 136; Stockholm, ILSMH symposium
on legal rights and, 20–21; UN
participation of people with, 136; WPA
on support for people with, 133
Mental Disability Rights International
NGO, 122
Mexico City 2002, 143; Ad Hoc Committee
of UN General Assembly and
international convention proposal by, 32,
82, 97–98, 121, 124; community
emergence, 128–32; equal recognition for
the law, 124–28; independent living right,
122, 139–42; International Convention to
Promote and Protect the Rights and
Dignity of Persons with Disabilities in,
121; new human rights diplomacy,
122–23; persuasion for UN drafting of
convention, 123–24; right to exercise
legal capacity, 122; right to live
independently in community, 122; UN
observances during 1980s, 132–34; UN
unpopularity of CBR, 134–39; WNUSP
and, 121–22
Miles, Mike, 136–38
Millennium Development Goals, 32;
disability insufficiency in, 56, 82, 89, 123
Millward, Gareth, 5
Minkowitz, Tina, 13, 121, 125
minority language, Deaf community on
recognition of, 12
Missing Pieces (Zola), 30, 148–49
model of truncation and fulfillment, of
Moyn, 6–7
Moyn, Sam, 6–7, 22–23, 82, 83; Anghie on,
8, 98; Hoffman on, 8–9

Nakanishi, Shoji, 138–39
National Co-ordinating Committee, for IYDP, Singapore, 70
national policies: conference of RI and Serra on rights in, 40; disability internationalism entanglement with, 19
nation-states: CRPD and, 146; European social model and responsibilities of, 110–11; human rights law implementation by, 83; role in Standard Rules, 73
negative freedom, in reproductive rights, 29, 35
neoliberalism, 7, 10, 37, 83, 86
New International Economic Order (NIEO), 131; global equality vision of, 57; WPA vision of equality and, 50
New York 1987, 99–100; consolidation of social development approach, 91–94; going to UN, 86–88; international law and utopias, 79–84; North American disability rights, 84–86; potential turning point in global disability policies, 88–91; steps toward human rights convention, 94–98
NGOs. *See* nongovernmental organizations
NIEO. *See* New International Economic Order
Nirje, Bengt, 20–21
nongovernmental organizations (NGOs), 9; Burke on, 146; CRPD sexuality word deleted, 34; European disability, 116; frustration with UN hierarchy, 96; human rights and, 85; of Mental Disability Rights International, 122; run by persons without disabilities, 38; in social development framework, 83; on Vienna conference inaccessibility by disabled, 102; World NGO Summit on Disability, of IDA, 123
normalization principle: Bank Mikkelsen naming of, 21; Danish and Swedish policies for, 21; R. Dybwad and G. Dybwad on, 21–22; Grunewald on, 21; as institutionalization alternative, 20–21; of Nirje and Wolfensberger, 20–21; Sterner on, 21; US-Scandinavian exchange on, 21
North American disability rights, 84–86
Not Enough (Moyn), 169n74
Nothing About Us Without Us (Charlton), 61
Nouwen, Henri, 152–53

Office of the High Commissioner for Human Rights (OHCHR), research Quinn and Degener for, 119
O'Flaherty, Harold, 85; on neoliberal agenda of Reagan, 86
OHCHR. *See* Office of the High Commissioner for Human Rights
Oliver, Mike, 4, 117

Pakistan Association of the Blind (PAB), 43
participation, in Singapore 1981, 71–73
Patibatsarakich, Narong, 61
Pérez de Cuéllar, Javier, 87, 88; Reich meeting with, 92
persons with disabilities: deinstitutionalization of, 29; DPI on basic rights for, 60; Dury as, 1, 144, 147; human rights of, 1; inequality of, 3; lack of participation in WPA, 72–73; societies view of inferiority of, 3; umbrella term of, 19; Universal Declaration of Human Rights lack of attention to, 20; vulnerability of, 57; WHO on human rights of, 20; WPA concerning, 47–51, 134
physical disabilities, rehabilitation for, 38–43
physical violence and vulnerability, of women, 30
politics, CRPD and, 146–47
positive freedom, in reproductive rights, 29
Priestley, Mark, 116–17
primary health care, CBR and, 138, 140
Principles for the Protection of Persons with Mental Illness and the Improvement of Mental Health Care, UN (1991), 133–34

"Proposal for a Decision on Action by the European Social Fund to Assist the Social and Occupational Integration of the Handicapped," 108–9
Protection of the Rights of Handicapped Persons by Different International Instruments, of UNESCO, 80

Quinn, Gerard, 32, 122; on CRPD Article 12 and independence, 142, 152; doing research for OHCHR, 119; on Standard Rules, 31, 53–54

Ratzka, Adolf, 16–18, 148
Reagan, Ronald, 85–86
rehabilitation, 111; Cold War and, 38–43; disability internationalism and normalization, 19; focus on adaptation to society but not adapting society to them, 11; focus until CRPD negotiations, 11; global disability policies, 38–39, 56–57; global policy as apolitical issue, 56–57; Global South efforts for, 42; Manila Statement, 41–42; for physical disabilities, 38–43. *See also* Community Based Rehabilitation
Rehabilitation International (RI): Acton as secretary of, 40, 89; Chandran-Dudley active role in, 70; DPI dissatisfaction with policies of, 59–60; Groce on, 39–40; as IDA member, 123; international conference on disability legislation in 1971, 40; Manila conference of, 41–42
Rehabilitation Unit for the Disabled, UN, 23
Reich, Alan, 12, 86, 96, 97; attempts to influence secretary-generals of UN, 87–88; as chairman of World Committee for UN Decade of Disabled Persons, 93; global disability policies development, 84; meeting with Pérez de Cuéllar, 92; on move of UN disability unit, 90; as US delegation member to WHO, 84; Yolah letter to, 89, 175n35

Report on Human Rights and Disability, UN (1993), Degener on, 115
reproductive rights: Article 23 of CRPD on, 24, 25, 33–34; idea to grant rights in 1990s, 10; ILSMH lack of confirmation of, 10; Jerusalem 1968 and, 24–25; negative and positive freedom and, 29; reproduction prohibition of persons with disabilities, 24–25; Standard Rule approach to, 35; Sterner on persons with disabilities right to marry, 24
Research Institute for Social Development, UN (1963), 82
RI. *See* Rehabilitation International
Rioux, Marcia, 94, 95
Roberts, Ed, 17, 66, 84
Rodriguez, Adaly, 62
Ruiz, Felipe Jaramillo, 34–35
Rules on Equalization of Opportunities for Persons with Disabilities (1993), 76

SAB. *See* Singapore Association for the Blind
Saulle, Maria Rita, 80; DPI Europe seminar on human rights, 115; DPI support of convention initiative of, 104–5
Schaaf, Marta, 30, 33–34
selective domestic implementation of human rights, CRPD and, 13–14
self-advocacy, 58; autonomy for persons with disability, 17; cross-disability organization for, 19; of Degener, 12; DPI support of, 11, 72; from Global South, 43, 44, 75–76; Global South organizations of, 43; human rights agenda of, 101–2; institutionalization of, 111–14; international level input of, 136; protests in 1981 by, 60; Ratzska independent living center, 17; tribunal organized to report human rights violations, 103; UN policy increased involvement by, 55; during World Conference on Human Rights in Vienna, 12

"Self-Help Leadership Training Seminars," of DPI, 61
Serra, Teresa, 40
sexuality rights, 29–30
Shah, Fatima, 11, 45, 74; Disabled Peoples' Federation of Pakistan cross-disability organization of, 46–47; as DPI board member, 46; Grant relationship with, 43; of IFB, 44; international conference of blind women and, 11, 43, 46; involvement in IYDP seminars, 46
Shakespeare, Tom, 29–30
sign language, 75
Singapore 1981: Chandran-Dudley mission, 69–71; diversity, 73–76; DPI during IYDP in, 11, 46, 58; DPI Human Rights Committee, 31, 77–78, 101, 103, 105; historicizing disability, 66–69; IYDP in Dutch Caribbean, 54, 61–67; participation in, 71–73; rights, rehabilitation and protest, 59–61; *A Voice of Our Own* conference title, 70–71
Singapore Association for the Blind (SAB), 69
social development framework, 3–4, 99, 117; consolidation of approach to, 91–94; Degener dissatisfaction with, 95; DPI support of, 11, 71; neoliberal utopia in, 83, 98; NGOs and businesses in, 83; replaced by human rights framework, 12; UN support of, 71, 89–90
socioeconomic equality, 37, 41, 56, 145; Chandran-Dudley on rehabilitation and, 70; CRPD including rights of, 57; Standard Rules addressing of, 55; WPA not central aim of, 50
special education program, of UNESCO, 19
Standard Rules on Equalization of Opportunities for Persons with Disabilities (1993): on community, 135; criticism of CBR, 135–36; CRPD comparison to, 33–35; on equalization of opportunities, 54–55; on equal needs and social development, 96; important step toward convention, 94; Lindqvist instrumental in adoption of, 68, 93–94, 106; mental disabilities limited protection and support, 136; nation-states role in, 73; Quinn and Degener on, 31, 53–54; reproductive rights approach of, 35; on rights framed as needs, 54, 107; Rule 9 attention to sexuality in, 29–30; Rule 9 family life and personal integrity rules in, 28–29, 31, 33–34; shift from welfare to anti-discrimination and human rights, 51–52; socioeconomic equality addressed in, 55; WPA compared to, 54–56
status equality focus, 3, 57
Step by Step policy instrument, for Declaration on the Rights of Mentally Retarded Persons national level implementation, 24
Sterner, Richard, 15, 21, 22, 23, 24
Stockholm: Global Meeting of Experts about WPA implementation, 52; WPA implementation in 1987, 28
Stockholm, ILSMH symposium (1967): G. Dybwad on legal rights of people with mental disabilities, 20–21; ILSMH *From Charity to Rights* rights declaration draft, 22–23; Sterner importance in, 15, 22; UNAPEI influence on, 22
structural approach to inequality, Anghie on, 98–99
Subcommittee on the Prevention of Discrimination and the Protection of Minorities, UN, 77, 104
Sweden, 49; emancipation of disabled people, 68; Lindqvist as blind activist in, 68, 105; normalization policies of, 21

Toledo, Pamela Molina, 74–76, 125
Torelli, Maurice, 80
Totolica organization, in Council of the Handicapped, 63, 65
Treaty of Amsterdam. *See* Amsterdam Treaty

UK. *See* United Kingdom
UN. *See* United Nations
UNAPEI. *See* Union Nationale des Associations de Parents d'Enfants Inadaptés
UNESCAP. *See* United Nations Economic and Social Commission for Asia and the Pacific
UNESCO. *See* United Nations Educational, Scientific and Cultural Organization
UNICEF. *See* United Nations International Children's Emergency Fund
Union Nationale des Associations de Parents d'Enfants Inadaptés (UNAPEI), 22, 23
United Kingdom (UK): Chronically Sick and Disabled Act in, 40; Millward on disability activism in, 5; social model of disability, 117
United Nations (UN): CBR unpopularity by, 134–39; Commission on Human Rights, 27–28, 52–53; Covenant on Civil and Political Rights, 19; Declaration on the Rights of Mentally Retarded Persons, 10, 23, 24, 41; DPI as acknowledged organization within structure of, 71–72; International Decade of Disabled Person (1983–1992), 26, 48; observances during 1980s, 132–34; people with mental disabilities participation, 136; persons with disabilities lack of accessibility, 102–3; Rehabilitation Unit for the Disabled of, 23; reluctance for convention in 1980s and 1990s, 12, 79, 81–82; Research Institute for Social Development, 82; self-advocacy increased involvement, 55; social development support by, 71, 120. *See also* Convention on the Rights of Persons with Disabilities; Declaration on the Rights of Disabled Persons; Economic and Social Council; International Year of Disabled Persons

United Nations Economic and Social Commission for Asia and the Pacific (UNESCAP), 112
United Nations Educational, Scientific and Cultural Organization (UNESCO): on children's rights convention, 80; *Protection of the Rights of Handicapped Persons by Different International Instruments* of, 80; publication on CBR, 136–37, 143; special education program of, 19; Torelli legal study extracts for, 80
United Nations International Children's Emergency Fund (UNICEF), 40
United States (US): CRPD lack of ratification by, 13; emancipation of persons with disabilities in, 115–16
Universal Declaration of Human Rights (1948), 49, 105; on interdependence, 140; Jerusalem ILSMH reference to, 22; lack of attention to needs of persons with disabilities, 20
Unlearning Eugenics (Herzog), 16
US. *See* United States
utopias: Het Dorp, 30, 148–49, 150; international law and, 79–84; Zola experience with, 148–49

Vienna 1993, 101, 120; considerable burden and, 108–9; disabled inaccessibility to conference venue, 102; DPI organization of conference, 103; European social model, 107–8; Europeans with Disabilities Act, 116–19; institutionalization of self-advocacy, 111–14; new awareness, 109–11; persons with disabilities integration into labor market, 108–9, 112; from tribunal to Standard Rules, 102–7; beyond welfare state perspective, 114–16
Vienna Declaration and Programme of Action, 106; on human rights, of disabled persons, 101; on rights of disabled person, 103

vocational rehabilitation policies, of ILO, 19
Voice of Our Own, A, Singapore 1981 conference title of, 70–71
vulnerability, of persons with disabilities, 57

Waldheim, Kurt, 87, 88
Waldschmidt, Anne, 118
WCWB. *See* World Council for the Welfare of the Blind
welfare state perspective, 114–16, 145
Werner, David, 131
WFD. *See* World Federation of the Deaf
Where There Is No Doctor (Werner), 131
WHO. *See* World Health Organization
WNUSP. *See* World Network of Users and Survivors of Psychiatry
Wolfensberger, Wolf, 20–21
women: Brégain on interest in issues for, 44; Global South and rights of, 43–47; Lakhani on physical violence and vulnerability of, 30; protest against men DPI dominance, 74. *See also* international conference of blind women
World Became My Room, The (Könkkölä), 68–69
World Blind Union, as IDA member, 123
World Committee for UN Decade of Disabled Persons, 93
World Conference on Human Rights, in Vienna, 12, 101
World Council for the Welfare of the Blind (WCWB), 43–44
World Council of Disabled People International, 113
World Federation of the Deaf (WFD), 38; as IDA member, 123; on sign language rights as human rights, 75
World Federation of the Deafblind, as IDA member, 123

World Health Organization (WHO): CBR approach to disability developed by, 131; DALY of, 139; disability definition of, 132, 139; "Health Aspects of Mental Retardation" memorandum of, 129; on human rights of persons with disabilities, 20; on medical model of disability, 51, 130; medical rehabilitation policies of, 19; publication on CBR, 136–37, 143; Reich as US delegation member to, 84
World Network of Users and Survivors of Psychiatry (WNUSP), 121, 124
World NGO Summit on Disability, of IDA, 123
World Programme of Action (WPA), UN, 11, 104; anti-discrimination law and, 51; Canada and Sweden on, 49; on community, 132; Concerning Disabled Persons in 1981, 27, 48, 96; concerning persons with disabilities, 47–51, 134; disabled persons lack of participation in, 72–73; DPI negotiations for, 72; European Regional Meeting on Implementation of, 81; following of WHO definitions, 132; inclusion of people with cognitive disabilities, 74; NIEO and vision of equality of, 50; O'Flaherty on human rights in draft of, 85; prevention of disabilities priority in 1981, 27; relevant action terms in, 49–50; socioeconomic equality not central aim of, 50; Standard Rules compared to, 54–56; on support for people with mental disabilities, 133

Yolah, Shuaib U., 89, 175n35

Zola, Irving Kenneth, 30, 148–51

GPSR Authorized Representative: Easy Access System Europe, Mustamäe tee 50, 10621 Tallinn, Estonia, gpsr.requests@easproject.com

www.ingramcontent.com/pod-product-compliance
Lightning Source LLC
Chambersburg PA
CBHW022054290426
44109CB00014B/1093